Safe Travels!

Mindi J-Elwole

Travel:
The Well-Known Secret

Travel Stories & Life Lessons

*I'll let you in on a little secret.....*You can travel, too!

Mindi S. Johnson-Eluwole

authorHOUSE®

AuthorHouse™
1663 Liberty Drive
Bloomington, IN 47403
www.authorhouse.com
Phone: 1-800-839-8640

First published by AuthorHouse 4/25/2011

ISBN: 978-1-4567-4521-9 (sc)
ISBN: 978-1-4567-4520-2 (hc)
ISBN: 978-1-4567-4519-6 (e)

Library of Congress Control Number: 2011904084

Printed in the United States of America

Any people depicted in stock imagery provided by Thinkstock are models, and such images are being used for illustrative purposes only. Certain stock imagery © Thinkstock.

This book is printed on acid-free paper.

TO:

Lamar William Stull

1922 - 2008

&

Amelia June

May you learn the *secret* earlier than I did!

&

Audrina Lynn

May you live life to the fullest and make the *most* out of every moment! You have earned it!

Contents

A Note to Readers

I AM NOT SURE what qualifies me to write this book. Could it be my 37 years of life, or the fact that I have visited over 100 countries? Perhaps it's my 24 years of writing in a journal that made it possible? Or is it the lack of ambition to get back into the "corporate" world that has pushed me towards this new adventure? When I tell people that I have spent the better part of the last eight years outside of the United States, backpacking, the same questions always arise: You travel alone? Is it safe? Do you ever feel scared? What are youth hostels? What do you pack? How do you plan your trips? How do you get around? How can you afford it? No one else goes with you? You only bring one bag? How many pairs of shoes? What about the language? What do you eat? How do you know where to go? What is your favorite country? After I answer all of those questions, I always hear, "Wow! You should write a book!" So in April of 2009, as I landed in Bali, Indonesia and met my goal of 100 countries, I thought it wise to finally get this project underway!

I am writing to future travelers in the hopes that I inspire you to get out there and travel a little yourself. I have written this book with you in mind. If this type of travel is not your thing, then my wish is to be an inspiration for you to live *your* life's dream, whatever that may be. I do believe, however, that the most valuable lessons about life can be learned through travel.

I am sure that current travelers (at any level) will get the most out of my crazy stories. I hope you can reminisce and/or get ideas for future trips.

Mostly I have written this book for my friends and family so they can see how I live "on the road," and also for me to have a complete compilation of my stories (well, almost complete). I have written this book at the PG-13 level; maybe someday I will be brave and write a second one with a few more of my scandalous stories - under a pen name of course!

In the interest of ease and functionality, I have divided the book into sections covering specific travel-related topics. I love to read short stories and thought it would be nice to give you a chance to read about any or all of my adventures in the order in which you are interested in reading them. So I apologize if I seem to skip around a lot. After this many years traveling I am surprised I even remember everywhere I have been!

I have had so much fun reliving these experiences for you. I hope you enjoy my stories and if you take only one thing away from this book, I hope it is this: by traveling the world, you will be able to better see how amazing your *own* life is, and how fortunate we are here in America. Please don't misuse our freedoms.

"No matter what happens, travel gives you a story to tell."
Jewish Proverb

And here is mine…please enjoy *my* take on the world!

Secret to: The List

"I haven't been everywhere, but it is on my list."
-Susan Sontag

ONE OF THE FIRST things I started to talk about with fellow travelers was "The List." This list contains the places I have been and my traveler's wish list as to where I would love to go in the future. I have noticed that after chatting with other people about traveling my list grows in those few minutes. The fun thing about "The List" is that it will never be complete. During the research for this book I have added at least another five places to my list. The problem with "The List" is that as soon as I cross off two or three places I add the same amount back to it.

I had to renew my passport in 2000 when I was hired into a position that would require extensive international travel. I was sitting there looking at my shiny new passport and noticed the expiration date of 2010. Ten years. This is when the math side of my mind kicked into gear: ten years, ten countries a year, I could visit 100 countries with this passport! The goal was set. In the beginning, it was about getting "my numbers up," but it slowly changed into covering regions of the world.

I remember reading somewhere that there are over 200 countries in the world. In 2009, I hit 101 countries and was happy to think I had seen about half of the world. In research for writing this book, I found a website for world travelers and they list 320 countries/areas. So, within one read through, I went from seeing half the world to only seeing a third of it. Guess I have to keep going!

Here is a year by year play of my travels: my international job took me to Chile, Peru, Argentina and Brazil, Barbados, Trinidad, Jamaica, Netherlands, Switzerland, China and Japan. I was off to a good start on the ten countries per year. In 2001, I took a three week vacation from my job in the U.S. and did my first backpacking trip around the United Kingdom. I visited England, Scotland, Wales and Ireland. My 2002 trip was a domestic one. We had just been through the wake of the 2001 attacks on the United States. I wanted to see more of my country and help promote tourism within the U.S., so I set out with my friend, Michael from work on a West Coast journey. We hired a car and traveled from Seattle, Washington to Tijuana, Mexico.

In 2003, my best friend David began calling every week trying to get me to go to Western Europe on a 35 day camping trip with him and our friend John with a group called Contiki. I tried and tried to be "sensible" and not quit my job, but the pull was too strong. After a Corona and Bacardi Limon day at the beach with my friend Adam, I was fully convinced that life was too short and I should do this while I still could. I went to work the next day and tried to quit. My managers wanted me to take this trip but come back to work after. So, six weeks off, unpaid, and return to my position? The stars were aligned.

This was my first real "backpacking" trip. Traditionally on a Contiki tour there are mainly Australian and New Zealand passengers with a few Brits and Canadians sprinkled in. Unlike the United States, these cultures have travel ingrained in them. They have something called a "gap year" where everyone is given one year after their high school equivalent and before they attend university to travel, see the world, or take part in an internship. So, when we started introducing ourselves at the beginning of the tour, the stories were very inspiring, but they also made me jealous. I found backpackers on the road for three or four months, and it had me re-thinking my measly six weeks. I was a hero at home for leaving for that long, but out there it was just a warm-up trip.

The tour started in London, crossed over to France and moved through 17 countries, including smaller countries like Vatican City and Monaco, and ending in Amsterdam. David, John and I travelled together for two additional weeks in Budapest and Czech Republic and then I spent one additional week visiting more of the United Kingdom.

I returned to my job in recruiting and spent the next year as a domestic recruiter in the U.S. visiting over 50 American college campuses, mainly in the southwest. By the way, I do count America as one country on my list, as I have been to 28 of our states. The summer was fast approaching and my newfound traveling friends were emailing asking what my next trip would be. I wanted to have a "next trip" so I started looking for opportunities to live overseas. A friend had started his own recruiting company in London, Yummy Jobs, and invited me to live and work in the UK. So in 2004, I packed up and headed to start my London life. I was not expected to start work until September so I took a 35 day Scandinavia/Russia trip, once again with Contiki, covering Denmark, Finland, Sweden, Norway, Russia, Belarus, Poland and Germany. The other passengers were on six or seven month journeys. The jealousy continued!

I was finally getting settled into my life in London, doing a few side trips to York, Normandy, and Amsterdam, of course! There had been attacks on the London Underground and the market was turning. This was not helpful for me to keep my position in London, so I was let go with one month's warning. I was "made redundant" as they say in the UK. Many times when big events like this happen in my life, it is easy to think that I will not come out the other side as happy as I was going in, but I can honestly say this change in location helped me to see my true life's purpose: to travel!

When I suddenly had to leave London, I organized a six month trip before returning to the U.S. I traveled from Estonia to Croatia sometimes solo travel, and other times with friends. I spent three weeks with David and his parents revisiting many of our favorite parts of Western Europe. I traveled with Natalie and Sally in a chain of rental car adventures through Estonia, Lithuania and Latvia. I did a tour of Spain and Portugal with Contiki, and finally, a Paddy Wagon tour of Southern Ireland. I thought with this trip, I would make it into The Big Kids' Club – but everywhere I went, I met other travelers who were doing a one year around-the-world trip, and needless to say, I was more than a bit envious!

I returned in time to be in my brother's wedding in October of 2005 and then began working for about 10 months towards changing my lifestyle completely. The big step; the life changing moment came in May 2006 when I decided to sell my house and all of my belongings, transfer my car lease to my sister-in-law and cancel my cell phone service. This was one of the best times of my life: I felt so free and so able to go anywhere in the world I wanted to go- and I did! I booked the first of my Round-The-World airline tickets from Northwest Airlines. It required that I have at least three stopovers of more than 24 hours each, onward movement, and it depended on the number of miles needed to make all of my destinations. I purchased the 40,000 mile ticket and decided to use my points to upgrade to a business class ticket. This allowed me to use the business class lounges and, most importantly, to fly my long-haul flights in the comfort of the business class cabin. I spent about 80 hours in the air on this journey and visited 33 countries. It was well worth the price for a little extra comfort.

A brief outline of my 10 month, around-the-world trip is as follows: London, Greece, former Yugoslavia (seven countries), a 35 day Middle East tour (Turkey, Syria, Jordan, Egypt), then on to Dubai, Ethiopia, three months overlanding through East Africa and down to South Africa (total of 12 countries). I spent 21 days traveling the east coast of South Africa with a company called Baz Bus and then flew to Thailand for a three week trip with my friend Brad on my way to Australia and New Zealand's South Island, where I did a tour with Stray, and finished in Tokyo as a stopover on the way home.

When I was in the Middle East, I bumped into a fellow traveler that was a "Lifer" and had visited over 100+ countries- and I was "amazed"! Now *I* am the "Lifer" and have traveled to over 100 countries- and yet the jealousy continues. I am now "jealous" of anyone who is traveling when I am not. I also get jealous of people if they have been to places I wish to go to. However, when you are jealous, it pushes you to see more.

Coming home and working for six months to save for a six month trip was now becoming easier and easier. I held two jobs and worked as many double shifts as both places would allow. In January 2008, I was ready to conquer Mexico and Central and South America for five months. This trip was the first that I booked with a one-way ticket from Michigan to Mexico, and had no plans on returning home until the money ran out! I traveled four of the five months of this journey with Christa, the American girl that was my guide on my tour of the Middle East.

Since 2008, I have completed two more six month expeditions to South East Asia and West Africa. I have spent a little more than five of the last 10 years *outside* the United States. This works out to be 62 months, 250 weeks or 1,750 days, give or take. The number one question people ask once they find out that I work six months and then travel for six months, is "what kind of job do you do?" Many are amazed to find out I am a server at Mulligan's in Cheboygan! Mulligan's is an Irish-American Sports Bar that is owned and operated by close family friends, the Ingersolls. I have been very fortunate to be able to have a job every summer to return to. It is a seasonal job that allows me to earn the *good money* when I am home for the summer, and it slows down in the winter, so they don't need me. I am not a big fan of the snow anyway! So, I usually travel each year from January to June. This is great on the budget too because it is low season in many parts of the world.

Once I began traveling for the better part of the year, people would try to suggest careers that would help me sustain my traveling lifestyle. Ideas of travel writing, volunteering and becoming a tour guide were at the top of the list. I did consider all of these options, but enjoyed the formula I had set for myself. Mine allowed me the freedom to move around and see many places. The other ideas would require me to be in one location for months at a time.

My South East Asia trip in 2009 claims the honor of my 100th country (Indonesia) and it was on this trip that I met my husband-to-be (Laos). We traveled around together for almost two months. I was happy to know he enjoyed traveling and would not try to deny me the happiness I find while traveling. Well, he has requested that I slow down a little bit. "Not until after our wedding!" I pleaded.

So, in January 2010, I planned a trip to include Iceland, Spain, and London with my cousins Timothy and Casey. I then organized another African Trails overland tour from Morocco into West Africa (another 14 countries). The original plan was to finish the 13 week overland tour in Cameroon; but during the trip, Femi and I decided to move up the wedding date and meet in Nigeria to get married with his friends and family as witnesses! Nigeria holds the prize for country number 114!

Traveling has not slowed down for me one bit since the wedding. I returned home for one last summer of working in Cheboygan. The

Ingersolls purchased a second restaurant in town, The Rusty Anchor, and it did very well its first summer, as did I. I saved money for my upcoming trip, but this would not be like the backpacker trips I ordinarily take. This time, I was traveling back to Nigeria to spend a bit more time "bonding" with my new Nigerian family, and then heading to Malaysia to see my husband.

During my flight to Nigeria from Atlanta, Georgia, a woman became very ill on board and the pilot decided she was too sick to make it to Nigeria and we would have to turn the plane around, and land in Bermuda. Flashes of the Bermuda Triangle and all of those superstitions now filled my head. Did I mention we were flying through a thunderstorm? Oh yeah! What is happening here? But, we landed without worry and then sat there for three hours. Extra time to catch up on my movie list! So, does Bermuda count as country number 115? Well, on some lists it does count as long as you just *touch down* at the airport, but I did not count it.

I was flying Qatar Airways from Nigeria to Malaysia and it only seemed natural to have a stop-over in Qatar on my way, adding the real number 115 to my list. Then as any *true* backpacker will tell you, "You have not traveled until you have been to India." So, I arranged to meet my friend David for a two week trip around the north of India (number 116). It was a quick trip and I would have loved to explore it more thoroughly, but I am happy to have had the chance to see it all the same. It was very fitting that one of my first backpacking trips and one of my last backpacking trips was with my oldest and dearest friend David. Don't get me wrong: our traveling together is far from over, just that I think the style and length of trips is changing.

So, what *do* I count as a country? The big ones of course- the ones no one would dispute: Germany, France, Morocco, Uganda. And the little ones that are pretty secure on most lists, Vatican City, Andorra, Monaco, and I do count England, Scotland, Wales and Northern Ireland as four separate countries. I count Ibiza and Majorca as separate from Spain, as I do The Dutch Antilles as individual countries separate from Holland and the U.S. Virgin Islands separate from the United States. There are many that could come up for debate like recently on my North and West Africa tour- the Western Sahara. It is recognized by the United Nations as a "non-self-governing society" and is mainly controlled by Morocco, followed closely with France. More people there speak Spanish (as it was formerly a Spanish Colony) and the people feel they are entitled to be a separate nation. I am always in favor of "chalking up one more" so to speak, so I counted it as a separate country.

The list I am currently going by is from the Traveler's Century Club website. Find out more on www.travelerscenturyclub.org I do disagree a little with the way they *count* countries visited. They claim that you are able to check a country off the list even if you have only been at the port-of-call or touched-down for a plane refuel. I like the idea of including the smaller places, off the beaten path, but will still hold true to *my* rules. I must have done at least one or more of these activities in the country for it to "count:"

- Crossed an official-border- whether I receive a new stamp or not
- Changed to a new form of currency
- Eaten at least one meal and/or spent the night
- Talked to the "locals" and *they* count it as separate from the other country in question

I noticed on the Traveler's Century Club Website they list multiple members with 150 to 200 countries visited. Oh, my jealousy rages on! At the time of publication I have visited 117 countries (finally made it to the Philippines!) Are *you* jealous? Get out there and start "earning your own numbers!"

There is always someone to be envious of! I have to give an Honorable Mention to three little girls that have made me *extremely* jealous over the years. Not just because between them they have seen the entire world, but because they were all so smart, cultured and beautiful. I met Abby and Hannah on my Galapagos cruise. They were traveling for 18 months with their mother and father and gaining the best "education" the world could provide. I traveled with Victoria for almost three months on my last African overland truck. Her father is a professor at University of Massachusetts and her mother is from New Zealand, so already she has a cultured life; but now include taking a year off from school (her second sabbatical in her 11 year old life) and she becomes the most interesting little girl I have ever met! She has visited over 65 countries (at least that was the count when I last left her), some of them when she was too small to remember, but she was still out there soaking it up one way or another. She definitely has plans to revisit a few!

Victoria and her family have given me a look into the next chapter of my life: what it could be like to travel the world with "little ones!" I have learned that even the "hard-core" adventures are not off limits to families! You rock, Subritzky-Katz family!

My only advice to fellow travelers when sharing "The List" of where you have been is to be careful not to brag. If you can, utilize the other travelers to find out tips, hints and opinions on the parts of the world on their list. My favorite part is to discuss future locations. This is how I will be sure to continue adding to *my* list!

I have included my "Future Travel List" near the end of this book. I am sure by publication I will have crossed out a few and added many more. I hope so anyway!

My Top 10 List!

*"Life is not measured by the number of breaths you take, but
by the places and moments that take your breath away!"*

– Anon

I PUT TOGETHER A TOP 10 List because after the question "How many countries have you been to?" always comes "Which one was your favorite?" I always like to answer "The next one!" Here are the places that I hold special in my heart and mind.

In no particular order:

- Nordkapp, Scandinavia - Land of the Midnight Sun
- Transylvania – Romania (Sibiu, Brasov)
- Dubrovnik, Croatia
- Ngorongoro Crater - Tanzania
- Wadi Rum Desert and Petra - Jordan
- Amsterdam – all 12 times!
- Pacaya Volcano - Guatemala
- Swimming with the sea lions in Galapagos, Ecuador
- Pisaq, Peru - Sacred Valley of the Incas
- Sailing from Panama to Colombia via San Blas Islands

Not Kalmar Exactly!

A few questions fellow travelers ask when they find I am from America are "what is your background?" and "where are your ancestors from?" Well, I can say with confidence: a little German, a little Irish and our strongest bloodline comes from my father's side, and that is Swedish. My great-great grandfather John Reinholt Johnson came over from Sweden in the emigration movement to help in the logging industry that was forming in Northern Michigan. To come to Cheboygan, of all places! Maybe I share his "Pioneer Spirit" and that is what drives me to continue to travel?

He went on to open a photography business that my Uncle David and Aunt Julie are still running today. I worked at Johnson's Studio and Camera Shop myself in high school and college and was there when we celebrated our 100 years in business. Pretty cool to be able to track our history back that far.

When I was planning my trip to Russia and Scandinavia, I wanted to spend a little extra time in Sweden tracing my heritage. So, before my trip I set off to my grandfather's house with an atlas in hand. We reviewed the section on Sweden and he told some stories that he remembered hearing from his father and grandfather. He pointed to Kalmar on the map and I circled it. How exciting: I was going to get to see the town of Kalmar where my ancestors had left from in the late 1800's.

During my trip to Sweden, I spent about five days in the city of Kalmar wandering the streets, checking out the Lutheran Church (the Johnson side is now Catholic), even walking through the various graveyards looking for our name. It was most likely Johansson then. I loved this little town, a bit more modern than I expected, but then again it was not 1887. I sent all the Johnsons a postcard from our original "hometown," showing off their winter scenes. It is amazing the snow that they get there in the winter. I guess that is why they were able to move to Northern Michigan without any worries.

Throughout my entire journey I was telling everyone about my pilgrimage to mother Sweden, and how I was excited to be the first person in my family to go back there. When I returned home and was sharing my photos with my grandfather and the rest of the family. I was very surprised when I heard my grandfather say "Well, we are not from Kalmar, *exactly*. It is a little village just *outside* of Kalmar." "WHAT?!" I can't believe I went to all the extra trouble to go to my hometown just to find out later I was actually 10-15 miles away from the real thing! Since I doubt I will return, or anyone else in my family will make the trek... we are now from KALMAR EXACTLY!

Secret to: Animal Adventures

Gorilla Trekking in Rwanda

WHEN I THINK ABOUT travel in Africa, one of the first things I think of is the animals. Where are they? How can I see them? How do I get close to them? Well, if Mountain Gorillas are the target, it is best to head for Uganda, Rwanda or DRC (Democratic Republic of Congo). The African Trails six week trip that I had organized regularly schedules their treks in DRC. At the beginning of our trip our guide got word from the tour's home office that there was civil unrest happening in DRC. Evidently they had just had a public election and the winner was not who the public was expecting and the locals were about to "kick off!" This was not an environment African Trails wanted to take Western tourists into. I agreed with them!

One of the reasons I decided to take an organized tour through Africa was because I was afraid this type of situation could come up, and in my little oblivious, non-news watching travel world, I might not hear of such a thing, or not find out until I reached the border, or worse yet, land myself in the middle of a riot! So, Rwanda it is!

Now, it is necessary to back up a bit and tell you about the "group" I am traveling with. Most of the organized tours I have taken have been Contiki and have had over 20 people cooking, sharing a truck, and setting up tents. This time we are only eight, and this included the two drivers, Gavin and Scott. They were both Australian guys who had been driving in Africa for a few years. The campers were: Jaimy and Marc, a married couple from the Netherlands; Julie and Tim from Australia and soon to be engaged; Paulina from Poland; and little ol' me! It was a lot easier doing dishes for eight people!

We all took very well to our small group. Some of the nights we would roll into camp late and if we were hungry we would want to start cooking rather than set up our tents. With only eight of us we decided there was plenty of room to "camp" inside the truck! The drivers thought we were crazy as they were out sleeping under the stars in nothing but a mosquito net. Yeah, I know a little vinyl tent isn't much to stop a hungry lion either, but if I was outside, I would rather be protected by a bit more than a flimsy little net! That is just me! We started to call ourselves "The Partridge Family" because we spent so much time in our "truck."

The roads in Rwanda were as bumpy and washed out as all of the other roads we had encountered throughout Africa. As part of the arrangement for the "gorilla trek," a local guide would pick us up and take us to the Volcanoes National Park entrance and get us set up with our jungle guide. At first, we felt very special to have all these people taking us from place to place; but then we realized they had just figured out how to make a living from the tourists. For example, our lovely guide took my $65 for the entrance visa for Rwanda and "processed" my passport with everyone else's. Come to find out later, Americans do not need a visa for Rwanda, but the other nationalities did. So, when I unknowingly gave my money with the rest of the group, he didn't say a word. I am sure my $65 paid his rent for the month.

We spent part of the morning at the base station learning about the trek and safety guidelines. Part of the "fun" of a Gorilla trek (so I am told) is the hike to get to them in their natural habitat. The jungle: hot, muggy and full of malaria ridden mosquitoes. It doesn't sound that fun to me. So, the guide gave us a choice: Easy - a one hour hike; Medium 2 to 3 hours hike and Difficult 3+ hours. We all decide that easy was "too easy" and difficult might be just that…difficult. Boy, are we smart! So we choose to hit the middle ensuring we don't see them right away and still have to work for it a little bit!

We were "DEETed" up and had found good walking sticks. We looked like we knew what we were doing! I wish our jungle guides did. Now, first of all, I have only ever seen a "silverback" at Busch Gardens in Tampa, Florida (behind some very thick glass) but I would think that you might need more than a rusty old machete to ward off a ten foot gorilla protecting his troupe. Okay, so they don't get that big- but you can understand my concern.

The gorillas are now protected by this National Park because of all the problems in the past with poachers. The poachers are still alive and well, and had most recently killed some German tourists that they came upon while trying to poach the gorillas. At the time we visited, the rangers armed with machine guns would bed down with the troupe to watch over them; then in the morning, they would hike back out and use a radio to tell the "jungle guide" where they left their troupe, so he can then bring in the tourists.

On our morning, I guess our scheduled troupe (The Amahoro Group) had a run in with another troupe and "battled" it out for territory - or so they say. I will tell you why I don't necessarily believe it. We began our two to three hour trek to find the gorillas and we were getting chewed up by mosquitoes, slipping all over in the mud and stung by these god-awful plants called stinging nettles. They actually burn more than sting - and believe me, it is a gift that keeps on giving. I think it is important to tell you that I really have NO sense of direction, but I am very observant. We were wandering aimlessly through the jungle! Isn't one of the benefits of the night ranger that the jungle guide knows *exactly* where to take the tourists?

"We are walking in circles," I whisper to one of the other trekkers. "No, they know where they are going," is the reply I get from at least two people when I voiced my concern. Finally, I have proof. I turn to Julie and I say "Look - THAT is the branch I hit my head on and THAT is the rock you tripped over!" I can't say whether I was happy to have been right or not. I decided to ask our guide why we were going in circles. "We are not, Madam." Okay, now I am getting mad, you mean he does this everyday and doesn't realize we are going in circles? My security level just dropped!

Finally, after I have my small group convinced, we all decide to sit down in protest. Within a minute he makes a call on the radio and then turns to us and says "Okay, we found them!" I am convinced that the troupe has always been about a one hour walk in and they just walk you around for a longer period of time if you the pick the medium or difficult trek.

We walked through the same path of stinging nettles for the third time - and lo and behold, there they were! I actually felt like at any moment I was going to stumble off the path and find a "Cast Members Only" door like at Walt Disney World! But, once you see those beautiful animals, it all melts away! I was in the jungle, in Rwanda, with a troupe of 18 mountain gorillas, and at that moment, I didn't care how I got there!

We had to leave all of our day packs with the second jungle ranger because the gorillas get curious and love to come after the tourists and take the bags. I wish I would have thought things through and remembered to have my extra camera batteries with me in my pocket. Oh well- with a small group, I knew I could get copies from the others. It was actually nice to just sit there and take it all in.

When they saw us, it was kind of like they knew we were coming. They are used to this parade of people now, and that kind of made me sad, too. We are using them as a tourist attraction, but at least our money (and it costs a lot, over $600 USD each for a permit) is going to help preserve their habitat and ward off poachers. The gorillas are so used to the guides that they can even communicate with them. They make this low grunting noise to ask "is everything okay?" and the guards reply in the same low grunt "MMMMMM HMMMM!" It was amazing to watch.

As with all wildlife, you cannot tell what they are going to do or when they will be tired of being stared at and want to make a move. After a few minutes of rolling around and playing, it was time for them to find lunch. We followed quietly and quickly through the winding woods, this time the stinging nettles were not a concern. All that was on my mind was keeping up with the group and not getting left behind to be some big gorilla's play toy.

I turned around and realized that I was the LAST one in the line-up. Oh crap! You know the saying "you don't have to be faster than the bear, just faster than the other person?" Well, I *was* the other person. I ran closer to the group and tried to stick close to Tim and told him he better have been paying attention to what that grunt sounded like in case they come near me! He says, "MMMMMM HMMMM!" Honestly, that didn't quite sound like the guide's version. I was worried he might be getting the sounds mixed up and instead of saying "All is fine, we are not here to hurt you," he was really saying "take her, she is willing," or "she is our weakest, we offer her to you!"

What is that noise? - Serengeti, Tanzania

Everyone who has been to Africa has most likely been on a safari, and those who have been on a safari definitely have some stories to tell. My guess would be about the amazing animals that they have seen while out driving around the plains. My animal story also takes place in the plains of the Serengeti, but it is narrated from the inside of my tent at our overnight camp.

We had a wonderful day on safari; we saw more lions than we thought possible. We even spotted a leopard, sorry for the play on words. Well, some people spotted her; I can't see ten feet in front of my face without my glasses on so I am taking their word for it. She was the last on my list of the Big Five. It is somewhat of an important list if you want to say you have truly been "On Safari." Okay, I won't leave you hanging: the Big Five are lions, leopards, elephants, rhinos and Cape buffalo. However, my story is about a few other animals you may run into in the wild.

I was settling in to my tent just fine after a long day in the fresh air. We had just relived the day's events over our group meal and campfire. We shared some digital photos from the day's safari and spoke of the animals we hoped to see on tomorrow's morning safari. My tentmate, Paulina, from Poland, was already snoring away when I came back to the tent from the campfire. I was hoping I could get that kind of sleep, too.

I had become accustomed to the sounds of the night after more than two months camping in Africa: the pesky mosquitoes, the crackling of the fire, and I was even getting used to Paulina's snoring. There was one sound outside that I was not used to and it sounded like "WHOOOP, WHOOOP!" The sound came from far away at first, and then I am not sure if it was my imagination, but the "WHOOOP, WHOOOP" was getting closer to camp. I was thinking through all of the things our guide had told us to ensure we were safe in camp that night. There are no tourist safety fences in the Serengeti. He said to be sure to stay in our tents after the fire was put out, and be sure to leave any and all food in the locked truck, not in our tents.

I am sure the animals can't smell Pringles in the can, could they? "WHOOOP, WHOOOP!" Can they? This is the least of my worries now as I realize I have to go pee. I looked at my watch and it was

12:15a.m.; we are not due up for breakfast for another six hours. This also means that the sun is not due up until then either. I laid there and tried to decide if I should brave it and head to the toilet block. Just then another "WHOOOP, WHOOOP!" The sound was so close I think the animal must be right outside my tent. Just as I was sitting up to grab my flashlight, I felt a large animal, much like a very tall dog, rub up against my side of the tent. Please let that not be a lion! I think it is a hyena. That's right, that WHOOOP, WHOOOP sound is what a hyena sounds like. Is a hyena outside my tent any better than a lion?

Sorry, Paulina, but I am not getting eaten alive while you sleep! "Paulina, wake up. I think there is a hyena outside our tent! - Oh, and by the way, I have to PEE!" She slowly opens her eyes and asks me, "Do you want my hat to pee in?" "What?" With about five hours to go until morning, I might have to take her up on her offer later! She sits up and tells me to unzip the heavy part of the tent and just have the screen portion still zipped so we can look out. The tension was worse than being in a haunted house - what if we do see the hyena?

Finally, I get up enough nerve to unzip half of the tent flap and peer out. My eyes are adjusting to the darkness and I didn't see the hyena. I think to myself, when *was* the last time I heard the WHOOOP, WHOOOP? I think it has left camp. Was I sure enough to actually go to the bathroom outside? Not on your life! As I was just about to close the tent flap, my flashlight captures a reflection of an eye from something a lot taller than a hyena and bigger, too. This thing was massive. "Oh my God, Paulina! There is a hippo in camp!" Now this is worth sitting up for, she gets out of her sleeping bag and joins me at the tent door. "See it, over there?" "No." "Watch when I shine the flashlight over there!" "See, I am *not* crazy." Paulina sees it too, but she asks why it isn't moving; it seems to be just standing there. We watch for a few more minutes and it really isn't moving, but we can still get the reflection from its eye every time I shine my light.

"Wait a minute," Paulina says "That is our Safari Truck, you idiot!" "Oh, so it is!" Well, good news, I didn't get eaten in my sleep, because I didn't sleep. I still had to pee and imaginary hippo or not, we were still in the middle of the Serengeti! I still haven't decided what is worse Lariam induced dreams or real life?

Python Eating a Jackal -Namibia

Near the end of my overland adventure we were visiting Etosha Pan National Park, in northern Namibia. We had finished all of the major game parks in East Africa and were now just making our way to Cape Town where the tour would finish. The campsite we chose for this leg of the trip was right inside the National Park. Most of the travelers, including myself were content with the animal adventures we had had so far, but there were still the few die-hards that made their way to the floodlit watering hole maintained by the park rangers each night. The watering hole was a great place to view animals most times in the day, but many of the bigger animals only came to drink in the evening when it was cooler. Overall, the showing at the hole was nothing to brag about.

The last morning of our stay, we had an exciting wake-up call from the rangers. They came running into our camp announcing that they had seen a Giant African Python strangling a jackal, and wondered if anyone would be interested in viewing this amazing event. Well, lions, elephants and giraffes were one thing, but a python and a jackal? I had not seen a snake this big in the wild before and thought it would be interesting. I grabbed my camera and put on my hiking shoes and started to look for the ranger's safari jeep that they would use to take us to the snake. When the two men just continued walking through the campsite, I nearly froze. This python was within walking distance from our campsite? The snake is big enough to catch, strangle and then eat a mid-sized dog and it is within walking distance? I had gotten up in the middle of the night to use the toilet and now was wondering exactly where this giant python was last night about 3a.m.?

A few hundred yards later and we stopped near some large rocks and saw the python with his prey. These snakes can get up to 16 feet long, but this one was only a measly 10 feet long. The snake catches its prey, crushes it and suffocates it until it is dead. Then it proceeds by eating the animal whole. We caught the python in the middle of this process, and the rangers said because there were so many of us around, nearly 30, that the snake could sense it and would hold onto its prey until it felt it was safe to eat it. It is ironic because jackals are known for hunting reptiles, but I think this jackal might have bitten off more than he could chew.

Antelope Park, Zimbabwe

Antelope Park houses a privately run Lion Release Program. At the time of my visit they were working on a release in Zambia. We spent three glorious days with all of the amazing animals on this property. I will try to share with you my experience, but this is one that you have to have yourself to really understand the impact.

We started our visit with a presentation about the property: the volunteers, the donations and the lifestyle these animals have become accustomed to. There were over 20 lions in the program they hoped to release into the wild. We signed up for all of the offered activities like we were enrolling in classes at a university, hoping there would still be enough room on the roster for each of us.

I started my first morning in camp at 6:30a.m.for a walking tour with the lions. There were 12 of us in the group and we took two nine month old cubs on a walk through the game park. We could hold their tails while they walked, pet them (once the guide got them settled on a perch) and watch them as they played in the tall grass. The guides tell you not to make eye contact with them or they might pounce on you. Also in the instructions was not to wear bright or busy clothes; it attracts their attention and they might want to "play" with you. Ren missed that memo. She had on a busy print skirt and the lions were mesmerized by it! Scary for her, entertaining for us!

Later that day we spent an hour playing with three four month old cubs. They were so used to the human contact that they came right over to me and climbed in my lap. Words cannot describe what it feels like to be holding such an amazing animal. Yes, their claws are sharp.

The evening was feeding time. You could sign up to be part of the feeding program. These lions were 18 months old and the biggest ones that we were able to interact with. With these ones, we stayed on the other side of the fence. You think? I was not so excited to go inside anyway. They did let us go in *after* they ate a few hunks of cattle! The volunteers were watching each interaction to see if the lions were behaving the way they should "in the wild," noting which lion was more dominant, and if they turned on each other when hungry - all important traits if they are going to be successful upon release.

Having our *cat* fix for the day, we were now able to play with elephants. Many of the group rode them and then took a bath with them. I was the official photographer and helped to capture the crazy event on film! The people sat on the elephant's back and then it would dunk itself under the cool water for its bath and the rider goes with it. The funny part is that the elephants can bring their trunks up for air; meanwhile the rider is still under water flailing around.

We also had the chance to help train them. One of the tasks was to kick a soccer ball; not sure that is a skill needed in the wild? I had a sneaky suspicion that they knew how to do this before I taught them. Interacting with these animals in this way makes me want to come back and volunteer here. Not sure I would be up for the butchering of the feed. Maybe not then!

Journal entry from Lake Naivasha, Kenya: Crater Lake Walking Safari

Today we arrived in Crater Lake Camp; the campsite was the departure point for our walking safari. What a beautiful place! There were monkeys jumping all around the trees above us. Every kind of bird noise you could ever imagine. We were happy to be settled in for a few nights.

We set up camp and put up our tents. Gavin came to the group to be sure that we didn't put our tents too close to the water's edge. He explained that the hippos come up on land during the night to feed on the lush vegetation near our camp. I have heard stories of how hippos can snap a canoe in half by coming up out of the water and crushing it. I was unsure the power a hippo would have fully out of the water and on land. These questions were answered quickly as Gavin shared the "urban legend" of the camp. Apparently two years prior to our visit, a group of German tourists were staying in the camp and could hear the hippos coming up onto shore. They headed out with their flashlights and cameras to get the "close-up" safari pictures that all their friends at home would be jealous over.

One of the German women accidently got between the mother hippo and one of her babies. The hippo charged her and literally bit her in two. Whether this story is true or not, Gavin made his point. I moved my tent and I am listening to the rules for sure this time! I came to find out much later on my tour with another African Trails guide, Mark, that this was not only true, but he was there to try and perform CPR on the lady. Sadly, she did not make it. When a guide tells you not to do something, you should listen, especially when it relates to African wildlife.

This camp site was a very memorable one for many reasons. The walking safari of the Crater was an amazing experience. We were walking along side giraffes and zebras, watching them run and play. They would run by us and almost taunt us. I kept asking our guide, "You sure there are no lions on this island?" He assured me we were safe! To reach the island you had to take a small boat. We used the boat to get close to shore to see the hippos bathing. I have to say I am still a little gun-shy regarding these powerful animals. They are ones I would much rather see from far away.

When we returned to the camp from our boat/walking safari, some of the group was going to take an additional village walking tour. I had decided to walk back to camp and rest a bit. I took the valuables from the others and promised to look after them at camp. As I was getting out of the boat, I lost my balance and started to fall out of the boat and into the river. I jumped forward and landed on the dock, but with all of my weight on my left hand. My wrist went between the slats on the dock. I was trying not to fall in the water as I had everyone's expensive cameras and their clothing. Chalk up a hand injury to the long list of "fun" in Africa!

The nights in camp were always a good time, recapping the days' safaris and listening to more camper stories from Gavin and Scott. This story happened to a fellow driver they knew: He had a two day stopover in this camp and was excited to have the local women do his laundry. This is a great service; everything is hand washed and almost looks better than when you first bought it. A few days after leaving camp he noticed some strange bites on his back and in the underwear region of his body. The bites grew bigger and more painful so he finally had to go to the clinic to see what was happening. They were some sort of fly larvae that had imbedded in his "private" region. The doctor said that you have to be careful of hanging your washing out to dry near these certain trees as the flies lay their eggs in your clothing and then you wear them and the new born flies bore into your skin. I think the removal of the bugs was the new issue. Needless to say, we were all checking our undergarments from then on. Ouch!

The next morning it was time to depart for our next adventure. I was still feeling a bit of pain in my wrist and I could hardly move it.

I had to take a shower and I knew it might take me longer than most because of my wrist so I was the first out of bed. Plus, it is not a bad idea to get one of the first showers of the day as they usually heat the water by starting a fire under the big drum of water, and the supply runs out quickly!

The shower block was a combination of about six little corrugated metal rooms at the far side of camp. I took the first stall closest to the water heater. I was struggling with getting undressed because I could only use one hand. I finally got organized and turned the water on. You know how you always hear people say "I could just feel someone looking at me?" That is the feeling I got suddenly, and was looking around the shower stall. At about waist height I see a little hole leading to the stall next to me. I bent over to look in, and saw a man's eye looking back at me!

My first instinct was to scream and cover the hole! I heard the door open in the stall next to me and someone running away. The funny thing is at first the guys in camp were laughing at me because they thought I saw a big spider or some kind of creature. Then they saw one of the workers running away from the shower block. Gavin and Scott chased him down and caught him. When the owner of the camp came over to apologize to me and check out the hole I spoke of, we noticed that ALL of the shower stalls had holes made in them. This evidently was a fun pastime for the groundskeepers.

So, my lessons learned in Lake Naivasha: don't go wandering near the water's edge at night; always check your underwear after they have been hanging on the line; and last but not least, look for little "peep" holes in all the shower stalls! Believe me, I looked in every shower after that!

Riding an Ostrich? - South Africa

During my six weeks traveling up the coast of South Africa, I found my way inland to a little town called Oustshoorn. I had heard from other travelers that there was a great hostel there and an ostrich farm where they actually allow you to ride an ostrich. My only experience with ostriches up until this point was at my friend Smitty's house in Michigan. Her parents raised ostriches on their farm and that happened to be the location of one of my Alpha Kappa Psi Big-Little Weekends.

We were under strict instructions not to interact with the birds as they get easily agitated. I still have visions of another friend of mine, Harris, trying to outrun one of them. They were not very friendly birds, so I was definitely nervous for my upcoming adventure.

I was using the Baz Bus for transportation on this leg of the journey. Baz is a great hop-on-hop-off bus service that runs the coast of South Africa. There is a little guidebook called Coast to Coast that gives the highlights of each area and lists various hostels along the path. One of the recommended stops was at the Backpacker's Oasis Shanti. What a relaxing place! They offered a wonderful "family dinner" each night serving vegetarian meals, but also the opportunity to taste ostrich steak. You would think that because it is a big "bird" it would taste like chicken, but it is more like a lean beef steak. I thought it was quite yummy!

The hostel had an activities board to help arrange the Cango Caves Tour and my much anticipated trip to the Cango Wildlife Ranch to ride an ostrich. I was a little worried because I had heard there was a weight restriction on who could ride the ostrich. When we arrived in the riding corral, I did notice a sign noting the weight restriction. I was a bit over the weight (story of my life). I learned a long time ago, especially when it comes to safety, it is NOT recommended to lie about your weight. Most adventure sports want to know how much you weigh so they can set the equipment correctly. If you are going to jump out of an airplane, why wouldn't you want them to know "exactly" how much you weigh? And in this case, the poor ostrich would not be able to hold my weight - or so, I thought.

When it came time for a volunteer, no one raised their hand. I was looking around, thinking, "I would love to do this if I could." The people next to me asked why I didn't want to try. I told them I did, but I thought I was too heavy. The guide said that I was able to do it if I wanted because this was a male ostrich, and he was able to handle more weight. So I was on my way down to the coral all the while trying to control my nerves and then thought: "Self - you dove out of an airplane, jumped off a gorge, bounced off a cliff face first; you can ride a little ostrich." Well - a big one!

It was in a little corral, and they loaded the bird in and put a bag over its head. If it can't see you, it doesn't realize you are getting on its back...really? I weigh a lot. Anyway, they are not the smartest birds, but they are the fastest. I climbed up the stairs and then jumped on. They had a little saddle blanket type thing for me to sit on and I held on to its wings as they eased him back out of the slot I asked the jockeys to stay with me because I didn't want to fall off and break anything. It was very different than riding a horse, but more memorable to say the least.

When I felt like I had had enough, about 10 seconds, I gave the signal to "Let me off!" and the jockeys pulled me off the back of the ostrich as it continued running. I received thunderous applause from the spectators, and I returned to my seat thinking to myself "Is it bad that I ate an ostrich omelet for breakfast this morning?"

Galapagos Islands - Ecuador

The Galapagos is another place that is hard to put into words, but of course, I will try! This is an excerpt from one of my group emails sent just after we returned from the islands:

We left for the airport early in the morning a bit nervous that our packs will be over the weight limit as this is the first flight we have taken since we landed in Mexico City almost three months ago! I just sent a package home with my extra guidebook and some souvenirs (2 kilos or 4.4 pounds) so my pack only weighed 16 kilos - not bad, but it still feels like it weighed a ton! Our flight was great, exciting to be finally landing in Galapagos after all the research and planning! We met 12 of our boat mates and waited for a bit for our tour guide as he was on a delayed flight. We had flashes of our 3 HOUR TOUR sailing experience in the San Blas Islands, but I am happy to say all was wonderful on our boat and we loved our cabin. It had little bunks but it did have air conditioning and our own baños privado (private bath)!

The food was good and plentiful, the crew was nice, and even a few of them were cuties. Such a hard life to be on a boat, in one of the world's most natural places with hot Colombian and Ecuadorian men waiting on you. Some of my highlights: swimming with the sea lions; it was like an adventure straight out of Sea World; if we would do flips, they would do flips. They must wonder what kind of animals we were with our masks and snorkels, but they didn't seem to mind. They loved having playmates!

I swam with a sea turtle, a reef shark, and many fun fish, if fish can be fun!?! We saw 50 or more dolphins around our boat while we were sailing, and four or five whales. We viewed bull sharks and rays from one of the islands. This place is a "must-see" if you like marine life.

I have to say that there are people in this world who love birds and those who...well, don't. That would be Christa and me! We would do nature walks every morning and it was really great the first day. One of the indigenous birds was called a blue-footed "booby". We would laugh every time our guide said "booby". I never claimed to be mature! We also enjoyed the Frigate birds, because said fast enough we might be swearing and that is what we wanted to do after seeing our 50th Frigate bird! Oh, don't forget the lava lizards, land iguanas and marine iguanas. Believe me; the other people on our tour took loads of photos like they didn't just see one just a few feet before. But we survived.... such torture seeing all this wildlife!

We enjoyed the island of San Cristobal and all its ice cream and internet and Twix candy bars. We acted like we had been away from civilization for more than five days.

I would say that the best part of the trip for me, besides the sea lions, were the people we met on board. One family stands out the most to me: Graham, Lorraine, Hannah and Abby. As all travelers do when they first meet, we gave our travel life profiles to each other and I was very impressed with theirs. They decided as a family to sell their house, cars, put their belongings in storage and take the girls out of school for 18 months to backpack around the world. They were all involved in the planning, each picking their favorite places from the atlas. They were from England and the mum and dad were "home-schooling" them as they traveled. What valuable life lessons! The girls were seven and nine and perhaps more adventurous than I because they were so young! They'd been hiking Machu Picchu, and swimming with the sharks! I truly hope that if I have children someday, I will be able to share the world with them in this way, too!

Whale Watching- Kaikoura, New Zealand's South Island

When I was a little girl, I dreamed of being a marine biologist so I could work at SeaWorld with the marine life. I was partial to dolphins, but loved the sea lions and whales as well. So, when the opportunity to go whale watching came up in New Zealand as part of my Stray travel pass, I jumped at the chance. Our tour bus was making its way north from Christchurch to Kaikoura for just this event. We arrived and went right to the tour company to secure a spot on the next afternoon's boat.

Our guide was sure to inform us about taking some sort of motion-sickness pills, as even in good weather the sea can cause a "little discomfort" in polite terms. I always carry Dramamine just for these situations. I noticed in the gift shop before we boarded the boat that they were selling whale-shaped ginger cookies. Ginger is great for an upset stomach, and quite yummy too, so I thought why not! I would be happy for this decision later.

The whale watching program's objective is to educate you as well as entertain, so they give a great slide show of past photos of the whales we might see. I am always up for some brain exercise, but my camera and I were ready to get "the money shot." The facilitator explained that we would mostly likely see Little Nick, the humpback whale that had been around for a few weeks. To give us an idea of just how big this whale was, she compared it to the size of the boat we were on. I looked out across the water to the second tour boat on the water and realized how enormous he was going to be. She also explained that humpback whales can stay under the water for over 40 minutes while "fishing," and this unfortunately makes it necessary to remain patient as we have no idea the last time the whale had surfaced, or if he was even anywhere around where the captain decided to stop. Luck was on our side! We saw him within 10 minutes.

The feeling is indescribable when you see the whale's back crest for the first time. Excitement tends to make the hands work less and the pictures are never as good as the moment. Although, I did get a shot of the tail as Little Nick dove back under to get some more lunch. We were happy to view some other wildlife on the trip as well. Birds! As you have learned I am not a big fan of birds; they aren't that cute or cuddly, nor are they exciting. But we were promised the Albatross: The king of the sea. These birds can have a wing span of up to 11 feet or 3.4 meters.

They look like giant seagulls; we call them "dump pigeons" at home. I am glad ours don't get that big! It was quite a sight to see.

The ginger cookies? The ginger cookies! Where did I put the whale-shaped ginger cookies? Wow, the guide wasn't kidding about this sea sickness thing. There were seven or eight people vomiting into little seasick bags and people with their heads between their knees. The poor summer volunteers were having to play nurse. Think about that next time you think your summer job is not so fun! You could be doing their work. Yuck! One lady was crying and another was closing her eyes and almost hyperventilating trying to settle her stomach. I was "on the verge," so even though I was happy to see Little Nick, I was even happier to see my new ginger friends.

Romanian Dogs - Timisoara, Romania

I was traveling alone in Romania and had originally only planned about two weeks in the country; but as it usually happens, I heard more from people who had been there and found more to see! So, the travel plans changed - one of the benefits of having an open-ended trip. I ended up spending almost one month in Romania traveling from Bucharest, through Transylvania and around through Timisoara with a return to Bucharest for my flight back to London.

Probably one of the most well-known budget tricks is to *never* take a taxi from the airport if there is perfectly good train/bus system. Usually the ride in the taxi equals the daily budget, so I do my best to find a train and take it to the closest stop to my youth hostel. On this occasion, I jumped off and realized I was still a few stops away, but was happy to be walking rather than sitting on a plane or a train!

The problem with being lost in a big city is the blocks are bigger too. So, to get to the next street sign, you walk one quarter of a mile only to find out it was the "other" way on the map. Lovely! Well, I *thought* that was my biggest problem. Once I got into the smaller streets, they were not marked *at all*. So, now I am just guessing that I am following the right roads. The locals are very helpful, even if they don't speak English, or know where you want to go, they still give you directions. "Drapa" means "go right." Everyone I asked would say "Drapa, Drapa and then Drapa." I know I am bad at directions but doesn't that put me right back where I started? After a lot of turning around and asking directions every ten feet, I finally found it. I dropped my bag down and crashed for the night. Lucky me, I woke up to a good ol' case of the bedbugs! It was not too difficult to check out of that hostel in the morning!

Because of the long walk with my heavy pack on the last leg of my journey (this was early in my backpacking career and I still carried way more than I needed) I decided that I would take a taxi to get to my next destination. I knew enough to try and ask the locals how much a taxi ride should be from this point to the center of town. I made my way to a little snack shop on the corner and bought a pack of gum and then asked the shop keeper about a taxi, the fare and best place to stay in town. The nice lady played a short game of "International Charades" with me and told me that the cab ride should be no more than 7 Lei, or about $2 US. I call it International Charades because when there is a language barrier the most natural thing to do is "act it out." I have found myself in so many of these situations - sometimes fun, sometimes not!

With my newly acquired information, I made my way to the taxi stand, hopped in the cab and started "negotiating" the price. He set the meter to 25 Lei to start. "No, I am sorry sir, but the nice lady told me 7 Lei." We argued for a few minutes, he wouldn't drive and I was staying in the cab! Finally, I said, "7 Lei," he says "7 Lei" and drives off. Whew, another rip-off artist conquered, or so I think! He drove down the long, winding road until the meter read "7 Lei" and he stopped the car, got out and handed me my pack out of the back! I was in the middle of nowhere! What to do? At this point, I was so mad I decided to be stubborn and take my bag and start walking. Turns out the hostel I wanted to stay at no longer existed, and I found a nice guy that walked me to a decent hotel. Thanks once again to a random Travel Angel!

So, with those fun Romanian transportation stories out of the way, you have a better idea of what my mind set was going into my trip to the train station in Timisoara. It is a little town in western Romania and a pit stop for me (on this leg of the race) on my way back to Bucharest. (Sorry, just a little Amazing Race humor.)

The town itself was pretty uneventful. I used most of the day as an "admin day": laundry, internet, upload some photos, called my brother for his birthday and ate at Mc Donald's. Just the sort of day you need to regroup and get ready for another leg of the journey. I got a good night's rest and was up at 5a.m. to pack my bag and head for the train station. My train was departing at 6a.m. and the guidebook said it was a two kilometer walk. After the con-man taxi driver I was not about to take a taxi. But it was *two kilometers* with a 20 kilo pack; for the non-metrics that is almost a mile walk with a 44 pound pack on! Oh, I am tough, I can do it.

I was walking down the quiet, deserted streets of this Romanian town. I was thinking of the upcoming leg of my trip, smiling about the money I was saving by not giving in to those thieving Romanian cab drivers and enjoying the fresh air. Just as I decided to cross the street to get to the side with more street lights, I noticed a "pack of wild dogs" wandering down the road towards me. My first instinct was to just be cautious. I am not usually afraid of dogs, but these are *wild* and *Romanian*. The little chant of "nice doggies" probably would go unnoticed as they don't speak English. So, I decided that I would just continue with my plan to cross the road and go about my business. Just as this thought was crossing my mind, a car goes by. These dogs didn't just chase the car; they caught it and were biting the tires. All six of these mangy dogs were running in a pack and actually catching the car! The driver realizes what is happening and speeds up to lose the dogs.

I was thinking the whole time that I hope they catch the car and leave me alone. Well, I spoke too soon. Now that they had lost the car, they were heading back in my direction and moving fast. I kept thinking crazy thoughts to myself: do I have any food in my bag that I could throw down a side street? Oh, but maybe they will attack me for it before I get a chance to throw it? Could I even run with this stupid back pack on? What if I miss my train? Should I turn down a side street but wait, then get attacked on a *side street* and no one could see me to help me?

I proceed towards the station thinking "no eye contact, no eye contact." Be confident, walk fast but not too fast. They were on to me. They followed a long for a bit. I was trying to decide which of these mutts was the leader. What was I going to do if I found out? Of all the crazy places I have been, and adventurous activities I have participated in, and this is how I am gonna go, getting attacked by a pack of wild Romanian dogs? As luck would have it, another unsuspecting car crossed our path and they were off again. And so was I, in the opposite direction.

Bedbugs-All around the world

Remember right before bed your mom would say to you "Good Night, Sleep Tight, Don't let the Bedbugs Bite!?" I thought bedbugs were in the same class as the monster in the closet or the goblin under the bed... not real! But, they *are* real and after traveling as much as I have, I was bound to run into the little critters a few times. My first experience was in St. Petersburg, Russia. I was on a low-budget hotel tour so we stayed in some pretty sketchy places. Up until this point I had only heard of other travelers getting bedbugs. The first morning in the hotel I awoke to bites all over my legs and arms. The bugs get hungry and come out of the mattress and use your skin as an all-they-can-eat buffet. They had a good eight hours to have their fill.

My bites were confined to my arms and legs, but my roommate, Tracy was not as fortunate. They must have been inside her pillow because she had bites all over the side of her face and neck. They itch and itch and there really isn't much you can do to treat them, other than not scratching them. We did ask our Russian guide to help us get some anti-itch cream. That was a fun one for International Charades.

The second time I got bedbugs was in Penang, Malaysia when I was traveling with my friend Anna. She was teaching in Abu Dhabi, in the United Arab Emirates and had a short break. I was visiting Femi in Kuala Lumpur and he had exams, so I left him to study and I met Anna for a "Girls' Beach Weekend" in Batu Ferringhi (Foreigner's Beach). We had a great stay there; the bedbugs came the last night before I met up with Femi for a trip to Langkawi. I had to take an early morning ferry from Georgetown, so I left Anna a day early and found a cheap little hostel on Love Lane, the popular backpacker area. It was called Love Lane because it used to be a brothel street when the Brits were in rule! Now all that rules that street are BEDBUG RIDDEN' HOSTELS. I should have known this might happen since my hostel bed only cost 10 Ringgit...maybe $3. I got what I paid for and more. I had over 100 bites all over my body.

I discovered the place had bedbugs after I spent the afternoon lounging in my bunk, reading and trying to avoid the heat of the day. I was out grabbing a nice meal at the street vending area, and started noticing the bites coming up on my skin. I knew the $3 accommodation was too good to be true. I should have listened to all of the write-ups warning travelers about the bedbugs on Love Lane! Problem now, I had already committed to staying there so now I have to tough it out. I spent the hours of 11p.m.to 5a.m.sitting up in a chair in the lounge, reading and dozing on and off. Throughout the night, the number of non-sleepers grew. I ended up sitting in the lounge with three others that were annoyed with these little pests.

So, I arrived to Femi sun burnt and flea-ridden. He was amazed at my bites and kept asking if there was anything he could do to help. The second day we were just relaxing in our hotel in Langkawi, and I was still feeling like I was getting new bites. We were in a nice hotel so I was pretty sure it wasn't from their beds. I soon realized that my pack and all of my clothes were infested with bedbugs. This is exactly how "clean" places get "dirty." So, if you suspect bedbugs, never use your own sleeping bag or travel pillow and as I now have learned, and don't lean your pack up against the walls or the bed. They make themselves at home in a new location very easily.

Getting them out of your clothes and backpack seems worse than having the bites. First of all, wash everything, I mean EVERYTHING in hot water. Since hot water can be hard to find when traveling, try to find a professional laundry service, I was fortunate enough to be staying in a nicer hotel that offered dry-cleaning. Yes, I broke the budget and paid the crazy prices. I also asked housekeeping for a large black trash bag (bin liner) and put my empty pack inside. We had a balcony so I set my pack outside in the sunlight for about eight hours. The little buggers can't stand the heat and die. I had one outfit and my bathing suit in my day pack from that trip and those were the only things *not infested*. Good thing we were at a beach and all I wanted was my suit! I am so glad I stayed in a $3 a night hostel to save money and then paid over $30 in dry cleaning. Lesson learned, but I am sure this won't be the last of these little pests!

Secret to: Adventure Sports

Skydiving - Titusville, Florida

LET ME SET THE stage: I am still living in Florida, working for Disney, but have just made the life-changing decision to go backpacking with my friends David and John around Europe in just a few weeks. My roommate and friend Meag asks me to start my adventures out right with a trip to Titusville and a 15,000 foot jump out of an airplane over N.A.S.A.'s Kennedy Space Center that boasts a 70 second free-fall. Why not, right?

We had our appointment and were telling everyone we knew. That is, everyone but my mom and dad. That call would be "after" the jump! We headed over to the jump site and filled out the crazy paperwork saying, "Yes, I know I could die, and yes, it would be my fault not yours if I do!" All we had left to do was meet our instructors, get suited up and board the plane. Oh, well and JUMP OUT OF IT! I can't believe they talked me into it. Our friend Adam was up for the challenge and this would be his first jump and Meag's second.

As we were waiting for the plane to land so we could board, we watched about four or five guys landing. "Doesn't look that difficult really," I think, just as a man fell from the sky, landed too hard on his legs, and they *both broke* under the pressure. "Are you kidding me? Is this a sign? Should I still jump?" This is the exact moment that I adopted a phrase I would come to use many times in my future travels: I figure, if it is my time to go, it is my time to go! But, what if I break both of my legs right before my big trip? "Let's get on this plane before I change my mind!" I shout over the noise of the engine.

It was pretty cool to see the space center and the coastline from this height. I kept reminding myself that I still had to jump from here. We had a few other people in the plane with us that were solo jumping with snowboards strapped to their feet. Maybe next time! Meag went first, and I remember thinking to myself how fast she fell. I was slowly walking to the front of the plane just as Adam and his instructor jumped. I watched him fall and he was nothing but a dot within three seconds. Oh crap! My instructor had told me two things: one - "Form is important; do what I taught you or you could force us into a spin." (Not cool!) and two - "We are going to do two summersaults out of the door and then straighten out. Remember to straighten out!" Oh, is that all?

"One. Two. Three!" The wind was rushing around my ears; it was so loud I could hardly hear him counting down. I was grasping the door with a death grip. I paid the extra money for a videographer to tape my jump and she was about to jump and then it was our turn. "Meag, why did I agree to this?" "AHHHHHHHHHHHH!" I remember smiling a lot and giving lots of thumbs up to the video camera and then I focused on the fall and the feeling of flying like a bird. This is by far the most outrageous thing I have ever done. Perfect way start to my new lifestyle!

It would be almost three and a half years before I would make my second jump, but I always knew there would be another jump. This time it was in Swakopmund, Namibia with Ground Rush Adventures over the Skeleton Coast. This was only a 10,000 foot jump with 35 seconds of free-fall but the price was right. Twenty out of 25 from our group jumped. As I landed everyone was there cheering me on and someone made sure that after each jump, the parachuter had a cold beer waiting. This jump was the best "after" the chute opened and we were "under canopy," the wind stops whistling and there is this eerie calm and quiet. Below, it was possible to see the Skeleton Coast. This water holds many shipwrecks deep within its belly. I enjoyed watching the waves crashing into the shore, and the sand dunes swirling under the sea breeze.

It was straight back to reality once the instructor reached back and unhooked something that made me lurch forward for a split second, and in that second I lost my heartbeat, because it felt like I was about to be cut loose and fall. I know now that it is just to make the descent more comfortable, but it is one feeling I will never get used to.

White Water Rafting- Slovenia

One of my very first attempts at adventure sports was in Slovenia. When I originally planned my trip in Eastern Europe, I have to be honest, I didn't even know there was a country called Slovenia, let alone what there was to do there. I was pleasantly surprised with all that was in store for me.

I had taken a train from Budapest and was on my way to Croatia, and Slovenia was a cool little "gem" to find along the way. I loved Ljubljana and Lake Bled, but was looking for something else to make this more of an adventure! So, when the hostel offered a full-day white water rafting package, I signed myself up. I was a little nervous because when you add rapids to the mix, things can get a little scary. I am a great swimmer, but rocks can be most unforgiving. The brochures bragged that this was an adventure for anyone, no experience required, only grade II and III rapids. Sounded like the perfect starting point for me.

It was a very hot day and even though we were squeezed into the one-size-fits-all wetsuits, we did have plenty of opportunities to jump over and cool down. The rapids were in fact quite small and gave us the feeling of rafting, yet not much danger. The guides were happy to give us another form of adrenaline rush that day in the way of jumping from a roadside bridge into the water. I remember realizing at that moment that my adventures "on the road" were just beginning, and I needed to make a firm decision about "these sorts of things" right here and now. So, even though I am very afraid of heights and wouldn't consider myself *super* athletic, I made a promise to myself that anytime an opportunity such as this situation came up in my many loops around the globe, I *must* give it a go! And I did just that, even surprising myself as one of the first to jump off. I look back now and think that I went first, knowing that if I waited too long I would probably have chickened out!

Adventure Sport Day - Zambia

When people think of adventure sports they usually think of a few major regions in the world: New Zealand, Slovenia, and Vic Falls, Zimbabwe. The latter is the location of my next adventure. Well, actually just next door in Zambia. Our campsite helped to arrange the Half Day Adventure or for the really crazy among us, the Full Day Adventure. This package included unlimited abseiling, rap jumping, the Flying Fox, and the grand finale: the Gorge Swing. It all sounded scary and like things I would have to force myself to do, but that is what you are supposed to do on a trip around the world, isn't it?

Did I ever! First of all you have to know a little about my personality to understand the significance of this day. I have never been a girly-girl, usually finding myself gravitating to the male company over a group of "cackling" girls. But, with hanging around boys comes the need to "keep up!" So, I signed up for the full day adventure mostly just to "hang with the boys!" Little did I know I would literally be "hanging" from many different apparatuses all day.

We started with the activities most easily recognized: Rap jumping and abseiling, rappelling backwards and forwards, using a rope-pulley system. Doesn't sound scary, but when you are out there it is harder to hold on to the ropes than you think. I ended the session with rope burns on both hands even with the protection of gloves. The mid-day activity was the Flying Fox, not a term that we are very familiar with in the United States, but in my many travels with Australians, I came to know what it meant. This Flying Fox was a zip line extended out across the gorge and you would run and jump off the cliff. You could fly like Superman; that is if you could bring yourself to let go of the chest supports. In all of my three tries, I could not!

We finished the day with the much-anticipated Gorge Swing. This is like a bungee jump but you can step forward or backward off the edge of the gorge rather than going head first. The fall is into a 91 meter (300 feet) gorge. I thought this might help me overcome my extreme fear of heights. Not so much. There are always a few guys in the bunch that do not have the "Fear Factor" and are the first to harness up and jump. Our group had five or six of those guys.

I know myself and I know I am afraid of heights, so I tell my guide that no matter what I say, I want to do this, "even if you have to push me!" It took me a few tries to get myself to the ledge. After a few short hyperventilating moments, I slowly backed to the edge. I weighed the options of forward vs. backward jumps. Forward looked just terrifying. Backward you don't have to look out over what you have to jump into, but you have to watch the cliff face inches from your face flash before your eyes as you plummet to the bottom. I was pretty sure my eyes would be closed so I decided backward had to be better. I was even more sure this was not going to be something I could do alone. The last thing I remember as I held my breath and fell back was the happy look in the guide's eyes as he *pushed* me over!

After you have stepped off the cliff, you drop rapidly straight down until the second rope catches your slack and you swing out over the gorge. Once you stop swinging wildly, you can soar over the canyon and enjoy the views. They have a second guy at the bottom of the gorge to catch you and guide you to the landing strip. Then, as with all the other activities that day, you have to make the 20 minute uphill hike out of the canyon. This gave me lots of time to contemplate jumping again. When I first landed, the adrenaline was running crazy and I got the feeling I could get hooked up again and sail out over the gorge right away. After the strenuous hike out, my mood changed a bit. All I cared about now was a big drink of water!

The crazy boys jumped many times. They started doing flips and twists and Ian even jumped with a beer and drank it on the swinging part! I was satisfied with the one jump. So I thought! When I made my way out of the gorge and returned to the "launch pad" I found out that I was signed up to jump tandem with Tom. "Yeah, it will be wicked; we will drop twice as fast and swing twice as far!" Oh, why, oh, why, must I pretend to be one of the guys?!?

I must say it wasn't so bad jumping while in the arms of a hot-buff British guy. One more time?

Zip Lines - South Africa

At the end of my first African overland tour, I allowed myself almost six weeks to explore South Africa and its amazing coastline. Along the path I found myself near Tsitsikamma Coastal National Park. The hostel I was staying at offered a zip line adventure with a local ecotourism company by the name of Storm Rivers Adventures. The day consisted of "zipping" along ten zip lines varying in length but all seemed to be hovering in the trees at a height of 90 feet above the ground. This is where I remind you that I am afraid of heights! The company was very professional and organized so I felt a little better that morning.

My zip line group was made up of nine of us, eight people who were traveling together and then me. I have to be honest here and tell you that the other eight people were all in their 60's and 70's. I am not kidding, these people were up for the adventure and at levels way beyond me. I think it was fate (or the guide's great instinct) to put me in the middle of the group, creating a sort of "peer pressure" situation for me, forcing me to continue on. I still find it humorous that throughout the day the "Grams and Gramps" were yelling to me and encouraging me that I could do it! Shouldn't it have been the other way around? I had finished the first three of ten zip lines and was pretty sure that was enough for me. The guide explained that the lines are all connected (as was I to the circuit) and there were only two solutions: one - disconnect, climb down the MASSIVE 90 foot tree I was standing in, and walk out; or two - "be a MAN, and finish what you started!" Well, the guide didn't use those words, but you get my point!

Numbers Four through Nine were a blur, filled with moments of me wanting to cry, almost wetting my pants and continuous chants from my adoptive grandparents reminding me to smile and look around. "Uh, no thank you!" I don't think I even smiled once until the last zip line. This one was shorter than all the others and it was the *last* one. Three or four people zipped before me with no challenges and now it was my turn. The guide that had been dealing with my drama all day was already on the other side waiting for me. I didn't know who would be happier now that I was finished. As I was just starting the cross, he started to jump up and down and sway the line so I was "bouncing" all over the place. I was screaming at the top of my lungs and the rest of the group was now peeing themselves, but in fits of laughter at my expense. I came to find out later that this was a common way of dealing with those "high maintenance" adventurers. I guess I had it coming!

Great White Shark Diving -South Africa

I was told you can't go to South Africa and NOT go Great White Shark Diving in Shark Alley off the coast of Cape Town. My camping tour with Oasis had just finished and many of the campers, myself included, decided to stay around the Cape Town area and check off some "tourist spots" from the list. One of the last group activities we arranged was the shark diving. If I remember correctly the whole day's event only cost around $100 US Dollars and it included a healthy breakfast, sandwich lunch on the boat and three dives in the cage.

I can't really explain to you the things that go through your mind as you are setting off for this type of adventure. I was doing the usual self-motivating speech "You have been zip-lining, rafting, and even skydiving, you can DO this thing!" The entire time the voice in the back of my head was saying "Yes, but all of these things did not include a SHARK!" Since I had already emailed home and told everyone I was going to do it (a secret strategy to stay tough) there was no turning back now.

After a nice breakfast and a few Dramamine for dessert I joined the crew on our shark searching vessel. The crew was very professional and helped us to better understand these dangerous creatures. The boat ride was cool, seeing the surrounding mountain views and gorgeous water. The problems came once we slowed down. This is the time they started "chumming" the waters by pouring in blood and fish guts to attract the sharks. This was not the problem; the problem was the boat was riding the waves and seriously rocking the boat. A few of the tourists added their own "chum" to the waters. Once again, Dramamine saves the day!

It took almost one hour before we saw the first shark come into the area. The excitement on the boat was electric. There were 15 of us and five people could fit in the cage at one time. We had somewhat successfully decided who would go when. Because of my bandages over my tropical lesions I was unable to wear a wetsuit, so I was able to get into the water with little preparation. As we were trying to get the first group in the water as fast as we could, I volunteered to be first. I was soon joined by four others and within minutes we were face-to-face with a nine foot Great White. The water was freezing, but I stayed quite warm with all of the adrenaline coursing through my veins; that and, I am a Northern Michigan girl and was raised around cold water! The cold water was the least of my worries - remember, I have open sores on my legs. Would the sharks be able to smell that? They were coming for us either way.

The crew uses a seal-shaped surf board of sorts to attract the shark, and once the shark sees the outline of a seal from underneath, it swims up and tries to eat it for dinner. As the shark is coming for the "seal" the crew pulls it toward the cage and the shark swims right for you. The point is to have your mask on and be underwater for this "attack," all the while trying not to let your hands or feet float outside the bars of the cage. Sound easy? It wasn't! I figured out a trick from the first round in the cage, if I stayed under water for the "attack," popped back up to grab more air, then dunked back under quickly, I would be just in time to watch the shark come back around under the boat. Watching these creatures swim is almost as amazing as watching them attack, almost!

Two highlights of the dive happened when I was not in the cage. The first was when, Sarah, a Canadian girl in the cage for the second round was so nervous when the shark came at the cage that she grabbed Ed, a British guy next to her and shoved him in front of her, toward the shark. You should have seen his face when he came up to get air. Shock! "Why did you do that?" "Well, I didn't want the shark to get me!" I am so glad she wasn't standing next to me in the cage! The second highlight came for the last group during the last pass of the "seal." This time, instead of the crew just pulling the seal toward the cage and then away from the cage, they lift the board out of the water, directly above the cage. This causes the shark to launch out of the water and land with his jaws wide open on the top of the cage. Great for pictures for the remaining ten of us on the boat, but imagine the view the guys in the cage received! Steve, who we lovingly called "Goober," was "lucky" enough to have the right corner and was within inches of the shark's teeth. When the shark tried to bite the seal, its teeth closed around the corner of the cage and got stuck for a moment. That is probably as close as anyone has gotten to a shark's mouth without losing a limb! One comforting thought: travel insurance doesn't cover this sort of activity!

San Pedro Prison - La Paz, Bolivia

I was told that Bolivia was the place to try *crazy* things, so I did! To me there is normal-crazy like skydiving or bungee jumping, and there is dangerous-crazy like trekking with Mountain Gorillas, and then there is just crazy-crazy. I would put bribing your way *into* a Bolivian prison in the last category. Have you ever seen the show "Locked -Up Abroad?" It is like that, but by choice.

Let me start the story with my arrival in La Paz: I had been separated from my little group I was traveling with and was now headed for the Wild Rover Hostel for a little reunion. Emily and Stewart were there waiting to share their stories from the past few days. They had their prison visit and Dangerous Road bike ride planned but I was happy to hear that each of their adventures was the day before I did mine. Even though I had heard it was possible to go inside the prison from other travelers, I was still a bit skeptical that it was possible, and more importantly, that it was safe. So, having Stewart go first and come back *alive* would help!

We bumped into a friend, Matt whom we had met in Quito, Ecuador and he and two friends were interested in going to San Pedro, too. We found two others from the hostel who were up for the adventure once they heard I was organizing a visit. I called the prison on the following morning; actually I called a prisoner's cell phone direct. A South African inmate, Stuart, answers. I tell him that myself and five others would love to *visit* him today. He says "How about 11a.m.? Good? See you then! By the way, please don't bring cameras, cell phones, passports or lots of money with you, but do bring us some cigarettes and candy for the kids." Yes, there are kids in the prison (more on that later). "Oh and bring 200 Boliviano each for the *visiting fee!*" That works out to be about $30 US Dollars. This was used to "convince the guards" that we were truly there for a visit.

Now, I know you might be wondering how I heard of this place and why am I crazy enough to *pay* to go inside a prison? I read the book Marching Powder about a British guy named Thomas who writes about his true accounts of being inside this Bolivian prison. I won't tell more, you will have to read it! The Bolivian government takes the stance that if someone has committed a crime and is being locked up for it, the criminal should have to take financial responsibility for incarceration not the government and the people. What a novel idea; one to think about for the United States for sure. The inmates have to "pay rent" for their cells, and since most homes in Bolivia are one income families with the men as the provider, when the man is jailed, the family comes with him. Their family can come and go as they please. The kids leave for school and return to San Pedro at night for their dinner. Meal options include pizza, take away, and dinner in one of the various restaurants inside, or their moms can grocery shop at the fresh market in "general population" and make dinner in the cell. So you can see the intrigue, can't you?

Around 10a.m., the six of us went to the corner shop and each bought a couple packs of cigarettes and cleaned them out of their supply of candy bars. We were all excited, yet nervous to visit our new friend, Stuart. We stood outside the prison gates trying to get up enough nerve to approach the guards. I thought we might have to do a quick game of "rock, paper, scissors" but since I made the original call, I spoke to the guard. We were told to come back at noon so we went to the nearest café. While we were there we met six other girls and three Irish guys that were waiting, too. This brought the total up to 15 *friends* for Stuart. There we sat with our packages of cigarettes and candy in hand! It was good to have others doing what we were doing, but then again, I was nervous that too many people at once and they might not let us in. Did you get that? I was nervous I might not get to go in, not that I might get arrested, or shot or who knows what! That is why this was a crazy-crazy idea.

At the gate they asked us for our passports, but we kindly told them that we do not have to show them our passports to visit an inmate. It felt a little awkward to tell a Bolivian prison guard his job. We got a stamp and one guard's signature on our wrist. I am still not sure what the point of that was.

Inside, it is like a little city with an entry courtyard that looks like a park, kids playing everywhere, men watching, well, mostly watching *us!* We were taken up a spiral staircase and into one of the *cells.* It looked more like an apartment than a cell complete with a bed, TV, bathroom, kitchen, and a table with lots of Gringos (white tourists) listening to stories of incarceration and how life is in this strange prison.

While we were inside, Stuart and two other prisoners were very hospitable and offered us all kinds of services. They took a tally sheet and went around the room, offering sodas, a meal of chicken and chips, cocaine, or beer and marijuana, but the last two are more difficult to get, and considered illegal, so they tried to convince you that all you needed was some cocaine and a Fanta. The cocaine is actually produced inside the prison and is very cheap, approximately $4 US for a gram. This was one of the most *surreal* experiences of my life. We spent the hour touring around the prison grounds, meeting ex-Colombian drug lords, playing games of pool with other inmates and then when it was time to go, Stuart showed us back to the front gates, thanked us for our *donations* and wished us all safe journeys. We heard a few weeks later that the guards were getting too much pressure from the Government regarding the large number of visitors to the prison, so they had to suspend the visits for awhile. Glad we *got in* when we did!

World's Most Dangerous Road - La Paz, Bolivia

So, as if the prison was not a crazy enough experience, I decided to sign up to Mountain Bike THE WORLD'S MOST DANGEROUS ROAD the very next day. It is called that because of the large amounts of deaths per year from cars and mountain bikes going over the 400 meter drop, that's 1,200 feet for you non-metrics! Why do this, you might ask? Why not? This has always been my motto: after all, you only live once. That is until you fly over the cliff on a bike!

Gravity Assisted was the company I used; they seemed to have the safest record, the best guides and the best bikes. I purchased the deluxe package ($75 US) and received all equipment, free t-shirt, lunch, water and snacks throughout the day. It is important to keep your sugar levels up to deal with the adrenaline rushes and crashes. Glad only my adrenaline crashed and not me!

My group was bussed up to La Cumbre, which is the start of the road. It is 15,400 feet above sea level. Once you are suited up, the guides suggest taking a practice ride around to get comfortable with the bike. It was so hard to breath at this altitude. Once around the parking lot and I was winded. The guides pulled us in from our training runs and had all of us stand in a circle to say a little pre-ride prayer. We went around the circle, taking turns pouring some special alcohol on the bike, the ground and in our mouths as an offering to Pacha Mama, Mother Earth, so she wouldn't take any of us as a *blood* sacrifice! Hey, if it helps! Whatever you say!

The road runs from La Paz to Coroico for 68 kilometers. The first 34 kilometers (20 miles) was all on paved roads, but all downhill so you could get going quite fast. I can still remember the smell of burning brake pads from my bike and everyone else's. Even without pedaling the bike would soar down the road at top speed. The scariest part is the second 34 kilometers, this was all on gravel. I was fine on pavement, but I have to admit that once we hit the *tester track* of gravel, I was scared. The little voice inside my head kept saying "YOU ARE NOT getting into the bus you little chicken, ride that bike" so I did. Although all the girls, including me, did get in the bus for the 8 kilometer ride UPhill, we were not risking it. We did not want to wear ourselves out *before* the scary bit! We had no problem letting the "boys be boys!" and race up the hill.

My only brush with death came when I blew out a tire. I was coming down around a curve, on a road that was as narrow as 3 meters (9 feet), in the left lane, closest to the edge, and was going fast. And to top it all off there was a little waterfall on the right hand side making the gravel wet and slippery. I had a good grip on both brakes when the tire popped, but it still scared the "you know what" out of me! There is one guide that leads the group and one that lags behind to pick up the stragglers, and behind him is the tour bus. I waited until they arrived and climbed on the bus. I guess I had to get on after all. I rode to the next check point where they changed the flat and I was back in business. The bus seemed scarier because I wasn't in control, and it was much wider and took up the entire road.

The guides stopped the group about 17 times throughout the day to told us about the next bit of road, sharing precautions and of course, telling us the stories about the people in the past who have died or had been seriously injured in that exact spot. "Just wonderful!" Hearing these stories did keep me *focused*! Some things to keep in mind if you ever find yourself on a steep, gravel road on a mountain bike: squeeze both brakes at the same time; grab just the front brake and you are over the handlebars and on your way down. Always get off your bike on the right hand side; why take the risk of losing your balance and falling over. And my favorite, as our guide warned, if you do go over, try to grab a tree or bush in the first 100 meters, because the rescue rope is only that long. Comforting! So, why do people sign up to ride this road? Pretty much so we can say we did and to get the t-shirt to remind people to ask us about it, so we can tell them how cool we are!

Paragliding in Colombia

Well, Adventure Mindi is back in full force. I tried to paraglide (jump off a cliff attached to a parachute) on my last trip in South Africa, but the wind conditions were not favorable...you need wind or you drop like a rock! Anyway, round two in Colombia. We tried the first day we arrived but the weather was not cooperating; too many rain clouds. We were lucky the next day. There were six of us from our hostel heading up the mountain by local bus, our ears popping all the way. "MAN, WE ARE HIGH UP!" was all we could keep saying. I promised myself: *No drama* today, just go up there get strapped in and JUMP! Well, I have a stronger power working against me sometimes and it is known as Mindi's Law, not Murphy's Law. It is never that simple!

There were four instructors and six of us, so the lightest got to go first, which left me and Stewart to wait as the others quickly got into their gear and took flight. I knew I should have kept up with my diet! Meanwhile back on the mountain, we are waiting for quite awhile because the others get a 30 minute flight and then land at the bottom of the mountain road. It takes at least one hour to get back to up us. In the two hours Stewart and I sat there I went from tough girl saying "No problems" to "WHAT THE HECK am I thinking?"and then, finally back to "Just get up here so I can go over the cliff already!"

So it's finally time! We signed forms saying: "Yadda, yadda, yadda, if we die it's our own fault!" The form said they gave us plenty of instruction to *not* die. This is more like how it went! "Habla espanol un pocco!" I only speak a little Spanish. "Oh, no problemo...you RUN, RUN, RUN y sit down!" Money well spent on training! But it was that simple, when the wind picked up the guide told me to run as fast as I could off the cliff and the wind carried us up right above where we were standing.

Instantly I was in awe. It's similar to the parachuting time after skydiving and we had over 30 minutes of it. The city of Medellin can only be appreciated from up here! The sun was out which made air warmer and our flight longer. The time was filled with twists and turns, and g-force on the cheeks. Amazing! All was wonderful until we were getting closer and closer to the buildings. I asked my guy "Donde?" "Where do we land?" He says "Aqui!" as he pointed directly below us. Oh great, in a field with horses and cows and little kids running alongside you as you fall - oh sorry, I mean land!

Just my luck the wind picks up as we are about to land and we go flying *into* the ground. The harness sent my pants so far up my butt, and we rolled over landing face first with my instructor on top of me. He kept saying "Bueno, Bueno!" Good, Good! Not so much! "Como si dice wedgy" which means "how do you say wedgy" in Espanol? OUCH! I never got the answer!

Fly By Wire – New Zealand

After my experience with the Gorge Swing in Zambia, I had decided that when I hit New Zealand I *wouldn't* be bungee jumping. It was hard enough to throw myself off a cliff "backwards" there would be no way I would be able to jump "head first." But, who goes to Queenstown and doesn't partake in some sort of adventure? Not me! So, I look through all the brochures and find one that is crazy and unique - Fly By Wire. It is a personal aircraft that you are strapped into on your stomach and hoisted into the air by a wire that cranks you to the top of a valley. Once you are as high as the apparatus will take you, it is now expected that you will release yourself from the hook, thus starting the motor. You have to steer yourself around the valley in big turns. They say it is like flying a jet fighter.

Sound exciting? There were three of us there that day, me and two guys. The instructor takes you through a few basic operating procedures and explains that if you do not release the "hook" at the exact moment you reach the top, then the motor will not start and you will just drop down, back to where you started. No ride and you lose your money! Okay, so no pressure! If you do remember to release on time, then you are going to be soaring around the canyon. The rider can control the speed of the ride with an accelerator similar to one on a motorcycle.

If you let go, the motor will stop. I was so scared that because I was nervous I would end up "gunning" it and go too fast. If you felt out of control or wanted to stop the ride, there was an "emergency stop" button in the center of the steering console. This, of course, would require you to let go with one hand to PUSH that button! Not a chance!

I was too chicken to go first; I wanted to see someone else in action. You know, to gauge their speed, and learn from their mistakes. Plus, I didn't know these guys; I could pretend I was a "wussy-girl." Oh wait, I sort of am! The ride with the motor gives you about five or six turns around the canyon. In order to make sure you get the *best* ride, the instructor is down below with large signs, telling you to "speed up," "slow down," "turn more to your right" and they throw in the occasional sign reminding you, "smile, remember you are having FUN!" Yeah, you really have time to read a sign when you are ZOOMING around hundreds of feet above the ground!

After about five minutes the motor cuts out and you use the momentum to fly around in the quiet valley, taking in the view. This is the pay dirt. What an amazing feeling. It was quite cool that day, so there was extreme cold, mixed with the strong winds whistling in your ears added to the excitement and adrenaline coursing through your body, and it all combines to a *rush* like no other. This must be what it is like to be a bird, flying through the air, well, minus the crank, hook and motor.

Sand Boarding - Peru

This experience wasn't so much of a dangerous one, as it was a unique experience. My friend Christa and I had been in Central and South America for over three months now and were working our way south through Peru to get to the culmination of my journey, Machu Picchu. We were still traveling with Stewart and Emily, the crazy Brits we met in Panama and they had a suggestion for a place off the path a bit. We were on schedule, so when Stewart explained Huacachina as an oasis in the desert, where you could swim, climb the sand dunes and catch amazing sunsets, I WAS IN! He failed to mention probably the coolest thing you could do there, which was a dune-buggy ride to go sand boarding. Sand boarding is like snowboarding but on sand!

I have done some downhill skiing in my day, but never did get the hang of having both feet strapped together. But, as always, I was up for a challenge, or so I thought! This is one of the many times I wished my brother was with me. He had always been great at skateboarding and snowboarding and I know he would have loved it. The ride through the desert was worth the price of the tour alone. I had been to Peru many times before with work and had never realized that it had such diverse landscape. Dunes, as far as the eye could see, and big ones, too. When we pulled up to the first "hill," the starter hill, I had second thoughts. The guide was assuring me that the sand is soft and all would be fine as long as I kept my mouth shut. Wait, was he trying to tell me something?

I waxed up my board, strapped in and…that was it. Fell within the first two feet. I gave it a go many times that day and honestly all I ended up fulfilling was "my underwears with sand!" Probably the best part, and no skill required, was the last hill. This was the largest by far and was usually conquered on the stomach, like the sledding I use to do as a child in Michigan, but on snow not sand. No need for wax on the board for this one, momentum alone was enough. Flying down that hill with sand flying in my eyes, ears and nose, I remember thinking, just another day in paradise. "Livin' the Life" as we travelers always say!

Fox Glacier Hike - New Zealand

I always enjoy when adventures include something of nature, like canyoning in the rocks and caves of Turkey. So when I arrived at Fox Glacier in New Zealand, I was ready for a glacier hike. I had done something similar in Norway on a glacier hike at Svartisen Glacier, but that was more hike than glacier. We were made to hike a long path and up many stairs. I remember I was as hung over as I had ever been in my life. This hike was part of a Contiki tour and we had a "cocktail party night" the night before in Mo I Rana, where we mixed all the alcohol everyone had in a cooler and drank from that! Ouch!

Not for Fox Glacier, this one was a serious hike on the ice with professional guides and equipment. The hostel we were staying at as part of my Stray pass was nice and cozy and had a self-catering kitchen, so I ate a nice dinner and then went to bed early, ready for my ice adventure the next day. We met at the tourist agency and check point to receive our "warm" gear and instruction on the day's events. We had an option of a full day hike or a half day hike. I look at these dilemmas in a few ways, one - what else will I see on the second half of the hike that is so different it is worth paying two times the price? Answer: more ice! Okay, two - what other things could I do in this area if I save some money on this trek? Answer: jet boating, cool! And three, do I really like being cold and wet so much that I would sign up for eight or more hours of hiking in sub-zero weather? Answer: you guessed it! So, half day it is!

As I was sitting there putting on my company issued boots, that were soaking wet already, by the way, I am already patting myself on the back for only committing to the half day trek. We had a good 40 minute walk just to get to the glacier. Squish, Squish, Squish, my boots were holding water. Once we arrived at the base of the glacier we were given talons (spikes to add to our boots to help with our footing on the ice). I felt like a real adventurer now. I was also quoting from Napoleon Dynamite: "Do the chickens have large talons?" No, but we do!

Our guide, AJ, was at the front of the group chipping away ice steps as we walked. This path is the one they use every day, but with the weather, wind and water always flowing, the path gets filled back in each day. It made me feel like I was the first to step there, how exciting!

For sure this is one of those places in the world you just have to see for yourself. The ice formations are spectacular and a simple camera does it no justice. I took a few nice photos, but will never forget being in awe of the colors and the sheer size of this act of Mother Nature! I will also never forget the feeling I had once we returned to the agency and I peeled off my sopping wet socks and drank a nice cup of steaming hot cocoa! Well deserved.

Switch Back Train Ride - Riobamba, Ecuador

This one was not really a sport as much as it was an adventure. There is an awesome train ride from Riobamba to Alausi near the mountain called Nariz del Diablo, Spanish for "devil's nose." The draw for this train ride, other than the spectacular views of the mountain terrain, was that you were able to ride on top of the train. The problem was that we had heard a few Japanese tourists had ridden on top a few weeks before and were beheaded because they stood to take a picture and there were downed power lines across the track. The government stopped the trains and was not allowing tourists to ride at that point. We wanted to take the chance and headed there anyway.

Rumor on the gringo trail said the train started running two days before we arrived. Although now they run these makeshift bus-trains, more like buses on train wheels. We didn't think we were going to be able do it at all so we were thankful for the chance to see this part of

Ecuador and ride on top of the train. It was a four hour ride on an old switch back train track. Tourists did get to ride one way on top and one way inside. We were smart and picked the right side on the way up and had the best views of the valley. On the way back, we were seated inside with the windows facing the steep mountain side; perfect time to take a nap. I loved this location because it is one of those unique places around the world. Not just another church, temple, or beach. After awhile they all blend together. As the saying goes in Europe- "ABC - Another Bloody Church." I have even stopped taking pictures of most of the churches because by the time I get home I can't remember the names of them anyway! But, I will remember the Nariz del Diablo ride for a long time!

Three Hour Tour - Sailing from Panama to Colombia via San Blas Islands

I know that sailing isn't usually considered an adventure sport, but once you read this story, you will probably agree that it contained an element of danger at a few points along the way! One of the travel adventures that many backpackers have while traveling through Panama is "getting off the road for a bit" and actually hitting the water by sailing from Panama to Colombia through the gorgeous San Blas Islands. The planning for this adventure began earlier in the month at Bocos del Toro, a group of islands just outside Panama City. We were staying at one of my favorite hostels - Aqua Lounge. Christa and I meet Emily and Stewart first and they were "extra" friendly trying to get to know us. We didn't realize right away that this was part of the 'not-so-secret' plan Stewart had to find their sailing partners before they hit Panama City.

The common thing to do is, arrive in Panama City, book into one of the three main hostels for two or three nights and wait; meet people, review the listings the boat captains post, ask questions, talk to other "sailors" and try to find people you *actually* want to spend the next four or five days with, in close quarters. Well, Stewart saved us the trouble of finding at least two-thirds of our boat. We heard that most boats take six people plus the captain and one crew member. Christa and I were really excited to know that these two crazy-fun Brits would be along with us. Did I mention that Emily lived in Chile for a stint and speaks fluent Spanish, and Stewart lived in Spain since he was 15? Yeah, talk about luck!

So, we settled into the hostel and the comforts of a big city: American looking supermarkets, air-con shopping malls, cinemas (in English), Wendy's and best of all, a place to do all of our stinky laundry. We met an Argentinean couple that would be the final piece to the sailing puzzle...so we thought! The hostel owner who claimed to know our captain (or know of him) told us that he had a boat with three cabins. Perfect fit, we thought! He then told us that a French couple was also joining the ranks. I have always been good at math and that "story problem" didn't add up: 3 cabins x 2 per cabin = 6 people: the French couple = 8. The hostel owner says not to worry because most of the time people are fighting to sleep out on deck under the stars, anyway. Oh, how exciting!

The plan on departure day was to head to Portobello to catch up with our El Capitan, Javier and his wife Esperanza, we were now ten people! Oh, and sorry to say one of the three cabins is for the captain and his wife. So, for those of you following the statistical side of this story, we are now eight people rotating through two cabins. As we are sitting there enjoying the boat, mapping out where we would sleep (rotate through the two cabins every other night), a ninth person shows up: Gerson, a Mexican guy! This will be the first of many times that the crew thought of mutiny on the Bounty, or mutiny on the Twilla. I tried to tell everyone not to be mean to him. It was not *his* fault our captain was greedy! Silly us, thinking that at $300 a person we might have paid for some comfort. This was not looking like a reality.

This is where the three hour tour line from Gilligan's Island started, "now sit right back and I will tell a tale, a tale of a tiny ship" only Gilligan's ship only had seven people on it and we had 11! "AHHHHHH!"

We left in the morning and everything on this trip was at an *island* pace so we had to learn early on to relax - "tranquillo" in Spanish. When it was uttered by our captain it made us all become anything but! Everyone was feeling a bit seasick and these were "supposed" to be the calm seas so we were all nervous about our next few days at sea, to say the least. El Capitan decided to give us a "free" night by stopping in Isla Grande overnight. We were happy for an anchored ship and the chance to swim and enjoy the sun! Emily and I were the smart ones that were popping Dramamine like candy. Sure, I fell asleep reading my book every time, but no puking over the side of the boat for me! Marina, the French girl, did not escape this fate, nor did Christa, who could hardly lift her head for half the journey.

The next morning we set sail for another island and then learned that we needed more water and that it wouldn't arrive until 5p.m.! Our fearless leader, El Capitan sends us to a Kuna Island so we could spend another day swimming and playing around a bit. Many were not happy to have the extra time but I had decided at this point to make the most of it. For crying out loud, we are in the middle of 400 islands with white sand beaches, hot sun and great water to swim in! "Relax...tranquillo!" When I am having a "bad travel day" I try to remind myself that some poor souls are waking up and getting ready to go to work! That always helps me to snap out of it! So, my attitude changed, but not everyone saw the beauty of it!

As part of the "fun" of this type of adventure, we were to help with the preparing of meals. The first few of us in the galley realized the supply of fresh water and more importantly, food was scarce! There might not be enough food on the boat for these "free" days El Capitan was adding, especially since Christa and I don't eat fish. If you happened to be a fish lover then the fresh tuna and barracuda that we caught everyday off the running lines from the back of the boat would have been heaven for you, but not for us!

We get to our next port of call - immigration. Because we were traveling from Panama to Colombia via water, it was important that we get stamped out so we can enter Colombia with no issues (or, a fact that later dawned on us, get sent back in the direction in whence we came). In true Gilligan's Island form, the immigration office was closed until Tuesday. Now is the time to tell you that it was only Friday. Please start humming the "Three Hour Tour Song" now!

The thing that I have learned after many mishaps on the road is that if I take a deep breath and focus on the positive then things will work out. Some times are harder than others to remember this. We got a signed document from a man who was probably only the grounds keeper of Immigration Island. The note said that the office was closed when we stopped and we couldn't get a stamp. Hoping that this was good enough, we set sail once again.

We spent another entire day at our own deserted island. It was so tiny; it only took about four minutes to walk all the way around. We spent the day swimming back and forth to our boat, snorkeling, eating fresh coconuts from the trees thanks to our very own Gilligan (Gerson). I even snorkeled. I have this insane fear of things touching me in the water and really don't like fish not only to eat but I also don't want to share the water with them either. With Stewart's power of persuasion and my crazy deal with myself to push myself every day, I got in with a mask on. He talked me into checking out this massive black spot in the water. "Are you kidding me?" There must have been over 100,000,000 little minnows! It was so amazing because if you moved your hand they would all swim away in all directions and then regroup. I can't believe I did it!

After the immigration delay, Captain decided it was too late to begin our two day sail so he said we could have *another* "free" day. THREE HOUR TOUR! At this point we were even starting to rewrite the words to Gilligan's theme song to fit our group and calling out who we wanted to be. Christa wanted Ginger, the movie star, so I guess I could be Mary-Ann; by default. I wasn't going to be Mrs. Howell. Gerson had won the Gilligan name because he could climb coconut trees and filet fresh fish and was totally "happy" about all that was happening to us!

So, this five day sail is already four days and we still have a two day sail ahead of us. We are down to a few eggs, canned tuna and lots of noodles. No need to add salt to the water for boiling because we were using sea water to save the fresh water for showers and drinking. Is that sanitary? I am still trying to convince the girls not to shower in case we get any more "free" days; we will have no water to drink. Meanwhile, hidden in my pack is a gallon of emergency water that everyone laughed at me for lugging through two bus rides and a crazy boat ride. I also have a packet of crisps, a few Oreo snack packs and a wheel of Laughing Cow Cheese. Who's laughing now? To make matters worse, the refrigerator was broken so everyone was eating the fresh food as fast as they could so it wouldn't spoil - not necessarily a good plan in my opinion.

With all that was going wrong Stewart came up with a very wise use of one of our empty wine bottles. He decide to send a "message in a bottle" and write in English and Spanish our names, emails and a short story of how we "hoped" to be in Cartagena and when. We said a little prayer and sent it floating away in the obvious sludge current. Yes, even in the middle of nowhere, not a sliver of land in sight, and we were floating by streams of plastic bottles and candy wrappers. Maybe adding a glass bottle to the mess wasn't the *green* approach, but we were talking about survival here!

So on to the rough seas we go, but here I must mention my highlights because there were many: catching fresh fish with the line off the back - no need to pay extra for a deep sea fishing excursion; seeing sea turtles, dodging flying fish; and having dolphins swimming right by our boat; eating fresh coconuts; and watching the neon algae light up at night when the water was disturbed. Not such a rough life after all, hey?

Our two days of sailing had turned into three as the winds died down on the last day and the engine cut out. Oh, the cast and crew were not happy sailors now! I have to secretly admit, I was loving the amazing tan I was getting and didn't mind the sailing days, maybe because I was so doped up on Dramamine; but now even that supply was running low. Our last few hours were the worst of the trip. Our big sail ripped and we were using only the small front one for hours (THREE HOUR TOUR!) This meant we switched the direction the boat tilted every ten minutes. Here Christa and I thought we were fortunate to have one of the cabins for the last night. We had to lie sideways, switching where our heads were every few minutes or we would be permanently spooning.

We could see the glow of Cartagena at about 2 o' clock in the morning. No need to get excited as with the small sail and light winds we didn't get to port until after 10a.m.! Okay, I promise this will be the last time I will say it but....THREE HOUR TOUR! Christa actually kissed the ground once we disembarked.

We were safe and sound in the city and looking forward to our South American Chapter. After a few days of eating in restaurants and sleeping in beds that were actually horizontal not vertical, I have decided that Gilligan did have it all figured out: island life does take time to get adjusted to, but worth it in the end! I have realized that when I look back on these types of adventures after a bit of time has passed, it always makes me wish I was right back in it again, kind of! I will sail this part of the world again someday, but to be sure it won't be on the Twilla!

Update on Message in a Bottle: Amazingly enough, the bottle found its way to a little town north of our port. The kids that found it sent Stewart a quick email to be sure that we had arrived to our destination. Wonder if they ever would have called the Coast Guard? Glad we didn't have to test it!

Secret to: Massages Around the World

THROUGHOUT MY TRAVELS I have probably had just as many experiences with massages as I have with animals and adventure sports combined. Treating myself to a massage is one of my guilty pleasures and one of the only reasons I will allow myself to "overlook" going over budget.

I don't set out to get a massage with the thought of it being anything other than a nice, relaxing massage to ease the tension in my poor, tired backpacker body; however, because of Mindi's Law; this is usually not the case. This is probably because the idea of privacy and professionalism is very different in American than anywhere else I have traveled. In America, we are fully covered with a full-size sheet that is draped and moved as the masseuse changes from leg to leg or from front to back. I can't even remember a time in any of my travel massages that I was even given a towel, let alone a sheet. Oh, I take that back, I had a massage in Brazil in my hotel room and after I told her I was cold she went into my bathroom and grabbed the facecloth. Okay, so now one breast was warm! At home, we are left alone in the room to undress and get under the covers to wait for our massage to begin; everywhere else, it is normal for them to stay in the room and set up for the massage.

After a few visits to the topless beaches in Europe, I started to get a little more comfortable just "stripping off." Next was to get used to having my breast and buttocks massaged. Kind of gives the term "full" body massage a whole new meaning. After about three minutes of the massage, I don't seem to care about anything other than trying to relax and have a great massage.

Because techniques are so different all around the world, it is always a little gamble as to what will happen to you "on the table." As the person begins to massage my left side, I think to myself: "Oh, this feels good! Cool, I still have the other side to go." But the opposite is also true if the massage is not feeling so good, I think: "Oh no, I still have the other side to go!"

In the beginning the massage experiences were very similar to a "Swedish" style massage, but as I branched out more in my travels, the styles became that much more "unique." When I was traveling through Vietnam I got a bit of a surprise when I felt the woman crawling on the table on top of me. I tried to reason with myself and came to the conclusion that this was done to give her better "leverage", just as the thought was crossing my mind, she *stands* on top of me. I had to open my eyes for this one! She was actually holding on to two parallel bars on the ceiling. I later found out this was called A-shiatsu, and her style was quite normal. Guess I missed that part of the briefing!

Just as I have a rule to try one of the local beers of each country, I have also come up with a rule that if the country has their own "traditional" massage technique, and even if the price is a bit high, I have to partake. I have had traditional Thai, Balinese, and Malaysian massages. I couldn't really tell you the difference between the three other than in the Thai massage you are given little pajama type clothes to wear, and they do a lot more stretching than massaging.

In Cuzco Peru, I signed up for an *Inca* massage after my nine hour trek around Machu Picchu. I could barely walk and was hoping that Inca just referred to the location rather than a technique. I just wanted an "old-fashioned deep tissue" massage. The massage took place in a dark room with about six or seven candles placed on posts and shelves around the room. I have a pretty crazy imagination so I started to envision that she might start by performing some ancient Incan ritual involving the candles. I was happy to find out they were only for ambiance - or were they for warmth? Cuzco is 11,217 ft above sea level and it was pretty cold in there. The lady did an amazing job and I actually booked a second one the next day as I knew I would be feeling worse, not better. Good thing the massages were only $7 for one hour.

Because many massages are done right on the beach, or in a little hut, they are offered at rock-bottom prices. I have paid as little as $3 for an hour massage on a beach in Cambodia. All it cost my lady was her time, so she was happy to have the money to support her family. I guess she could have given me a horrible massage and I would have still been okay with it, because I was getting a massage for the price of a coke and candy bar; but she didn't. She really made sure all of my muscles were thoroughly worked on and even gave me my favorite "ear massage." Some of the best massages I have had were on the beach on a musty old cushion with some sand mixed in!

One of the most unique massages was in Nicaragua. Christa and I were in Granada for a few days and were definitely ready for a massage after all of the bus rides we had suffered through, so we were on the lookout for a massage parlor. We went into a little coffee shop to investigate what pastries they had on selection and found ourselves a great chocolate cake and an interesting massage technique. The Seeing Hands Organization was offering massages by blind masseuses. The organization has helped train the sight impaired to give massages and learn English to communicate with tourists. This program has created a livelihood for the blind, who might otherwise not be able to find work to support themselves or their families. Not only did we have a wonderful massage, but we felt happy to have been able to support this amazing organization. I have since come across a few of these organizations on my travels and am always excited to hand over my massage dollars to such a great cause!

I have had some otherwise normal massages that have turned into memorable ones mainly because the girl doing my massage felt the need to answer her mobile phone, yell at her little brother and talk non-stop to the other girl that was giving my friend David a massage. I almost had a "moment" and then remembered I was in China and I was getting a $6 foot massage. At least we didn't know what they were saying, and after a while, we just tried to pretend it wasn't annoying. After all, in my opinion the best foot massages in the world are given in China.

The most genius massage location is at the airport! What a better way to spend your layover than in a massage chair! I have frequented the spa at Detroit Metro throughout my travels, but enjoyed my two hour spa package at the Kuala Lumpur International Airport the most. They even have free massage chairs that you can use. When you enter the massage chair room you tell them what time you need to be leaving for your flight and they are sure to wake you if you happen to fall asleep.

Genius! Thailand and Philippines are also great places to get a massage at the airport, and for cheap.

I would like to think I could be considered an expert on what makes a great massage. Let me share with you a few of the features that make a quality experience in my book: I like a darker room; if it is too light, it takes away from being able to relax; a proper massage table with a place for your face is helpful, but as I mentioned before some of my favorite massages were on the beach. (Note: you can dig out a little space in the sand for your face and put your sarong over it!) Pressure, and lots of it! I would rather have to tell someone to "go softer" than to have someone who does not have the strength to "really get in there." No massage should ever be considered over if I haven't had my hands, feet and head massaged! I never care if it is lotion, oil or dry, as long as it feels good.

I have recently found my favorite style of massage: "couples!" My husband and I have lived in South East Asia together for almost a year if you combine our time in Cambodia with the time in Malaysia, and we loved to get massages as part of "date night." I think I have literally seen it all in the massage department, so now when I get a massage, I am happy if I don't feel any *pain* and there are no *awkward* moments!

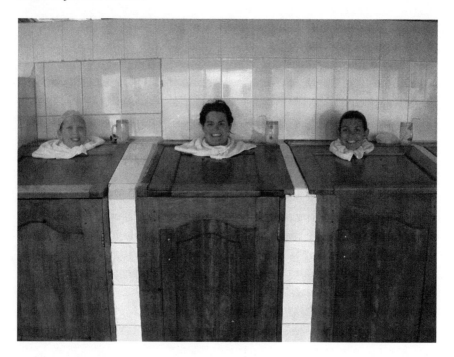

Spa Day in Baños, Ecuador

We arrived in Baños after a four hour bus journey, nervously holding our day packs in our laps the entire time as Emily and Stewart had emailed us that Emily had her camera lens stolen from her pack on the floor in front of her a few days before. Someone had cut open Emily's pack with a knife. Emily said she even felt the bag move under the seat, but thought the guy ahead of her had just kicked it.

The main event for Baños was the 20 kilometers *downhill* bike ride to visit 15 waterfalls. Two of my favorite things: waterfalls and downhill! The ride was over four hours long because you could stop and enjoy various activities along the way. One of the waterfalls was on the opposite side of the river and it was necessary to take a cable car across. We finished the ride in Puyo, had lunch and threw our bikes on a local bus to ride back up to Baños. The buses are designed for multiple bikes as this is a common tourist attraction. I know the ride was mostly all downhill but it was still quite a workout, and coupled with the stressful bus ride the day before; we were ready to relax. This turned out to be easier said than done.

Once we were settled into our hostel, we started to look for a place to get a massage. We found a brochure at the front desk that looked interesting, so we called to see if we needed an appointment for *"the unique spa experience!"* No appointments were necessary - just head on out! A $1.25 cab ride split between the three of us and we were there. The ladies that work at the spa explained to us all of the options: mud bath, steam cabin, massage, and an herbal *detox*. They even offered us enemas - we will give that one a miss, yuck!

We decided to do the combination mud bath, steam cabin and massage, and all for under $30. We thought we would just do those three things, and then head back to the hostel for a nice nap. We were at the spa for *five hours* total! Before we could even think massage, we were told the experience starts with "spiritual cleansing." Here are the five steps to a clean spirit:

1. Take your shoes off and walk across the car park full of sharp rocks to a place they called PURGATORY. Walk around the fire pit three times thinking of all the bad you have done in your life.

2. Walk through a flower garden to a house (the House of Screams) where you climb to the top of a hill and scream out all of the stress from things people have done to you. Walk down a grassy path (as you are closer to forgiveness, the path is softer - coincidence, I think not!)

3. Walk further to another screaming point, where you cleanse yourself of all the bad you have done to others.

4. Reflection Wall - stand there and hold hands, ask for forgiveness while looking into each other's eyes. Christa decided to scream here too just for good measure. We think she has found her calling as a voice-over in horror films.

5. Walk down a long grassy path, until you are back at the car park; yes, over the same rocks. When you return to the spa you must get on your hands and knees and crawl around the rose bush three times, all the while thinking of your *new* path in life! I think all I gained was grass stains on the knees of my pants. WOW! So when do I get this massage? Soon!

We now changed into our bathing suits and were sent to the "MUD

ROOM." This is where you apply a mud that helps to maintain your youth. They were very strict that you apply only with your right hand; you could have no help from others and could only use your left hand to do your right arm. This was an interesting process. So how did we spend the time drying you ask? *Merengue*! Yes, a dance video. We did an aerobics tape, covered in mud in our swim suits while looking out over the beautiful mountains. I moved a lot just so the mud would dry faster. What a sight we must have been!

Next, we were instructed to shower off and head to the steam room. Our treatment included 40 minutes in a steam cabin. They were actually individual steam rooms that your head sticks out of. The amount of steam is controlled by using a little lever inside the box and they feed you water, more of a tea color with floaties, through a straw because you can't use your hands. Then, just when I started to warm up, they opened the box and tossed freezing cold water all over me. Sorry, but I am ready for that massage now!

This goes on for a while, then they ask us to sit in a tub of freezing water and then rush us back into the steam cabin, throw more cold water, add more steam, and finally it ends! The three of us tried not to laugh too much. The spa workers were so serious about "the process," but all we could do was see how over-dramatic they were being. We were moved to a rocky area where we stood and got hosed off. I forgot to mention that all directions all day have been given to us in Spanish! Good thing we had Emily! T he Spanish course I took in Quito didn't cover this situation. Finally, we were told to dress in our robes and go to the SHHHHH section, literally signs above the doors say SHHHHH! We all laid down on the massage tables, surprisingly, in a really nice room. Okay, now maybe after all of this, it will be worth it. My body feels like dead weight and I prepared for the massage of a lifetime, or not!

Now, nothing crazy happened like some of my past experiences, just a decent massage finished off with a hot rock treatment, but kind of anti-climactic really. We all just laid there laughing because they left us alone all oiled up with hot rocks on our backs and legs. My rocks were all sliding off and they took my pillow away so my neck was in a knot! No worries - when you are finished you get more brown water and some fruit! As we were waiting for our taxi the receptionist gave each of us a dab of smelly stuff under our noses and we were told to breathe in and out three times. More dramatics! All in all, it was a really crazy idea of relaxing, but such a fun *girls' spa day*. We laughed about it for weeks after.

The Art of Threading: No, not a guide on needlepoint... much worse!

First of all, I have to tell you what a typical day on the beaches of Cambodia looks like: Sihanoukville has become tourist-central. The beaches are lined with bars and restaurants that all look the same from the front. If you are smart you can save 50 cents by checking all the menus; otherwise, just pick a place because they all offer the same menu! They all have nice beach chairs with cushions and umbrellas. In some countries you would pay to rent them for the day, but not here because they know if they get tourists to sit there for the entire day, they will earn more than by charging a $3 rental fee. Plus, it makes a budget-traveler like me feel like I am getting something for *free*. Although, a beach day in Cambodia is definitely not *free!* On average, I spent about $20 a day while on the beach and here is why...

The number of chairs far outnumbers the tourists, so it is some guy's job at each restaurant/bar to get you to sit in *his* chairs. Once he has you hooked, he waits to see if you really sit down. Be careful, all the chairs/cushions look the same but there is an imaginary line in the sand for each restaurant and the guy will tell you for sure if you have picked his competition's chair and move you back to his restaurant...two feet away! Let the fun begin! There are women/children wandering the beach offering (selling) a selection of the normal fresh fruit, bracelets, and various seafood cooked while you wait. There are also people offering the creature comforts: massage, manicures, pedicures, and threading!

My favorite part of these interactions is the sales techniques the girls use. Let's be honest, there is no sense getting upset about them approaching because they will, over and over again, and to be fair, we have created this environment as tourists, but that is a whole other chapter. I have taken marketing classes at university and at the Master's level; my professors and fellow students knew nothing of how to get the "gringo" to buy something they had no interest in! Things you don't need, want or would even have for free are offered, and the girls somehow persuade you, and you buy it. Well, I buy it!

You can start out by being 'hard-nosed', saying to yourself, "NO! I don't need any of this", but it is a secret society. They wear you down. They act like they are in competition: "You buy from me, promise, later? If you buy, you buy only from me." Kind of looking at you like there will be some super *hex* on you if they find out you bought from someone else! Heaven forbid you forget which 14 year old Cambodian girl you pinky swore to buy fresh fruit from. The fun begins when you think you have the right girl and buy the over-priced pineapple, mango, and melon combo only to find out you were wrong, because the original girl comes back and lets you have it and I don't mean let you have the fruit for free! How can you feel guilty when you only bought the damn fruit to be nice?!

The ladies that do the manicures, pedicures and massages have various notable techniques too. Some approach simply asking: "Massage today or change color of nails?" However, the most amusing to me were the ones that walk up, look at your feet (at least mine) and say "WOW! You have lots of dead skin, feet real bad, I fix for you!" Yes, I am a pedicurist's dream...or nightmare but two days later my feet look the same again. So I will save my money for macramé shrimp that the girl assures me "she" made herself. It is pink! I am sure my niece will love it - $1! The point of this story: you get worn down, worked over and they play you. Basically, they do their job! They are professionals!

I read about this threading thing in the Cambodian guidebook and have seen other women on the beach having it done. Not really sure why women must put themselves through all of this; maybe it is because they have all been worn down too. My lady's approach was: "Lady, do you have a boyfriend?" Oh, how sweet! How did she know I wasn't feeling good and was missing my boyfriend? It was so sweet of her to ask. "Yes, yes, I do!" "Where is he?" Opening dialogue non-related, then ZAP! "He would like you to have smooth legs, no?" Surprise, surprise, she can help. Just so happens she has a long piece of thread right here! Only $10 to have each hair individually ripped from its root. Oh, and it takes one hour at least. "You have lots of hairs, lady." "They are thick; it hurts more because you shave!" How come I didn't see all the other women on the beach wincing in pain? Some ladies even had their armpits done. OUCH! Still not the end of the story: now one of the ladies has you "prisoner" on your bed for at least an hour; send out the "wounded deer" signal! "We have trapped tourist! Approach! Approach!" You think maybe you've warded them all off, but by finally caving and getting something done by one of them, they all know YOU ARE A SUCKER with US Dollars and they want their share.

As I laid there trying to pretend this didn't hurt anymore than getting my various tattoos, young girls would approach and say "Oh, it hurts doesn't it? Well, if you talk to me it will hurt less!" What they really mean is "if you talk to me and let me make you a bracelet, you will make me very happy!" Older ladies approach and say "Oh, lady, it hurts? Maybe I give you massage while she do that, then you no think of pain." What I want to know is, if everyone on this bloody beach knew IT HURTS, why didn't that make it into the sales pitch?

A half hour later, my left leg feels like a war zone for defeated leg hairs and I have bought two bracelets, one macramé shrimp, more fresh fruit and was almost talked into a manicure from a lady boy and I am thinking to myself "And that is only the *first* leg...one more to go!" Oh, the things we do as tourists!

Fish Massage- Batu Ferringhi, Malaysia

One of the strangest massage experiences I have ever had was when I met my friend Anna in Penang, Malaysia. We stayed in Batu Ferringhi which means Foreigners Beach, named for the hippies that used to hang out there. It was a quiet little beach town with lots of cafes and a cool little street market. There were no major plans for our "girls' beach weekend" other than to get some sun and a massage. We had enjoyed the sun that afternoon; me a bit too much so I was lobster red and I couldn't imagine having a typical massage. We had seen advertisements for a "fish massage" and thought it sounded interesting. Boy, was it ever! The salon had six pools out back filled with various sized fish. The objective was to soak your feet in the first pool with the smaller fish, allowing them to *nibble* the dead skin from your feet, then move up to the larger fish. Anna was braver than I, sticking her feet straight in, but I had to take mine out several times because it really felt strange. They suggested we try our hands as well. I just kept thinking, "anything for the story." I am happy to say, "been there, done that, no need for repeating!"

Turkish Bath House

This is the group email that I sent out just moments after returning to my youth hostel in Istanbul from one of the craziest "massage" going experiences I have ever had!

Subject: Turkish Bath House
October 15ᵗʰ, 2006
This one just couldn't wait!
I am in Istanbul for a few days before my 35 day Middle East Camping Tour of Turkey, Syria, Jordan and Egypt. I thought it would be nice to get a few of the big sights taken care of before the tour. I visited the Blue Mosque and the Souks (for shopping) but I knew that one way to start a long camping tour would be to get a massage. Many of you know that I enjoy a really good massage and I try out the techniques around the world.

I have had a Japanese woman give me a Shiatsu style massage in Brazil. I have had "sand massages" on the beaches of Greece, Colombia and Vietnam. I have had a Hungarian massage in Budapest, a psychic massage in Brazil, and I have even had the Chinese foot massage where they make music by beating on your legs and feet, so naturally I thought I had seen it all.

I arranged the massage from my hostel because they pay for the taxi and assure that I arrive at the right bath house. One side is for females and the other for males. I assumed this would be the case, especially in a Muslim country.

I was a little hesitant because I had talked to an Australian girl in my hostel that had gone a few days before and she said "it is fine as long as you don't have any hang-ups about being naked! No need to bring your swimsuit!" Okay, here we go! At the bathhouse, I was asked by the woman I was assigned to, through a hand motion, to strip off. Everything! I know this because she was standing there almost naked herself, only wearing a pair of black panties. She tugged at hers and then looked at me and said "NO!"

The rest is a blur. I remember getting my towel, having her rinse me off with water from a basin, and lying down on a cold marble slab in the middle of the bath house. Did I mention

I was completely naked? The woman was pouring water and soap all over me exfoliating me with a big mitt, and when I say exfoliate, I mean it. My skin was coming off all over the place! I even have bruises already. I was sliding all over the marble slab and my inability to hold still was making her very angry so she was rubbing extra hard to prove she was the boss.

The "not-so-relaxing" part was over and now it was time to get my hair washed. She sat me down on a stool and washed my hair for me and gave me a head massage. I started thinking about being a kid and having my Mom or my Grandma wash my hair for me and remembered how good it felt. What a great memory. Ahhhh! Now, I flash forward to the present. I am in a musty old bath house in Istanbul getting my hair ripped out by an 80 year old woman, in just her knickers! I had to keep one eye open the entire time in this grimy place because I had seen a few cockroaches the size of small mice running around. It is all about the "experience," right?

Anyway, it was time to move on to the sauna. I was in there for what seemed like forever and I was waiting for my crazy lady to come and tell me my time was up, but she never came back! I was afraid to go out and ask if I could be done because I had already made her mad a few times by not holding still, or by opening my eyes! After another 15 minutes, red faced and dehydrated I decided to leave anyway. She was out in the lobby, fully dressed and making her lunch on some type of portable gas cooker. Needless to say, I don't think she was going to come back and get me!

Walking out of the bath house I remember smiling and thinking: "Yep, this one is going to make it into my book someday!" Hope you enjoyed it!

Secret to: Surviving the Mishaps

THERE ARE SO MANY stories I could include here, but I didn't want this book to be 800 pages. In research for my book, I went to local libraries all over Michigan to check up on their travel sections, to see what was out there, to benchmark and to get inspired. Due to the unpredictability of travel, there are entire books on the subject of mishaps. You can treat this section as the "Dangers and Annoyances" section of most travel guidebooks, although I would like to use a little more humor than they seem to! After all, travel wouldn't be any fun if everything went as planned all the time. How boring!

It's Not Murphy's Law, it's Mindi's Law!

"Why me?" I have had so many strange things happen to me during my travels that I have stopped asking myself that question and now just laugh and say, "Of Course!" Murphy's Law states: "Anything that can go wrong will go wrong." I guess this could be said for all areas of travel, but for me, it is a daily occurrence. I no longer get upset when these things happen, because I almost expect them to. The cure for this affliction is laughter.

Not only do I believe that Murphy's Law, which you have already heard me referring to as Mindi's Law, is a real phenomenon, but I am also superstitious. I get very uncomfortable when people say things like, "I have never broken a bone before," or, "I always find a place to stay." I feel like they are just testing the Travel Gods to drop a surprise on them. I try my best not to speak in absolutes, especially when discussing travel.

I have so many examples of missing trains, taking the wrong bus or standing in the slow line, changing lines only to have my new line move slower than the first one. Mindi's Law is a combination of Murphy's Law of mishaps and my own version of unexplainable crazy events that I feel could only happen to me. I think I attract these situations because of my crazy aura. I find myself saying, after a strange incident, "Only me!" or, "what are the chances?" Read on and you will see what I am talking about!

Croatian Opera Singer

I was meeting a friend in the main square in Zagreb, Croatia. He was running late and I was sitting near the statue in the center of the square. I am very content people watching and was enjoying the music that a busker was playing nearby. I found myself looking around at each guy that passed, thinking they might be Danijel. This action proved to be very dangerous as I made eye contact with an interesting guy. He approached me and asked if I was alone. Not a very comforting first line really! I explained briefly that I was waiting for my "boyfriend," a technique I have found works to ward off what would be his natural next question. He asked a modified version "Are you happy with him?" I found this very odd for a stranger to ask as a second question, but then again, it is Mindi's Law! We talked for a few minutes, he told me about his life, and job and secret wishes to be an opera singer. He pulled a few small bottles of vodka out of his pocket and offered me one. I looked to see if the seal was still on it and it was, so I decided to partake. Danijel was now 30 minutes late and I was getting annoyed, the vodka would help. I was drinking lemonade so I added the vodka to the jar. My new drinking partner drank his straight from the bottle.

We continued to talk, all the while I was hoping Danijel would arrive and save me from this crazy man. I had a feeling he was a little weird at first and then my suspicions were confirmed. He started to sing opera at the top of his lungs! Many people in the square were looking at us and wondering what this man was up to. I felt embarrassed and I was not even *with* him. He was singing directly to me, awkward smile, nodding and fidgeting and he was still singing. I receive a text from my friend that he was at a café just down the street, could I meet him there? Saved by the bell! I graciously excuse myself and try to make my way to the café. He says he knows the way and will walk me there. Just wonderful! So, we start in the direction that I know and he says I am going the wrong way. As you may have realized by now, I have absolutely no sense of direction so I am torn between thoughts of him really knowing the way or having an alternate plan to take me down some back alley and murder me. Well, I decide to follow him on the main street until we come to a covered walkway. He explains he brought me this way so I could hear his singing in better acoustics.

This crazy man starts singing opera again, and now the vodka has kicked in and my patience has run out! "Listen, mister, you are on my last nerve! Do you know where this café is or not?!$ He stopped singing and quietly walked me up the street to the café. Only Me!

Gorilla Warfare

I have written the story of my Gorilla Trekking in Rwanda but left out one small detail. During the briefing with our guide, we were told of the rules and practices we must follow to make sure we were safe and the animals were respected. We found out that we were to leave our day-packs with another guide once we found the Gorilla troupe so they would not be tempted to take them or play with them. They also explained that we needed to turn off our flash and sound from our cameras so we would not aggravate the gorillas. The last thing I want is to have a Silverback upset with me.

At one point in the journey I was quite upset with the way the trek was going and I was talking to Tim, the Aussie, and he said out of the blue, "I would hate to see how upset you would be if your batteries die while we are with the gorillas!" "Tim, why would you say that?" Lo and behold, minutes later my low battery light flashes and I have a hard time getting the pictures I want because I have to keep turning the camera on and off to save battery. I could not figure out how to silence the "low battery" signal and the guides were furious with me for making my camera "beep!" Once again, only me!

Unwanted Help

During my trip to Central and South America I found myself in

Montericco, Guatemala after landslides blocked the roads and made it impossible for us to get to El Salvador when we had planned. This was not really a concern of mine because things happen that change my path all the time, so Christa and I were happy to have an alternate side trip to take. When Mindi's Law is in full effect, look out! This trip was a comedy of errors. Our mangrove tour was cut short by a case of traveler's tummy on my part. I had to have the guide turn back to find a toilet before we even reached our destination. Our horse riding excursion was uncomfortable because we were riding on bare wooden saddles and in the heat of the day down black sand beaches. There was no trail, just 30 minutes down the beach and 30 minutes directly back the way we came. And to top off the weekend getaway, we found out as we were waiting for our bus back to Antigua that the hotel that organized this trip for us had never arranged seats for us. This was the *only* bus going back to Antigua the day we wanted to leave.

Okay, I can take a deep breath, practice my combination of Spanish and International Charades, and see the positive in this situation; but does the Universe have to send me the local drunk to interrupt me every few seconds while I am trying to arrange future transportation? I am trying to tell the ticket salesman that we have already paid for transportation and could he please call the hotel in Antigua to confirm, all the while drunkard is talking to me, telling me I am beautiful and that he is happy I am visiting his town. Smile. Grit teeth. Smile! We are making a bit of progress when we are joined by three other travelers that are stranded here and do not have a way back either. Misery loves company, so we band together. The drunken man is now offering solutions to our situation. He can drive us. Oh, yeah, sorry sir but you can hardly stand let alone drive. "Please be quiet Sir! Please!" My patience was shot. Christa was just standing back laughing and saying, "Only you, only you!" I guess because I find myself in these crazy situations all the time, I just stay as calm as I can and look for a solution. The ticket salesman got in touch with our hotel in Antigua and they were sending their personal driver. We made sure he had room enough for our three new friends. Funny how things always work out! This time the Travel Gods used their power for good and not evil! Thank you, Travel Gods!

An Oversold Situation

I had been traveling with David and John in Hungary and I was on my way back to Prague on my own. I needed to get to get to Prague so I could catch my flight back to London, and then fly home after my six week break from Orlando. This should have been a pretty straightforward train trip, one that many people take from Budapest to Prague. I decided on an over-night train to help save on my accommodation budget, so I went to the train station booking office and did my best to purchase a ticket. I walked away thinking I was all set for the night train and I would arrive in Prague early the next morning. I booked just a normal train seat for this train, as the sleeper beds were a bit expensive and I thought I would be fine sleeping in a seat (just like on an airplane, right?).

I had gathered a few snacks for the train; a habit I long ago discovered is a good one since they hardly ever serve "edible" food, if any, on a train. I was at the station early; another of my Mindism's that other travelers sometimes tease me about. Being early usually means you are the first to board the train and first to secure the storage space for your rucksack, but not this time. As I start to make my way down the skinny corridors of this Eastern European train I am realizing that all of the first class cabins are jammed with passengers already and many of the second class cabins are taken.

I frantically looked at my ticket hoping that this is one of those times that I have been assigned a specific seat number. Even if this is the case, it is never a sure bet that you will actually be the only one with that seat number; you just have to be the first one *sitting* with that seat number. I looked over my ticket and noticed that I did not have an assigned seat number. I pushed on back through the train, trying to stand aside if someone else was passing in the opposite direction. I had my big pack on my back and my day pack on my front, the typical "turtle backpacker" look, and was trying to move as fast as I could to secure a place before they were all taken. It is common practice to oversell a train and then those without a seat must stand, no matter how long the journey could be!

I bumped into a large group of young French speakers that were all jammed in a hallway in front of me. I was trying to push through but there were just too many of them and no option for any of us to step aside. The group leader of the clan asked me if I had an assigned seat number or was I just trying to find a place like the rest of them. He explained that they thought they all had assigned seats too, but the train official said that the ticket office oversold by 50+ people and the hallways were all that was left for space. Oh, difficult decision time: Do I get off, forget the $10 I spent on the ticket and buy another one tomorrow? Find another place to sleep tonight and make my way back to the train station again the next day? Or do I hunker down with the French crew and survive by power in numbers?

You see, although the hallways were the only space left for all of us, it is still illegal to sit, stand and especially sleep, in the hallways - kind of a catch 22 really. I decided that I would band together with the French crew and get to Prague. The leader of the group said he found place for all of us to store our packs, so we all began to have a backpack assembly line heading down the train. My instincts were to keep my bag, as I had no idea where the assembly line ended, but went along with the group anyway. It was kind of nice not to have the bag to worry about. Out of sight, out of mind!

We settled onto the floor, alternating which direction we were each facing to maximize the space. Oh, why didn't I study more in French class? At least they were all pretty versed in English. We played many games of cards and laughed at our horrible attempts at "International Charades." As the night past, we were only asked to move along once, and we all pretended to be picking up our stuff as the man passed through checking tickets, then quickly settled back to our spots when he moved to the next carriage.

The train made a few stops in the night and at one point I was awakened by one of the students and asked if I wanted an actual seat. The first class cabin that we were sitting outside of had emptied and the French group had called "Dibs." The group leader had told the kids it would be nice of them to offer a seat to me. "Merci Beaucoup! Why, I thank you very much." A little better off the floor but now we had about 14 people crammed in a seating space for eight - more cramped and less breezy.

I dozed on and off all night, not wanting to miss my stop. The worst train rides are the night trains where your stop is NOT the last stop. No one wanders through to make sure you make your stop, so it is up to you to be awake and organized when the train stops. I then realize that I have NO idea where my backpack is. I tap the group leader on the shoulder and ask in a combination of French and Spanish where he put my pack. He assures me that we are all getting off at the same stop and he will give me my pack then. Alright, I hope he understood me well enough.

The sun is coming up and the passengers are slowly waking. I decided to head down to the toilet and brush my teeth before our stop. As I approach the toilet, I realize the door is slightly open and there are packs sticking out of it. The leader had stuffed all 30 of our packs in the toilet. "Oh, please let mine not be on the floor, or worse, on the toilet - Yuck!" As I am turning around to head back to my "seat" I realize that the French crew is moving frantically, getting their day packs together. They are getting ready to get off, that means it is my stop, too! The train stops for what only seems like two minutes, there are packs just flying off the train onto the platform.

I watch carefully at each one, I am not getting off the train until I see my pack fly by, in case it never made it in the toilet with the others. Half way through the launching, I see mine get heaved out the door. I jumped off, collected it, said some quick "Au revoirs," and then looked to see where I could exit. Just as the train was pulling away, I happened to look up at the sign stating what station we are at. It did not say PRAHA CENTRAL it said PRAHA SUD. I was just literally thrown off the train at the wrong stop.

Now, it would be up to me to make my way into the center of town on my own. The lady at the ticket counter told me that I was only two kilometers outside the center and I could walk it if I wanted to. So, sleep in my eyes, semi-wet backpack on my back (still don't know the origin of the wetness, nor do I want to find out), I set out on the longest two kilometer walk of my life. Turns out the underground station was two kilometers away - and the center was a few stops beyond that. I took the next tube and found my way. Oh, how I love to travel!

Taxi Ride in Paris

We were riding around in a big Contiki tour bus through the middle of Paris and catching the sites on the "fly by" and thinking to ourselves, there has to be a better way to see Paris. This was my second time in this wondrous city but I was now traveling with David and John and this was their first time here. We were happy to have the bus to take us around as the local metro was on a workers' strike. I would come to realize in my future travels this was a normal event in France. The bus, unfortunately, was not really stopping anywhere and we had our own ideas of what we wanted to see. As the tour guide was telling us that we were now on our way back to the Contiki campsite a few kilometers outside the city center, we quickly decided we would get off the bus, stay in the city and find our own way back to camp later that evening.

I still remember the look on everyone's faces as the three crazy Americans departed the bus. They were all wishing they were gutsy enough to jump off too, but were afraid to separate from the tour. We were proud of ourselves for making the move and made our way to the Latin Quarter. We had heard this was an artsy part of town and thought it might be nice to check it out. We had dinner *el fresco* (outside) on a wonderful little side street, enjoyed some cheap French wine, and of course had great conversation. When it was time to head back to camp, we decided not to waste our time with the infrequent metro and just grab a taxi; split three ways wouldn't be too bad – or so we thought!

We hailed a taxi and here is where the fun begins. We showed the driver the address for our out-of-the-way campsite. He smiled and started the car. Not quite an assuring smile, but a smile nonetheless, and that is a lot for a Frenchman. As we made our way out of the city center, I noticed that he checked his map, called another taxi and then he finally turned to me and asked a few questions, in French. I studied French in high school, I even went on the French trip when I was 15, but I could not understand anything he was saying. David has a grasp of Spanish from living in Los Angeles for so many years and between the two of us, all we could get was "no comprende!"

The taxi driver was driving in circles, the meter was slowly creeping up to a massive amount of Euros and we were all getting frustrated. At one point he tried to drop us off at a deserted train station. When he slowed down, I realized what he was doing and tried to explain that the train station was closed so we would be stranded. This might have been one of my first attempts at International Charades. It was not working! One good thing is that I remembered the name of the train station, and it was the one listed as close to our campsite, so we pressed on. The driver was getting very aggravated and his smile was long gone, as were ours. A glance at the meter and I realized we could have stayed in the city in a nice hotel and met the group the next day! A few minutes of Spanish-French-English charades and we were headed down a dark forest road.

By this time I was starting to doubt our driver's integrity and letting my mind wander off to a movie scene of him calling another taxi to come and meet him; we get robbed, murdered and our bodies flung out into the forest for some hiker to find days later. Just as the scene ends in my mind, I realize he is on the phone again with another taxi driver and I see headlights coming at us on this deserted road. It was another taxi. My heart was pounding and the little buzz I had from the wine was long gone. John had a strange look on his face but all the while David was saying, "it is going to be fine!" The other taxi pulled up just as our driver stopped and got out to open the trunk. I was so scared to see what he was going to get out of the trunk. Just then, David hopped out of the car and said "Oh good, we are stopping, I have to pee!" "YOU WHAT?" I am now back in my movie scene and thinking we should definitely stick close together. The taxi driver walks to the other driver and has a little chat. I am watching all of his facial expressions from the car hoping for a tip off to run!

This is the first of many times in my travels that I would think to myself "Who do you think you are?" and, "What if I have gotten myself in over my head?" These are times when I realize that I just have to use my head, remember my past experiences and have faith it will all work out. The driver had gotten a flashlight from the trunk and asked us to walk with him through the woods. David is all for it and John and I were just looking at each other in disbelief – this cannot be happening! I reluctantly followed the group onto a forest path all the while thinking of how I could escape if I had to. We walked for a few minutes and then emerged right at the entrance of our campsite. What are the chances?

We paid the guy, walked slowly to the front gate of the campsite and stopped. I was a ball of nerves. David says "See, I told you we would be fine!" I just started to cry. David was telling me that I overreacted and all I can remember about the end of that night is hearing John tell David, "Oh David, let her have her moment!" That was a very stressful night for all of us but we did agree on one thing: No one in the group was to know we had problems getting back! We still wanted to seem like the "cool, crazy Americans that went off on their own." Now the truth is out!

Paris is not the only place I had a crazy experience with a taxi driver; actually, I could probably write an entire book about them. First of all, I would like to know, are taxi drivers allowed to tell you NO!?! I think it is a strange phenomenon when you get a taxi drivers attention, explain where you would like them to take you, and then they just simply say NO. I thought that was the point of taxis; the randomness of the city, just waiting to pick someone up and drive them, let's say…anywhere!

This is where the positive attitude really comes in handy. I would say that in general I am not a very cynical person, so I try to see the good in everyone, even taxi drivers! Well, I have my guard up, but start the negotiations with a smile. Here are a few simple rules to keep in mind:

Rule # 1: Always ask if there is a meter. This is usually a good bet as it is somewhat difficult to alter that (although it has been done). Read the signs carefully. Femi and I got socked for a 50% surcharge on one of our taxi rides because it was after midnight and before 6am. I was not a happy camper then!

Rule #2: Have the address of your intended destination. Of course, it helps if the taxi driver can read English. If not, this makes for a fun game of International Charades. Unless you are in Ghana - then the game gets stepped up a notch. They do not know the street names because they use landmarks to find their way around. This makes for a very interesting and long ride when all the parties involved don't have a clue where they are going. When my friend Kayelene and I were on a mission to renew her passport in Accra, we had a heck of a time finding the Australian Embassy. The driver was really helpful and stopped to ask every single person we would come across. We finally found a businessman crossing the road that knew exactly where it was. Thank you, Travel Gods! Ghana was a tough place to pre-negotiate the rate, so, after an hour of turnarounds and reverses, we just had to come to a compromise.

Rule #3: After you negotiate the fare, don't pay it until you are safely at your "requested" destination. They sometimes take you to where they want to go. Watch out for the *commission* trick, like in India. We found a wonderful taxi driver that filled us in on the "secret to tourism" in India. The taxi drivers can give you a *cheap* taxi ride as long as you don't mind stopping at the hotels *they* pick, or the shops they suggest. They get paid a commission at these that is well higher than the measly 50 Rupees you might pay as the fare. There are some restaurants where the drivers eat free if they bring tourists. We told our guy to *Hit the Jackpot*. We ate in the restaurant he wanted, we shopped where he got 300 Rupees just to drop us off and we were with an Austrian girl who bought some killer gems at the factory he suggested (they get 5% there). He really loved us in the end!

Rule #4: Don't be in a hurry! I have had more taxi drivers than not pull over in the middle of the journey to "gas up." Many times they are running on fumes until they picked you up and it is impossible to continue without more petrol. If you are in a hurry, plan to leave a few minutes earlier than necessary. In Thailand I even had a driver pull over at a roadside temple to pray, yes, in the middle of my journey. Guess this is when you just smile and say "I love to travel!"

Rule #5: And probably the most important...Don't pay the fare until you have your bags out of the boot and onto your back. This is a very simple trick the cabbies do to try and extort more money out of you. They strategically raise the rate and then refuse to open the trunk until you pay the new fare.

I remember a time when I was traveling with Christa in Cairo, and since we had quite a long taxi ride ahead of us, we negotiated the rate and then proceeded with our journey. The traffic was horrible and the driver had to take an alternate route, a longer route mind you! So, Christa and I were whispering in the back seat to each other that we are not going to pay extra and we planned to have the exact change ready in case he tried to increase the rate. I had visions of Christa jumping out of the car and throwing the money at the driver as we ran off. We both broke out in a fit of laughter as I explained that with my luck I would get my pants stuck on the door handle and she would be half way down the block. The driver did try to get a bit more, but we were firm and friendly and only paid the going rate. Kill 'em with kindness, as the saying goes!

Now, with all of this being said, I have also had my share of amazing taxi drivers. They have been friendly, knowledgeable about the area, helpful with local customs and cultures, and overall a highlight in the city or town that I was visiting. When Femi and I were staying in Phnom Penh, Cambodia, we had a little tuk-tuk driver (with a turquoise helmet) that waited for us night and day outside of Femi's apartment just in case we wanted to go anywhere. He never understood our English, or the exact location we were hoping to go to; we never understood anything he was saying back to us, but with each interaction he just kept a smile on his face, so we kept a smile on ours. We figure that we single-handedly helped support him and his extended family that month while we played happy tourist in Cambodia. Not to mention it was quite convenient to have a tuk-tuk driver all to ourselves.

Femi and I both seem to have been "cursed" when it comes to finding competent taxi drivers. A great example of this is the time we were hailing a taxi to find the Philippine Embassy in Kuala Lumpur. When we are together it seems our chances are *doubled* that we will have a "situation" with our driver. We had a letter that we were to give to the Embassy in order to apply for a tourist visa for Femi and me to travel over one of his breaks from university. The letter had the Embassy's address printed clearly on it, so we thought this would be pretty fool-proof. We showed the driver, he looked at it and nodded. We negotiated a rate and off we went. Wow, that was easy. We started driving around for a bit longer than we had anticipated and so we asked him if he knew where he was going. He replied with some answer we didn't understand and then pulled over to ask the next person we saw. They sent us off to the area of the city where most of the embassies are clumped together.

He pulled up in front of the Canadian Embassy and smiled, "Canada!" "Yes, we know but we are going to the Philippine Embassy!" He says again, "Canada." "Okay, now what?" I say as I turn to Femi. We insist that this is *not* the place and we were off for round two! A few more minutes and we arrived at…the Indonesian Embassy. He says, "Embassy!" "Yes, we know, but we are trying to get to the *Philippine* Embassy, it is a different set of islands!" "Embassy!" So, as our last ditch effort, we asked the driver to show the guard at the Indonesian Embassy the letter that we had given him in the beginning, maybe he could tell us where it was. Finally, third time is the charm and we arrived at the Philippine Embassy. Trying to only pay half of what the meter said (because he was the one getting us lost all over town) was not so fun. We paid the driver quickly and ran inside the Embassy hoping he would not be waiting for us when we came out!

Bogs in Africa

Everyone remembers their first "bog," right!?! A bog is getting your vehicle stuck in the mud, usually for an extended period of time. In Africa, both mud and time are plentiful. We were leaving our campsite in Jinga, Uganda early in the morning because we needed to get to the Uganda/Rwanda border to meet the guide that would be taking us to the gorilla trek. The night before our departure we saw quite a bit of rain. This is never a good thing for the slippery, muddy roads in Africa.

Still half asleep, we settle into the back of the overland truck and begin dreaming of our trek with the Mountain Gorillas. Just as we are leaving the long road from camp, we feel a little slide, then a bump and then hear spinning of tires. I have to say, in the beginning I was a little excited for my "first bog." When I researched this type of tour online, I noticed that everyone wrote about the crazy bogs they were in and I was happy to have my own story about to unfold. Okay, ask me again four hours later when we were still there and thinking we would never get out.

Gavin and Scott are both great drivers, they both stay calm in these situations and were pretty creative as to how we could get this truck out of a two foot hole. Our truck literally looked as if it would tip over sideways at any moment. The thing I love about Gavin is his sense of excitement when we are bogged. He was making an African film and was thrilled that he could catch this entire bog on camera!

I need to paint the picture for you. It was not just our group trying to push and pull the truck out of the hole. The entire surrounding village came to watch, help or beg. If they did help you to push out the truck, they would insist on money or food for helping. If they were too small to help push then they just watched and smiled, and many were staring at us just hoping for a handout. We had to put one person on watch in the cab of the truck as this is where all of our passports and travel money are located We don't want to get so caught up in the bog and then realize later that we have been robbed.

I had brought over some toys and suckers from the Dollar Store and felt like this was as good of time as any to share. I think that in the future, giving away toys and candy should be accomplished from a moving vehicle, or one that has the option of moving. I didn't consider what would happen when I ran out of supplies. We have a picture of the kids literally hanging off the bottom of my pants begging me for more!

We tried to rock the truck, use grates for under the tires to gain traction, even brought banana plants to fill the holes in hopes the truck could just drive out of the mess we were in. We would summon passing four wheel drive trucks to help, but the ropes would snap under the pressure. We even had two or three other vehicles get stuck around us. At one point, all of us were helping to push out other cars and trucks. At this rate we could be here all day! Our spirits were high for about the first three hours and then it started to become obvious to us that this bog was bigger than all of us, and we might actually miss our meeting to cross the border for our gorilla trek.

Gavin asked a local villager if he knew of a bigger truck than ours that could help get us out. "Yes, come with me!" was all it took and they disappeared into the horizon, only to return within a few minutes with a massive truck. They hooked up the chains and in two minutes we were out of the bog. The fee was 80,000 Ugandan - wait, let me do the math: 3,000 Ugandan shillings to the USD, so about $26 to get us out. "GAVIN, why didn't we do *this* three hours ago?" "Ah Mate, then I wouldn't have such great bog footage, eh?"

There would be no shortage of "bog footage" on this next leg of the journey. We were not in Africa for the rainy season, but it was a pretty rainy week. We were hearing reports from other drivers that the Masai Mara National Reserve was washed out and many trucks were stuck inside (for days) and many more were not allowed in for fear that they would get bogged. We were a bit worried our time in the Mara would get cancelled because of the washed out roads. We needed three things: dry weather for the next few days; a smaller 4 x 4; and a local driver crazy enough to take us in. Gavin went on a search.

We found a driver, Sam, and his 1976 Land Rover we lovingly called "The Beast." By hiring a local man to take us in, we were supporting him and his family. The problem, however, was he was taking us in no matter what. He was not turning down that kind of money. So, while he was not necessarily the best driver, he had a 4 x 4. Here we go again! Just a few things went wrong with the Land Rover before we got "inside" the Mara, like the brakes going out. We had them fixed twice and they still were not working so well. So, we did half of the game drive without brakes. Silly me - I was thinking brakes were kind of important when there were roads washed out and you only realized it when you were two feet from the drop off.

Gavin was loving the trip in because he was now a passenger and didn't have to worry about the driving, or did he? Sam was such a cool guy, but was crap at getting through the really muddy spots. We were bogged within minutes of entering the game reserve. At times I would see a mud hole coming up and just think to myself, we are going to get stuck again, and we did. One point, as dusk approached, we almost drove off a 15 foot drop where the road was washed out and completely gone. We had to "go around," which sounds easy enough, but other trucks had gone around to the left and to the right, just adding to the washing out of the roads. All that was left was an actual BUSH crossing. The truck had to get through tall grass that was growing out of two feet of water. We decided that it would be better for the truck if we were all out of it and we would walk through to meet up with the truck on the other side. Maybe I should mention it is getting dark and we are surrounded by WILD animals?

Our shoes were caked with mud, socks were soaked, but hey, we were inside the "closed" Masai Mara. The "pay dirt" was worth it: two brother lions just posing for us on the side of the road, a cheetah eating her morning kill, a herd of over 22 elephants, a family of hippos bathing in the river, and more birds than even Gavin could handle.

The Masai Mara was an amazing place and I hope to return someday, but "Heaven on Earth" is located at the Ngorongoro Crater. A 600 meter descent into a lush animal playground, it is like being in the Super Bowl of African Wildlife - the largest concentration on the planet and it spans over 96 square miles. Everywhere you look you would see giraffe, zebras, wildebeests, and water buffalo. The BIG FIVE, no problem: elephants, buffalo, black rhino, leopard, and lion. CHECK! I was happy to be able to see them, but I was here for the BIG CATS. Bring on more lions and cheetahs!

We stumbled on a pride of lions resting in a bit of tall grass. There were about seven or eight other tour groups inside at the same time, and if something exciting was happening, all the trucks were in one place, surrounding the animals. This took away from some of the "authenticity" of finding lions in the wild. The lions were not complaining about the trucks; they would get up from their tall grass and walk over to the shade of the truck and lie down. One truck was literally stopped from moving on because the lion was under their vehicle and its' tail would wag just under the tire.

Highlights of the day for me: Seeing the male lion lying on the crest of a hill and posing for all that passed him; watching the cheetah in the middle of chasing down a poor helpless gazelle; lesbian zebras; and riding through the Crater playing Disney's "The Lion King" soundtrack. Cheesy, but it had to be done! Oh, and our driver's taste in music: Bob Marley. Now I love me some Marley, but he only had one cassette tape and we listened to it over and over and over. Two words: AFRICA UNITE!

Tourist Tax

One of the stories I seem to tell over and over is the Albanian Border Crossing. I think it is because they ask what it is like to travel as an American, or as an American Woman. I do give it thought when I am out there, but mostly just plug along and deal with the strange and unusual when it is presented to me. This border crossing was one of those times.

I was on an overnight bus traveling from Montenegro to Albania in 2005. I remember boarding the bus and looking around to see if there were any other travelers on board. This section of the world was just opening up to backpackers and the road was the "less traveled" - not quite the same as jumping on a bus from Lima to Cuzco. I noted that there were three others that were non-Yugoslavian. I settled into the back seat, plotted my next few days and drifted off to sleep.

I woke up at about four a.m. to a border official moving through the bus and asking for travel documents. As I was in the back of the bus I was the last person to be checked. He asked me to follow him off the bus and into the office. He started asking some basic questions: how long have you been traveling; what are the last few countries you have visited; what is your intended length of stay in Albania? The question that got the biggest reaction was, "Why are you visiting Albania?" I answered, "Tourism." He followed up with, "what are you here to see?" I tried to give a simple answer, "Your beaches!" By this time, all the men in the office were laughing and saying, "Croatia has better beaches!" I had not seen their beaches yet, but now as I look back, I can agree. They finally had enough fun with me and the bus driver was now inside requesting that we move on. They put a stamp in my passport and wrote "10 Euro" on the stamp. I was made to pay the entrance fee that I suspect was money for their breakfast.

Belarus Border Crossing

Even though I had a bit of inconvenience at the Albanian border, it was overall a quick crossing. The cross from Belarus to Poland was my longest crossing. We spent almost four hours at this border. We had heard in advance that this was not a "quick cross" and decided to capitalize on the opportunity to use our foreign currency. We all put in a handful of leftover coins that we had and put our name down along with the best guess for the time we would be released from the border. Winner takes all! My guess was somewhere around two hours.

We knew it was not going well when they asked our driver to open the undercarriage and remove all of our bags for individual inspection. The inspection, bathroom visits and duty-free shopping still only filled an hour or two. We thought maybe they were letting the small cars through first and just waiting for the bus because it was more work, but the family in the little car next to us was there all the time we were. The Aussies and Kiwis have now started a pickup game of Cricket. I have never had the time to learn how to play this sport, and even now with all of the time in the world, I realized I still don't ever want to learn how to play that game.

We passed the time by telling stories and playing the "lolly" game. (In Australia, they call candies lollies.) One of the passengers had a bag full of gummy candies and we each took a piece and tried to see which one of us could make the candy last the longest. What can I say? We were bored. The guide told us an urban legend of a passenger who went through this exact border and used the drop toilets while waiting to be approved to cross. He had his passport in his back pocket for easy access, but when he went in to use the toilet, it fell in the pit. I will save all of the details on how he retrieved it, but he did. He wiped off as much as he could and let it dry in the sun. He then placed it in a zip lock bag. Bet he was glad he had one of those. When it was time to present his passport to the border officials he tried to explain that they shouldn't open the bag. They didn't listen, and the group was then processed very quickly and released. Oh yeah, when our time reached almost four hours, the thought crossed our mind to have a redo! But, who was going to sacrifice their passport? No one in the group volunteered, by the way!

Not a Good Night's Sleep - Turkish Campsite during Ramadan

For almost the first full year I was living in London, England, I met people that had done the 35 Day Middle Eastern Explorer tour. It was finally time for me to do the tour myself. There were 22 people on our overland trip, including our driver and the guide. Funny how some groups can just hit it off and start having a blast from the first day. That was us!

Most of the tour was Aussies and Kiwis, but there was one other crazy American girl, Christa. She was the guide, and I was the *storyteller.* We clicked right from the start. We were both loud, but honestly, she is louder than I am. We were both freaks about "how we travel" and had a similar way in handling difficult situations, so, it was easy to see we would be hanging out a lot.

We would sit around the campfire at night and people would pick a country and I would try to tell a funny story that I could remember from there. I should have been taking better notes as to which stories I told back then; maybe I would have had an easier time to develop the stories for this book!

I usually don't do a whole lot of planning in advance for my trips, especially if it is a group tour. I did overlook one small detail on this one. It was Ramadan, the holy month for Muslims. This meant fasting from sun up to sun down. Well, not for us, but it meant that the restaurants were closed the entire day. Needless to say, we had a lot of supermarket meals.

The lack of accessible food was not really the hardest thing to adjust to; it was the call to prayer. They are required to pray five times a day and were reminded when they needed to go to the mosque by a loud call to prayer. Every morning, we would awaken to the screeching and howling of the Arabic Morning Prayer – so, early mornings, to say the least! Then, in order to signal the start of the fast again, there would be a drummer sent through the village pounding and pounding and pounding to tell the families they could not eat again until the sun rises the next day.

During this trip we did a fair bit of bush camping, which means no electricity, only your tent and sometimes simply on the side of the road, in a field. We found our campsite late one night in what I thought was the middle of nowhere. I was smiling to myself as I went to sleep that night thinking there is no way we would be able to hear the drumming or the call to prayer where we were camping.

The group settled in and prepared for this to be a peaceful night's sleep. As I drifted off, all I could hear were a few of the guys snoring a few tents away which, was now like music to my ears. Then I hear crunch, crunch, crunch right outside my tent, literally right by my ear. There were stray dogs digging in the garbage from our dinner.

I rolled over and decided at least it was not...drum, drum, drum. The thought came just as the three a.m. drumming began. Where was this drummer coming from? I kind of smiled and thought, well, at least we will get to sleep in. Nope! There was a man riding on a dirt bike with a basket on the front. He was carrying a portable boom box and a megaphone and blasting the morning call to prayer. So, much for a good night's sleep!

About a month later I had moved through the Middle East and Egypt and had made my way to Kenya. Other than a few random, loud roosters, the nights had become much more peaceful. I took a week away from Nairobi and traveled to the island of Lamu, off the coast of Kenya. I arrived to the main dock on a rickety old dhow that was taking on water the entire ride. As with most places that tourists arrive, there are always a group of people offering you tours, accommodation and transportation. I found a cute little hotel and settled in. A quiet night? Not so much - 5:30a.m., the call to prayer was belting out over the island. I did not notice in my research that Lamu was a Muslim island.

I have to say that as I was lying there, remembering all of my travel mates from the Middle East tour, I realized I was actually happy to hear the call to prayer. It goes to show that when you are immersed in a culture, you begin to adapt.

Worst Room Ever - Livingston, Guatemala

Christa and I were heading to Livingston, Guatemala to explore and find out more about the population of the Garífuna people. They are descendants of escaped would-be slaves and have created a Caribbean subculture. We left Placencia by water taxi to the mainland, then caught a bus, and went on to catch three more boats to get to Livingston. We had hoped to stay in a very popular youth hostel, Casa de la Iguana. The problem here was we had such a long journey and were unsure what day we would arrive. The hostel is very popular and that means sometimes you need to make reservations. They were all booked up for the night, but could get us in the next night.

We decided we would just walk down the road and "stay anywhere" for cheap and then move hostels the next day. We found a small hotel up the street for about $3 a night. From the moment we walked into the room we doubted if we could actually stay there. I will try to explain the room. The bathroom had hot pink tiles, splattered with mold and mildew. The toilet seat was barely attached, as if we would actually sit on it. We left the door open when we went so we wouldn't get locked in there.

The mattresses, if you can call them that, were thin sheets of foam on top of cement blocks. The electric outlets and light switches had bare wires. I guess it would have been better if we hadn't inspected the entire room, and found some very large spiders living in the corners. All of the other things are forgivable, but there is NO WAY we would be able to sleep if those monster spiders were crawling around. No worries, Christa to the rescue. She volunteered to kill them. The problem with this plan was Christa screams really loud just *before* she swings the shoe to kill the spider, thus alerting the spider that the shoe was coming. She missed, and it fell behind my bed.

I still can't believe to this day that we didn't check out and stay somewhere else for only $5 more. We toughed it out! Solution: Gallo Beer and lots of it! Christa and I slept in the same bed using our own linens. I couldn't bring myself to be on *my* bed closest to the M.I.A. spider. You need to know how strict Christa and I can be with our accommodation budget. Maybe not the ice cream or nacho budget, but accommodation, look out, we will sleep anywhere. Maybe not SLEEP! Wait, didn't we end up spending more money on beer to deal with the

$3 room? At least I have the story and a winner for the award for "the worst hotel room ever!"

The natives were restless and so was I - Nairobi, Kenya

To go along with the theme of NOT sleeping, I bring you to Nairobi, Kenya at the start of my first African overland tour, to a hostel simply named Nairobi Backpackers. Now, I am not telling this story to "diss" the hostel. I loved this place and have since recommended it to many other travelers; but on this particular night, the natives were restless. The mice that is, and lots of them. I had stayed here a few nights before in a room down the hall, but had left for my Lamu adventure and had now returned to find myself moved from the quieter four bed dorm to the louder, more crowded eight bed dorm, named Hotel California. I enjoyed a wonderful meal that night at the organized group dinner, fit in a quick internet session, showered and was off to my bunk to read until my eyelids were so heavy I would just fall to sleep. Well, that was the plan anyway. I had just decided to call it a night, turned off my head torch and snuggled up with my travel pillow when I heard a little rustling under my bed. There was no fan so it had to be something else causing the bag to move. I laid there trying to get up enough nerve to peek under my bed.

What if it *was* a creature? Did I really want to see it with my very own eyes? The noise persisted and became a bit louder and closer to my head, so it was time to investigate. I grabbed my head torch that was hanging on the bed post and peered under my bunk. Oh, why did it have to be MICE? Three of them, and they seemed to be sharing a few bread crumbs or something they found under there. When I shined the light at them, they all froze and stared at me as if to say "Yes, can we help you?" So much for sleeping tonight! I know, I know, there are those of you that are saying, "Oh, they are just mice, cute little creatures, they won't hurt you. They are more afraid of you than you are of them!" Yeah! Yeah! Yeah! I have heard it all before, and it still never helps me to deal with these situations. I decide that the 24 hour internet desk was where I would camp out until the morning light. Not the most comfortable chair and I would dose off every few seconds. This is the *only* time I can remember wishing I would have drawn a top bunk.

I was pretty much left alone throughout the night except for the guard dog. He did come into visit me once, prompting me to think that maybe the hostel should get a guard CAT instead. The overnight security guard also stumbled on me during his rounds and found it very hard to believe that I was THAT afraid of a few little mice. "Yes, I am, kind sir, now move along and let me NOT sleep!" I waited until the first sign of light, tiptoed to my bed, checked that the mice had moved along and when I was sure they had, it was off to dreamland for me. I think the words to the song should be changed for this Hotel California to: "*you can check in but you can never sleep*"....

Mr. Wu's in London - All-you-can-eat Chinese Buffet in China Town

I was traveling with David and John in London, and as you do in London, you watch your pence. So, we were in search of a cheap meal that had staying power. We found Mr. Wu's for about seven pounds ($13 US) for lunch and settled in. The tiny restaurant only held about 20 people; some were even sitting at makeshift tables in the entry way. Cheap eats in London are hard to find - looked like everyone else had the same idea.

We ordered three buffets and began to eat. When Mr. Wu asked us if we wanted drinks with our meals, we kindly said no and snuck drinks from the Cokes/water we had hidden in our bags. Budget! We were nearing the end of the stuff fest and realized Mr. Wu was getting closer to our table. "YOU GO NOW, YOU EAT TOO MUCH RICE!" I think he just wanted to turn the tables to get the next people in to make more money, or maybe we *did* actually eat too much rice!

Beware of the Manager's Special: The Bait and Switch

We were on the Greek Island of Paros enjoying a typical warm Greek evening. The thing to do was to walk along the shore and look at the menus for a place to have an evening meal. You don't have to worry about being able to read the menus as they have greeters posted by the menu stand and it is their job to shout out to you and entice you to dine in their restaurant rather than the identical one just up the walk. Many people tend to get annoyed by this tactic and to be honest, it used to get to me, too; but once you embrace it, the opportunities are endless.

We had wandered down the "zone" for a few minutes turning down free Ouzo and fresh fruit desserts and finally found a fun greeter who wanted to do business in a serious way. He was offering: Free wine; free appetizer per two people; entrees; and free dessert. When asked what the dessert was on the offer, he said they had the best ice cream sundaes on the island. WOW! SOLD!

There were only three of us, so we did two of the "manager's special" and one individual meal. The food was great, our server was friendly and the night breeze and sunset were priceless - so we thought! It was time for the dessert and of course, we ordered "the best ice cream sundaes on the island!" And, they were very good. The bill comes and this is where the fun begins. Instead of the 15 Euro combo meal like we expected, we were asked to pay the 15 Euro plus 12 Euro EACH for the ice cream sundaes. Now, they were good, but not $18 USD good!

I guess because my background is in Hospitality and Restaurants, I was voted to try to explain to the waiter. I did and he said, "No, ice cream is no part of manager special!" We then asked to see the man that told us to order the famous sundaes, and he, too, now had the same story. He said we must have misunderstood him, "the manager's special comes with a plate of fruit." Now we start to raise our voices because we realize what has happened. All of the manager's specials along the walk came with fruit, too; he just used the old "bait and switch" on us - told us one thing and then gave us the other, while still charging us for the original item.

Well, this was not going to happen to us! By now we have other customers involved who, by an outstanding margin, also understood that their meal was going to come with the "best ice-cream sundae on the island." We shared the lesson with a nice couple that hadn't gotten to the dessert course yet. We told them to get the fruit! We tallied the bill *minus* the two sundaes that we thought were included, still left the outrageous 12 Euro for the third sundae and started to walk out of the restaurant. Now Greek Mama was after us saying that we didn't leave enough money.

Oh, what a sight we must have been, screaming at each other, telling all the people that we passed by NOT to eat at that restaurant, all the while still being chased by the "Manager" who started this all.

Luck was not on my side

My friend Natalie always teases me with "Americans will throw a penny into *a puddle* just to make a wish." Maybe this comes from the large amount of people with Irish heritage in the United States, but I know there are a few times throughout my travels I should have done just that!

I was passing through San Pedro La Laguna on Lago Atitlan in Guatemala on my tour of Central America. We were planning to spend a few days in this gorgeous place. San Pedro is located on a volcanic lake with views of Toliman and San Pedro volcanoes. We didn't find out until our arrival on the island that the weekend we were there was a national holiday. Most of the time it is not much of a problem, especially in a place like this because locals usually travel out of town to see relatives and celebrate. This seemed to be the case for us as we found our accommodation quite easily, and cheaply I might add. At this point we were traveling with a fellow traveler, Gustavo, a Mexican-American guy and we paid $3 between the three of us for our room. Didn't they know they could have charged double seeing it was a national holiday and all? Just kidding - we were happy for the cheap accommodation.

Our first order of business was replenishing our supply of quetzals (local currency) as all of us were running dangerously low. We asked a few locals about a bank or an ATM machine in town. We were informed that there were two. We chose to check out the closest one, but found it to be *unplugged*. Alrighty then, so we made our way up to the little town center and looked for the small bank. We could see a line of people out front that looked like it included more people than the town could hold. I wandered up to another "gringo" in the line and asked what was happening. She explained that because of the holiday, the bank ran out of money. I had never heard of such a thing. Apparently, all of the locals had withdrawn money to take away with them for the national holiday which left the bank with no money.

We queued up and waited. We were told there was a delivery coming from a larger bank in a matter of time. That was just the problem; what *matter* of time were we talking about? We waited for over an hour and then decided that we would just have to leave the island sooner. It was a Saturday and the banks were closed the following day anyway. So off to Antigua we went. Next time, I am going back with a *wad of cash!*

Another time I found myself worried about getting local currency was in Romania. I was hanging out in Brasov, one of my favorite little towns in all of Romania, but needed to move on. I had decided to go to Sulina, which was on the Danube Delta. I had heard from other travelers that this was a beautiful area of the world and there was a beach. I had been traveling around Eastern Europe for a while and was in need of a "beach day." I was also excited as this would be my first time to swim in the Black Sea. I had told a fellow traveler, Ljupka, from Serbia, about my journey and she wanted to join in. She was a biologist and wanted to explore the delta firsthand. Cool! It is always nice to have company for long journeys, and *long* it was. We had to take a two hour train, then a bus for the 195 kilometers to Tulcea, and then we waited over an hour to catch a ferry, which took almost two hours to reach Sulina. The surroundings were amazing, so we spent the travel time taking in the scenery and chatting about our lives.

As you will find out in the Traveling Planning (or Not) section, I usually lean toward the *or not*. I knew that there was a 50 bed hostel in Sulina because our hostel in Brasov recommended it, so I was not too worried about finding a place to sleep. After all, this was a tiny town. How many tourists could actually be there at the same time? A LOT! Just so happens there was a large group that had reserved the entire place, all 50 rooms. What would we do now? We decided to walk back to the dock area and try to find the guy we "totally blew off" who was offering a place to stay in his mother's house. Time to make nice!

We passed him on the way to the dock and he quickly showed us the extra bedroom in his house. Not great, but not horrible, so we decide to take it. We were both short on Romanian Lei so we ventured out to find a bank or money exchange. There were only two major roads in the town, the one nearest to the port and the one parallel to it, on which the bank was located. I tried my MasterCard in the machine and quickly found out that it only accepted Visa cards. Maybe I can go inside and take a cash advance on my card? Maybe it was the lack of Romanian I spoke, my horrible International Charades act, or the fact that this was an out-of-the-way town that has never even heard of a "cash advance," but I was unsuccessful.

Last resort: try to change some traveler's checks. This was *way* back in the day, and I don't carry those anymore; useless as you are about to see. The expression on the teller's face was priceless. She had never even seen such a thing before. I was visiting Romania before they had joined the European Union, so I am sure a lot has changed now, but that didn't do me any good at that moment. We headed to the main street defeated! Between the two of us, we had enough to pay for our room, and if we budgeted carefully, we could eat one big meal and each get a ferry ticket back to Tulcea the next morning. It was a Saturday and nothing would even open in Tulcea on Sunday, so the plan was not foolproof, but what choice did we have?

Then we met "Andre," he was a local guy sitting in the café with two French backpackers having a few beers. We asked him for suggestions on how to get money and he had a "great idea." We could just stay at his aunt's for as long as we wanted; he would cover our spending money until Monday's ferry, and if we wanted to stay longer, we could take the ferry over to Tulcea, collect money, spend the day and then return to Sulina together. A man with a plan - I like it! Now, we just had to go back to the first house and back out of the contract. OUCH! We just played dumb tourist and told them we couldn't get money and had to leave that day. They seemed sad to lose the business, but understood. I felt bad now, because we were totally lying.

We did spend that night and the next night with our new French mates and the ring leader, Andre. He showed us where to find the one and only bar in town and we liked that. He even convinced the bartender to give us a tab at the bar that we could pay in a few days when we had money. I was loving the small town trust. The catch was that he was also putting *his* beers on our tab, and helping himself to the French guys' cigarettes; seems they were in the same predicament and had been staying at his aunt's house since early Friday. I still, to this day, can't decide if he was a travel angel or an opportunist, but either way he saved the day!

The next morning, I was cleaning out my daypack and found two 20 pound notes from the UK in a little side pocket. At the time, this was over 300 Lei and plenty to get us through to Tulcea on our own and we could stop paying for Andre's party life. Ljupka decided to head out the next morning anyway and head back. She was short on cash overall and needed to get back to Bucharest to catch her flight. She asked if she could borrow the equivalent of 20 Euro and get it back to me on my way through Belgrade when I visited Serbia later in my trip. Normally, I would have happily given it to her but at this moment I was worried about me having enough to get back to "civilization" without stressing. I couldn't leave a fellow traveler in the lurch, so I gave her the money; we traded information and said our farewells!

I found myself in Belgrade a few weeks later on my birthday. I was not so worried about getting the cash back but did think it would be cool to meet up and have a local show me around for my birthday night out. I called Ljupka and we made plans for dinner and a dance club. Not only did she pay me back in full, but she *and* her friends all brought me birthday presents, bought my dinner and took me to the coolest night club, which happened to be a boat floating on the river! What a memorable night! Here's to good karma!

Police Reports

Let me start by saying, if you are a traveler, I hope you always have safe and happy travels and don't have to file a police report of your own. Perhaps by sharing my stories with you, you will learn a little from my "bad luck" and avoid them all together! If you count the time that I worked in international recruiting, I have been traveling for over ten years. In those ten years, I have only found myself in a few situations. I feel lucky to only have three stories to tell!

My first experience with crime-on-the-road was when I was traveling by train in Italy with my friend David and his parents. We were taking a night train into Florence and had booked into a six person sleeper cabin. We were pretty confident that we would have a safe and quiet night once we realized the other two people in our cabin were an elderly Italian couple going to visit their family. That is what we thought we deduced from the quick round of International Charades. Well, that combined with David's "amazing" Italian: "Grazie, Grazie!"

The train was chugging along throughout the night. David and I were on the very bottom bunks, and very claustrophobic I might add, while his parents were in the middle bunks, leaving Mr. and Mrs. Italian on the top bunks. The night was pretty uneventful, except for Mr. Italian getting up every 30 minutes to go out into the hallway and have a cigarette. I found myself waking up and looking around to be sure everyone was okay the first few times he got up, but then quickly dismissed the noise and tried to get some sleep.

About 5 a.m., we felt the train slowing down and were thinking we might be at our stop. As David and I are standing up, we both notice that Mom's purse was unzipped. She had been holding it on top of her throughout the night to be sure no one could get into it. David instinctively asked her to check inside to be sure nothing was missing. We all thought everything would be fine because we couldn't see how someone could unzip the purse, take something out, all the while Mom (Peggy) having a firm grip on the bag. She searched for our passports first, all accounted for! Then she looked for her wallet and realized it was missing.

Well, now we have some questions. Could it have been Mr. or Mrs. Italian? Or possibly anyone else wandering by while Mr. I was out smoking or using the toilet? David does his best to explain to the couple that we have been robbed and that they should check their things, too. Everything else in our packs was accounted for, just not the wallet. She had hidden about $600 US Dollars in an inside pouch of the wallet for safekeeping. David and I snap into "detective mode," he went to check the bathrooms down the hall and I went to get the train security.

As I was returning with two train guards, David emerged from the toilet with Peggy's wallet in hand. I breathed a sigh of relief until I saw David's face and realized the wallet was there but the money was missing. We spent the next 20 minutes trying to explain the ordeal to the guards, with not much luck. They were trying to tell us to get off at the next stop (one before our scheduled stop) and to fill out a report with train officials, but we were adamant that we needed to make our way to Florence, and promised to file the report with the police there. The entire time we were chatting to the guards, Mr. I was standing next to us, looking quite guilty, with his hands fidgeting nervously in his pockets. I have a sneaky suspicion that if we had asked him to empty his pockets he would have had roughly $600 in there. It was not like we could have proved it was *our* US Dollars anyway! If you ask me, it was Mr. I, in the toilet, while smoking, on the train.

We did spend an entire day in Florence finding the police station and filling out the required report for my travel insurance. We had a slim chance my insurance would cover the lost cash, however, with so many travelers committing insurance fraud, the companies are now super strict and had requested money exchange receipts or a bank statement proving we brought that cash with us on this trip. Not easy to prove, so no money was recovered. In the end, we were thankful that we were safe and, most importantly, had our passports.

The second robbery took place at one of my favorite hostels in Panama - Aqua Lounge. We arrived in Bocas del Toro, Panama and arranged to take a water taxi to our hostel that was built out on stilts over the water. This is where we met Emily and Stewart (our new travel partners for the next two months) and made other friends from our 11 bed dorm. Needless to say, we spent the next few nights having fun. There was Ladies Night on Wednesday at our hostel, Ladies Night on Thursday on the main island, and 50 cent beers on Friday. We were planning to leave because Saturday was another ladies night at our place, and frankly, our livers couldn't handle it!

While we were there we visited some of the surrounding beaches. Wizard Beach was my favorite because the waves would come in at all angles and it was like a *wizard* was controlling them. The current was too strong so not a lot of swimming there. We went to Red Frog Beach, where we were greeted by a little boy showing the ever famous, toxic Red Frogs; luckily they were on a leaf! You could take photos for the low, low price of $1. I snapped a few photos on my disposable camera, as it is very unsafe to carry your *good* camera to the beaches in case you want to swim...people like to come by and snag your bag while you are in the water.

All was well at the beaches; it was our hostel we had to worry about. The last night we were there we all left the Aqua Lounge island and headed to the main island. It was a pretty quiet night at our hostel, so they closed the bar and came over to party with us in Bocas. The problem was they left our hostel at 10:30p.m., and security didn't come until 11p.m. and in that half hour someone broke into our room, and cut the padlocks off four of our lockers. There was a combined loss of $720 US Dollars. I lost $110 and my travel partner, Christa lost almost $400. Thankfully, they left our passports, our cameras and my iPod. I had my money hidden in two places and luckily they didn't find the additional $250 US Dollars I had hidden in another location.

Flip a coin, leave the valuables at the hostel or take them with you, either one is a risk, as you could get robbed at the hostel or worse, mugged on the street? We had taken all the precautions that we could in this type of hostel. All of us used our *own* padlocks. Travel Hint: Be careful with locks that a hostel provides, as I can guarantee they have extra keys they can use while you are away. The types of locks most backpackers carry are not super strong, but as my mom always said, "They keep the 'honest' people honest!" If someone wants in, they will get in, and they did. It put a big damper on the fun we were having in this area of the world.

That night, before we had crossed back to the hostel, my travel partner Christa and I were having our first traveler's fight - I wanted to stay in Bocas one more night and she wanted to move on. I had used all sorts of "strategies" to try to convince her to stay on and not create the awkward situation of us having to split up. I had come up with an idea that we were able to *each* have three times in the next three or four months to throw down an "extra day free" card, you know, like the "get-out-of-jail-free" card in Monopoly? Well, she wasn't having any of it. So, she had gone back ahead of me to the hostel upset, and I was dreading the conversation I was going to have to have to say I had decided to stay!

But, as you now know, when I arrived I was quickly informed that we were robbed. We were all just sitting around talking it out, playing detective and Christa asked the ever-popular questions "Why me, why us?" I only had one answer to give: fate. It was fate that this happened, because if it didn't, I would have walked in that room that night and told Christa I was staying on and it might have ruined our trip together, or even worse, our friendship. My mom also always says, "Everything happens for a reason!"

I was really sad that it had to happen here as I would have loved to recommend it to everyone I could. The owner was very apologetic and even waived our three night stay including bar and food tabs. This brought my losses down to only about $40 - not the end of the world. In researching for this section of the book, I had gone on Trip Advisor to check out some other travelers' comments about Aqua Lounge and found multiple stories, many worse than mine, regarding robberies and even muggings at this hostel. It seems to be getting worse, not better in this part of Panama, and so if you brave a visit there, please keep your wits about you!

Oh yeah, let's just say the police report with our *un poco espanol* was funny to say the least! The detective even thought I was born in Peru - what part of CHEBOYGAN, MICHIGAN sounds like PERU? The most memorable part about filing this police report was the *Miami*

Vice style ride on the police boat back to the hostel to show the officers the damage to the lockers. (P.S. International Charades is much easier when you have props!)

The last story in this section is from my latest overland trip and takes place in Essaouira, Morocco. An overland trip is a low-budget, usually camping style trip that mostly lands you in bush camps along the way. A bush camp is just that, camping in the bush, not at a campsite with facilities. As a seasoned overlander, I had come to expect these. As the tour neared the Moroccan coastline, the bush camps became "beach camps." I loved this idea because there is nothing better than falling asleep to calming waves, or feeling the cool sea breeze in *hot* Africa.

Mark, our driver, did explain the dangers of sleeping on the beach and suggested that maybe we put off setting up our tents until just before dark, as to not draw attention to ourselves. Well, I think the BIG GREEN MONSTER TRUCK we were cruising around town in drew enough attention already! We had set up camp, made a fire, did some laundry and started to prepare our evening meal. My tent mate and I decided to put our tent up early, but agreed not to put anything in it until we were ready for bed. The entire crew decided that was a good idea, so we set up our little "boom town" of tents on the dunes above the truck. Mark and a few others had planned to sleep on the truck to protect our valuables and the rest of us would just tough it out on the beach.

Because of the way the dunes were set, my tent mate, Kayelene had to turn our beds sideways because we were sliding down on our sleep mats. This put me length wise at the door with her behind me. It was a really still night even near the sea, so we had our fly open to catch any breeze possible. I was just lying there, gazing out at the moon, thinking about life, love and well, my favorite thing at this point to think about - truck drama. As I was deep in thought about who I would "vote off the island" so to speak, I watched the fly to our tent close slowly over me. I got a strange feeling in my stomach, like someone was outside my tent. Within seconds I felt someone pushing on my tent, just above my head. I thought maybe it was one of our group getting up to take a wee in the night and maybe they lost their footing and fell against our tent. I gave the tent a swat and yelled, "Hey, go around!" At the same moment I hear Lara yell from down the way, "Someone slashed our tent and stole my backpack! My passport is missing!" This was enough to get most of us up.

We did the rounds and checked to see if anyone else was a victim to robbery. Final count: five tents slashed; the family lost their sleep sheets and two pair of boots; with Lara losing the most having her entire pack taken: passport, credit cards, camera, and iPod - the lot. We all began to search the area around the tents. Lara's passport and credit cards were found in a bush near the truck and one pair of boots were abandoned. Because they left Neal's boots and took his daughter Victoria's boots, we figured the thieves must have been kids.

Upon closer inspection in the morning, I noticed that our tent was also cut in two places. The part where our feet would have been had a big cut, but I had the tent bag there and it was too thick for them to get through. The second cut was where my head had been, like they were just starting to cut when I felt them leaning on the tent and scared them away. The feeling I had was right, they were just outside my tent and had I been sleeping they might have gotten into our tent, or worse, cut the top of my head. Count this one too close for comfort!

The only thing you can do in situations like this is to look at the bright side - at least we got Lara's passport and credit cards back. Those are the hardest to replace. We learned a *big* lesson early on in the trip, not to bring *anything* of value into the tent - no matter what. And no one was hurt! I will be honest, it is easier to say than to actually believe, but you can't turn back the clock, you can only push forward or go home. We chose to push forward.

So what happens when it is the police/security that are the ones trying to rip you off? As a young child I was taught to trust a policeman, to search out someone with a badge, these are the people to go to when you need help. I am not arguing this is untrue, I am just providing a case for the other side of the argument. Here are a couple of times when the law was not so lawful:

Riga, Latvia

During my time living in London I made some great friends and even better travel mates. I met Natalie on the Russia/Scandi tour and since we were both ending the tour and living in London it was natural to stay in touch. I loved hanging out with Nat in London because she was always up for a fun time and weekend getaways. If you are a traveler and living in London the opportunity to do short "bank-holiday" weekends away are endless. Nat and her group were always sending out group emails asking who was in for a trip to Normandy, Oktoberfest, or even just a big day out at THE CHURCH, a nightclub that is open from 12 – 4 p.m. every Sunday.

When I found out, without much notice, that I was losing my job and work visa due to the economy, there was only one thing I could do! Travel! I called Nat and told her that I would be leaving London in the end of May and would be traveling with David and his parents for a few weeks, but after that I was thinking of heading to the Baltics (Estonia, Latvia and Lithuania) and would she like to come along? She grabbed another mate Sally and we were off.

We took advantage of the cheap prices to rent a car in each of the three countries. This gave us the opportunity to see more of the country and make it to the far off places. One day we were driving around Riga in Latvia and trying to find our way to the shopping area. Road signs and traffic rules were a little hard to decipher. Just as we realized that we were going the wrong way down a one way street, we see a police car pulling up behind us.

Not good! Natalie was driving on this day and rolled her window down to chat with the Latvian officer. He said to her in broken English, "You have broken law, you need to pay 40 Lat." I am doing quick math in the backseat and with the exchange rate of almost 1 Lat = 1 GB Pound = 2 USD, that would be about $80. Now, we are getting into serious money! Natalie listens nicely to the man tell her that she needs to pay him cash now. Oh, so this is the situation! Natalie holds her own and says, "Okay, I will pay the fine, but you have to write me a receipt for the money that I am paying." He looks confused a bit and then says, "Okay, you only pay 20 Lat!"

Natalie was far from paying for the two officers' lunch, dinner and probably half their monthly rent for their home. She told him firmly, "No ticket, no money!" "Okay, please you pay 10 Lat" "If you give me a receipt" "Okay, go, go, go!" The lesson I learned that day, from Natalie, was priceless. I have saved so much money by not being afraid to talk back to the police.

Athens, Greece

One of these unlawful episodes was in Greece when I was traveling with two friends I had met prior on a tour. I was starting my ten month trip around the world and they had six weeks holiday. We joined forces and planned a common path. One of the places that had always been high on my list was Greece. We had about three weeks to spend in this region of the world and headed off to the Islands. On our way back from our "island hopping" we landed in Athens.

Athens is a great city with lots of history, rich foods and gorgeous people. We took in the sights and ate lots of gyros, but now it was time for us to depart. We went to the train station and purchased our tickets to the airport. I know you should never assume everywhere you go that everyone will speak English, but you would hope at a touristy place like the Athens Train Station at the window where you buy tickets to the airport that the man behind the glass would understand English. One would guess. After a short interaction and three tickets printed we were off to platform 2.

The train was shiny new, air con and fast-all compliments of the Summer Olympics initiative. We settled in for a 30 - 40 minute journey to the airport. I glanced down the train and saw two train employees coming along and checking tickets. I gestured to my travel mates to get out their tickets. We noticed some sort of hold up at a group of young, German backpackers in the next car. It was hard to hear exactly what was happening but from the gestures, it seemed as if the group did not have the proper tickets for this journey. The officials wrote them a ticket and made them pay a fine on the spot.

I was not worried at this point as we went to the "airport" window at the train station, and this train was in fact going to the airport. Here come the ticket checkers and they did not appear to be friendly. They motioned for us to get out our tickets, we do and they looked at them and turned to us and said, "You have wrong ticket, you pay 25 Euro!" I was not sure which of the three of us should handle this, but felt as the woman in the group, I might be less confrontational. I tried to explain that we thought we bought the right tickets and felt the ticket seller was to blame, not us. After all, we were not trying to scam out of paying, we were just issued the wrong ticket.

"You have wrong ticket, you pay 25 Euro each!" Oh, now my two travel partners are involved with the conversation and voices are raised and tempers start to flare. I explain that I think it would be fair to pay the "difference" but not the full fine! They were not having any of it. We explained that we would not pay their fee and we would like to discuss it with their superior. Not a problem for them, at the next stop they would take us off the train and take us to the police station. This is a common scare tactic, because they know we are going to the airport and we are on a time schedule that we would not, in fact, take them up on their offer to get off the train.

Now, I am thinking back to the German group and realized I only saw one of them pay and receive a pink receipt. The chances are the entire group bought the same type of tickets, so they must have come to some sort of agreement. I offered one payment of 25 Euro and said I didn't need a receipt; this meant that they didn't have to document that they received the money. I guess they were tired of arguing and wanted the 25 Euro for lunch so they agreed. Sometimes you gotta scam the scammers!

Malaysian Haircut

As I was mentally developing this story, I was unsure which section to place it in. As it is a haircut and head massage story, my first thought was in the Secret to: Massages Around the World. I was getting the haircut and massage at a Hair College and it was only costing me $2, so my next thought was in the Budgeting section, but as the experience continued, I realized quickly that it most appropriately belonged in the mishaps section and here is why:

As far as haircuts go, I am pretty cheap anyway. I usually get my haircut very short before one of my six month trips and then let it grow out until my return home. This saves me money on the road and the stress of finding a place I feel comfortable getting a haircut. Since Femi and I had met, he requested that I keep my hair a little longer. Since my next scheduled trip was Iceland, Spain and London, I reasoned that longer hair equals warmer head and we were traveling in January and would be seeing freezing temperatures, so it sounded like a plan. Directly after my trip with my cousins, I was flying to Malaysia to visit Femi for one month before then heading on my African overland tour from Morocco to Nigeria. Femi and I traveled around Malaysia from the north in Langkawi, to the south in Melaka and Port Dickson. We spent a lot of time touring the cities and relaxing on the beaches. The weather in Malaysia was hot and muggy and I was not enjoying my new longer hair.

I decided that before I left for three months in *Africa*, I had better get a trim at least. One day Femi and I were staying near the Bukit Bintang area of Kuala Lumpur. On our walk back to the hotel I saw a sign for a Hair College and it was offering a haircut for 6 Ringgit (About $2 US Dollars). Sounded good to me, so I sent Femi back to the hotel to rest and I was ready for my salon experience. This was definitely a no-frills place. The front was clean and sparse in decorations. The receptionist was efficient and smiling, getting me the next student within minutes. All was going well! I guess I should have been more nervous that a student was cutting my hair, but after all I was only there for a trim.

I've played International Charades for many things, but this was the first time I had tried to explain ½ inch in sign language/English to a Chinese student in a Malaysian hair salon. Everything was bound to go wrong. She just kept nodding yes, and in my experiences in Asian countries, the nod can be very dangerous. Asian people want so much to please you so they say "yes" even when they have no idea what you are talking about. I did think about trying my "purple elephant" trick. In the middle of an exchange with someone that does not speak English as their first language and I am going round and round and am unsure if I am getting my point across, I sort of test them. I just say, "purple elephants," and see how they react. If they just keep smiling and nodding, I know they have no clue as to what I am trying to say. I did not test this poor girl, as we were having a heck of a time already, in hindsight, I probably should have.

When I thought that we had agreed to the cut, she began washing my hair. Most salons bring you to the sinks and wash your hair while you lay back and relax, but here they actually wash your hair while you are sitting up in the chair. I guess this is more efficient when they have over 20 customers in the shop at the same time. She was a cute girl, Lin was her name. She was Chinese and shy but always smiling. "This can't go too wrong, can it?" She used a mustard type squeeze bottle filled with water and another filled with shampoo and slowly from the center of my head outward, she shampooed my hair. I remember sitting there completely relaxed thinking "Heck, if this goes alright, I will ask if I can just pay the $2 to have another shampoo/head massage again tomorrow!"

Amazing! She washed my hair for about ten minutes. I was getting my wish because I kept thinking I never want this to end. I realized she was just stalling. She washed my hair for another ten minutes. At this point she won't have to cut my hair, it will all just fall out. After a time, she must have finally gotten up the nerve to begin and walked me to the sinks to rinse out the gobs of shampoo in my hair. Let the fun begin! I could hardly believe it; we spent ten more minutes in another round of charades, and then the scissors finally came out!

I could not bear to watch. Normally, when I am getting my hair cut at home with Lori, my hair stylist and friend, we talk so much that I don't even notice she is cutting my hair. With Lin, I felt every cut. She combed my hair so many times, each time putting a different section of my hair into large clips. I had about ten clips in my hair, and it really isn't that long. The first chunk falls to the floor and I realize the "growing out" stage is over.

Throughout the process she would just stop and stare at my head, not doing anything. The instructor overseeing the students was also Chinese. She was a very stern lady and she was not impressed with her student's lack of cutting so she would come over, rant something in Chinese, grab the scissors away from her and CHOP my hair in a very Edward Scissors Hands sort of way. Then she would walk away and leave it to Lin again. This happened a few more times. I felt so bad for Lin that I almost forgot it was MY hair getting chopped off.

I have been in the salon for almost an hour and a half so I started looking forward to the times the Chinese Nazi instructor would come over and cut my hair, at least we were getting somewhere. A total of two hours and five inches off my hair and I was finally done. Poor thing, I did not have the heart to act as shocked as I was when she spun me around to show me the hack-job I had received. I did only pay $2 for the *trim*. Guess it is true "you get what you pay for!" Well, on the upside, I had three months in Africa to grow it out before I had to return home. I should have put a note on the feedback form telling them to do the head massage *after* the cut, and then maybe the customers would leave the salon a little less shell-shocked!

I am not sure what bothered Femi more; the fact that I had no hair left or that I was gone for over two hours. I knew at that moment he would be a good husband because he just smiled and told me that I looked "Great!" I knew he was lying, but he passed the test.

Wow! That is a lot of examples of how things don't go "just right" while traveling. So with all the headaches and hassles, why continue to go back out on the road and do it again the next time? The challenge it gives me - seeing if I can make it through another trip smarter and stronger than the last time. The rewards - meeting exciting people, experiencing diverse cultures, and seeing what Mother Nature has given us first hand. And, if for nothing else, for the story!

Secret to: First Aid Abroad

American Clinic in Russia

LET ME START OUT by saying, BUY travel insurance! I have never been one to purchase the extra insurance on a rental car, or up my coverage on my personal insurance, but once I started traveling to faraway places, I changed my tune a little. It was the beginning of summer and I was off for a 35 day Scandinavia and Russia Tour with the ever-popular Contiki Tours. This is the same tour company David, John and I used when we did the camping tour in Western Europe, so I kind of knew what to expect.

There were long nights of drinking and even longer days filled with sleeping on the bus. Some might argue that this is not the way to travel, but at this point in my adventures, partying and meeting boys was top of my list. I mean, it has to be better partying in a campsite outside of Oslo than back in Michigan, right?! The tour was broken into two sections: 17 days Scandinavia and 18 days in Russia/Belarus/Poland with the tour ending in Berlin. The tour group was also split into those that were Scandi only, and then the diehards, my group, the Scandi-Russia crew.

The group got on well for being such a large group, about 35 people. We made the most of our time with the Scandis to say the least. But my core crew, Marc and Damon, an Australian gay couple, and Tracy, another crazy Aussie, and I took this partying thing to a whole new level. We were in Scandinavia during the summer solstice and the sun never sets this time of year, which means you have no point of reference for time of day. The sun doesn't set, so you never want to sleep and it also doesn't start to rise again, so you don't realize it is 6a.m. and you are still awake partying!

We did have fun playing with the ones who decided to sneak off and try to get some sleep. One night at a campsite in Andalsnes in Norway, we noticed that Mark and Damon had slipped away to their private caravan (camper). Our group was so large that we took up all the traditional tents and cabins so all that was left for two of the group was this old camper trailer off by itself near a ravine. Mark and Damon were the unfortunate ones to get the camper and the wrath of drunkenness that followed. We got the great idea to "rock the caravan" and scare them. Oh, it worked. We rocked it so hard that the dishes were falling out of the cabinets and the boys were inside zipped up tight in their mummy-style sleeping bags and couldn't get out as the camper was tilting, so they fell on the floor while still in their sleeping bags.

Oh, this would be funny enough if that is where is ended. Mark came out screaming and yelling and we promised "never to do it again - that hour!" We all went back to the campfire to drink more and laugh about our little prank. About an hour later, just when the guys fell back to sleep, we headed back over to the camper and did it again, this time harder and faster and never stopped even when we heard the screaming! We have it all on video. Too bad this was all before the days of YouTube!

We split from our group in Helsinki to pick up a new group that was doing the Russia only tour. Since we had gone through the Lappland Mountains of Sweden and had seen the reindeer and spent "Christmas in July" near Santa's Main Post Office in Finland, we wanted to keep with the holiday theme and have a "New Year's Eve Celebration" in Helsinki as our final farewell to our much loved Scandis.

You get the point right? We like to have any excuse to party! This sure didn't change once we crossed into Russia and the vodka got cheaper. It was only two Euro for a small bottle, at this rate it was cheaper to buy vodka than bottled water! Decision made! There were all kinds of "dodgy" businessmen that met the groups along the road and in dark alleys to sell pirated DVD's and discounted bottles of vodka. I said no to the DVD's, but bring on the vodka! Our tour group bought 86 bottles. By this time we have wrangled in another guy, Joseph, to our crew and with him, the five of us bought 40 of the 86 bottles. Now there is a math "problem" for you!

We arrived in St. Petersburg and started the touring and the drinking. Our tour guide, Anna, was a funny lady that brought along her own supply of Champagne or as she called it "Champansky!" We would stop to see a sight, drink a gulp right from the bottle and all yell, "Champansky!" We were also making Polar Bears – vodka and Champagne. It was actually better that we drank so much because we all woke up the next morning with a horrible case of BEDBUGS. Mine were confined to my arms and shoulder, but my bunkmate Tracy must have had them in her pillow too, because her face was covered in bites!

That night we went to the Russian Ballet and watched "The Swan Lake." Now, I am the first one to want to participate in the arts but with lots of vodka, bedbugs, little-to-no sleep and people from our group dropping like flies from some strange sickness, I was ready for the swans to fly off the stage! I spent the second half of the show lying on the cold floor of the public bathrooms. Yes, I said the floor. I wasn't alone. There were three other girls confined to the bathrooms, if you know what I mean. Finally, the swans all flew away and the show was over. On the ride home, there were about 13 of us very ill. We all spent the night in agony waiting for daylight. Yes, it gets dark in Russia. By morning, 16 of us were so sick our tour leader had to take us to a clinic.

The Clinic was called The American Clinic so that made a few of us feel a little better. I thought we were being taken to the Russian hospital. Just because it is called an American clinic doesn't mean they actually speak English. Now I am NOT trying to be an annoying American tourist here, but when you are this sick (105 degree temp) the last thing you want is to have to play International Charades. At least the sign for pooping and puking is the same in Russia!

We arrived at the clinic after a 15 minute bus ride - 15 minutes is forever when you have diarrhea. We must have been a sight. We entered the clinic and immediately lined up for the bathroom. There was only one toilet and 16 of us in dire need. As soon as one person would come out of the bathroom, they would go to the back of the line hoping they could make it until it was their turn again.

This was a small clinic for eight to ten patients and we rocked up with 16. They added a few makeshift beds and even had cots in the storage closet. Poor Joseph couldn't get any rest because they kept coming into his broom closet to get more medicine and supplies for the rest of us! The first full day in the hospital was a blur. I remember thinking I have to call my mother. She is going to get a call from my insurance company saying "your daughter is in the hospital in Russia!" I also remember the male nurse coming into my room that first night and asking me if I was warm enough. "Yes, thank you!" He left…with my blanket for another one of my partners in crime. "Too many patients, not enough blankets," he said as he walked out of the room.

One of the girl's husband was not ill but risked staying with us, because he loved his wife so much, but also to watch out for all of us. We were all mostly zoning in and out of consciousness. He was also there to play those dodgy DVD's on the second day when most of us were out of the woods with this rare sickness none of the doctors or nurses could figure out. They would come in and glance at your chart and say, "Vhat wronng vit you?" The second day, half of the group was released. I was in the unlucky half that couldn't pass the "can't poop for four hours" test. I was happy if I could go without for even one hour.

The group that remained was in good spirits as we had DVD's, contraband raspberry lollies from an Aussie girl's backpack, and rooms better and cleaner than where we would be staying with the tour group. We sat in one room and joked, "Mindi, they probably had to put vodka in your IV!" I responded in my best Russian accent, "is that Wodka in my Weins?" I would have rather had vodka in my IV than have to drink that grey, cement-like liquid called, something like, "SCHMECKTA!" We were going to get our group t-shirts made to say "Team Schmeckta" to remember our time in the hospital.

When dismissal time came the next morning, another girl, Amy, and I were the only ones that could not pass the non-pooping test. We knew this because after you are that sick in that small of an area, you know *everything* about each other. If most of the second group got released then for the good of the tour group, they would move on to Moscow by plane to meet with the group already there and leave those who "don't check out" to find their own way home or to the meeting point for the tour. So, Amy and I decided to head with the flight and risk the still annoying restroom issues we were having! So, we lied to the nurses and said we had not been to the bathroom in over four hours. So not true, I had just come from there!

Other than having no strength to carry my backpack around the airport, I have to say flying the one hour flight wins out over a 15 hour bus ride with diarrhea. That time the "math" was in my favor!

The biggest lesson I learned from this hospital adventure came when we returned to the group. My partners in crime, Mark, Damon and Tracy were not among the ones admitted to the hospital and had wasted no time trying to get me back "on the drink." As alcohol is the last thing I needed for my sensitive tummy, I tried to resist. Being one of the sober ones in the group now allowed me time to analyze the behaviors of my crazy drinking partners. WOW! Was I that annoying? I guess it is all perspective, and alcohol clouds the senses! Sorry to those I must have annoyed on the first half of the journey!

Tropical Lesions in Africa

I can't even remember a time in Africa that I didn't have the tropical lesions all over my legs. They officially began in Victoria Falls, Zimbabwe at Shoestrings Campsite. What an amazing campsite! Maybe it wasn't such a spectacular place, but it was the first time we could just lie around and chill and not be hiking mountains or flying over waterfalls. We could enjoy the pool, hang out playing music or lying in hammocks. I made friends with the "jewelry guys" and hung out with them at night around the campfire making beaded necklaces. I have bought more homemade jewelry than I could ever wear in my lifetime.

The night I got bitten was a night like the last few, sitting up on the picnic tables playing cards and waiting for night to come. We had little incense candles lit to keep the mozzies away, but in Africa and especially in a malaria zone, you have to DEET up. We were finishing a game of cards and kind of forgot to do the nightly ritual of walking to the tent to cover ourselves in bug spray. It only took a minute and my legs were covered in bites.

Tropical lesions are just bug bites that get infected, and now I had many of those bites. I had gotten penicillin over the counter, mass amounts of anti-bacterial creams and salves and nothing seemed to help. I finally found a proper clinic in Cape Town. The doctor there said that I had some kind of crazy bacteria that was growing in my body and the infection was coming out through any open sore. He instructed me not even to shave. He dressed all of my wounds and told me to stay out of the water. "Oops, I am sorry hot, South African doctor, but I am going Great White Shark Diving tomorrow!" He was not impressed. I would have to come again and get the sores redressed again after my crazy adventure. Good thing he was cute!

I fought these lesions for the next three to four weeks up the Garden Route in South Africa. I even had to forego the surf lessons in Jeffery's Bay because I still couldn't get wet. The doctor in Durban wanted to give me antibiotics through an IV. Yeah, I am not really up for that. No needles in Africa. I actually had my own needles with me. One of my travel partners was heading home and gave me her sterile pack of needles. Crazy to think you need to carry your own needles. I met a couple along the way that had an entire blood transfusion kit. I guess it is better to be safe than sorry!

My lesions healed over three years ago and I still have the scars on my shin to prove it! The travel souvenir that keeps on giving! So, a few rules you should follow when it comes to Mosquitoes: always inspect your mosquito net to find any holes - those little buggers are clever. Shut the lid of your toilet at night, either that or look before you sit, no need to explain any further! DEET is your best friend, you can't use enough of it, and lather up even if you have a good net! The over-the-counter stuff we get at home is not strong enough; I have my pharmacist order DEET compound and then make me up little lotions and sprays - 50% or above for sure!

24 Hour Clinic- Cambodia

During my time in Sihanoukville, Cambodia, I fell ill. I was not sure what was wrong with me, but I had a high fever and was having strange shooting pains in my side. One does begin to wonder, "Where exactly is my appendix?" when it is the middle of the night in Cambodia and you are in the middle of nowhere. I was ruling out malaria (mainly because I was on anti-malarial pills) but thought it best I get checked at a clinic in case it was my appendix. Luckily the owners of my cottage were from the United Kingdom and also spoke Cambodian. It was midnight when I finally felt this trip was necessary. They arranged a tuk-tuk to take me to the 24 hour Clinic as there was no hospital for four hours. Let's hope it is not my appendix.

My side was sensitive to every twist and turn and every bump in the road seemed that much bigger. The poor tuk-tuk driver was trying to drive so fast, but it was really making it worse! We finally arrived after about a 20 minute ride. I see that the clinic is no more than a little shop front. When I entered the clinic I saw about four people sleeping on cots all around the room. Are these people patients or staff? My question was soon answered when the man nearest to me stood up from his cot, still semi-sleeping and put on a lab coat. Let the International Charades begin.

Try explaining shooting pain in your side, fever and diarrhea to a Cambodian man who is still half asleep. During part of my charades routine I mentioned malaria. Oh, he liked this one, he turned to the pill counter, grabbed the antibiotics you would take if you were tested and found to have malaria. The problem was I was pretty sure I didn't have malaria, but if I did, I sure would want them to test my blood first before taking any medication. So, now I was getting angry and asking for him to test my blood and to check my side. He said firmly, "No, new doctor come at 7am." He actually refused to help me! I even asked the tuk-tuk driver to come in and try to tell him in Khmer. No luck! And so I had another 20 minute bumpy tuk-tuk ride back to my cottage, with me crying the entire way!

Throughout the night the pains got worse, my fever would not break and I now had the shivers. "This is it! This is the time when my luck has finally run out!" I dosed off and on all night, waiting patiently for 7a.m. to come. I had arranged to be picked up by the same man in just six hours. That morning we took the same bumpy journey, this time I was almost passing out from the pain.

Dr. Hour was the man on duty this time. Very pleasant, ran many tests on me, gave me pain medication and allowed me to sleep in one of their medical rooms until I felt stronger to make the journey back again. I was enjoying the air conditioning. If you think that I was getting his "individual" attention, think again. The entire time he was doing ultrasounds on my internal organs, he was on the phone with the ambulance driver. Apparently, they had just sent an ambulance from here to Phnom Penh (four hours away) but on the way the ambulance had gotten into an accident. In Cambodia, the ambulance drivers are not actually trained paramedics and the doctor was walking them through some basic procedures to help the patient that was riding in the back of the ambulance, who now had sustained more injuries. Guess my almost taking malaria antibiotics when I didn't actually have malaria pales in comparison to that man's story!

Random Pharmaceuticals

One positive thing about first aid abroad is that it is much less expensive than in the United States, and you don't need a doctor to prescribe medicine. Anyone can just walk up to the many little pharmacy stands along the road and ask for what they need. If you do need to go to a clinic, the nice thing is it is a doctor visit and pharmacy in one location. There is no need to run across town to turn in a prescription and wait: instant medicine! Well, you have to be willing to play International Charades to get them, but that beats $100 doctor visits for simple antibiotics.

I was traveling through a city called Pakse, in the south of Laos and realized that I had a urinary tract infection (UTI). Oh yeah, "hurts when I pee" is a great charade to try to pull off in an Asian country. Luckily, some of the bigger pharmacies have a list of "symptoms" posted in English with the local language translation next to it and you just point to what is wrong with you, and they find the medicine that will hopefully heal you!

Of course, there is a risk that they misunderstand my charade and give me the wrong medicine. Well, for a whopping $2 for meds, I decide to risk it and start the course of pills the smiling lady gives to me. I took the pills for three days and my problem cleared up. Whew! I lucked out on that one. I had returned home after about five months on the road and was cleaning out my toiletry bag. I found a few of the pills left from this pharmacy visit. I wasn't exactly sure what they were for, so I Googled the pill shape, color, and coding on the internet and found that these pills were in fact for a urinary tract infection...but for BOVINE. Yes, these pills were actually for veterinarians to give to their cow patients if they had a UTI. WOW! Makes me wonder what *udder* pills I have taken in third world countries. So far, no side effects that I know of - MOOO!

Anti-Malarial Pills and The Infectious Disease Center

One thing I have always taken seriously is vaccinations and anti-malarial pills. I guess I can thank Disney for starting me off right with this one.

As part of my orientation to the International Recruiting Department, I was scheduled for a barrage of shots at the local Infectious Disease Center in Orlando, Florida. I got the typical Typhoid, MMR, Hepatitis A & B Series, Tetanus, and the ever popular Yellow Fever shot. This is one of the most requested vaccinations worldwide. Well, the stamp on your immunization card is what is required. Only about 10% of the people who get the Yellow Fever shot actually come down with flu-like symptoms. Oh yeah, count me in the "lucky" 10%. Remember it is MINDI'S LAW. The flu symptoms came alongside having both of my arms so sore I could hardly lift them. I spent a few days at home with packs of frozen peas on my arms.

It is recommended to keep your immunizations up to date throughout your travels and most insurance plans do not cover the Infectious Disease visits. However, this is one that I will recommend to "break the budget" on. Traveling abroad is hard enough; you don't want to add being deathly ill to the mix. Speaking of "death", that is a *fun* part of the travel insurance game. Some tours that you travel with may require you to not only have travel insurance and prove it, they may also mandate what coverage you have. Many ask that you at least have "repatriation of the body" coverage. This is not exactly the normal thought that comes to mind when you are flipping through travel magazines and glossy brochures: "What if I die while on vacation? What will happen to my body?" If you research any travel insurance online they have already accounted for this and it is usually included in most policies.

One of the popular topics of conversation amongst avid travelers is malaria drugs. Which ones you are taking, if any? How long you have to be on them, what side effects are you having? There are three main options and any long term traveler out there will know them. (Please see the Infectious Disease Center in your area for medical advice, I am just rambling here and would never want you to take medical advice from me). The three types are: Doxycycline commonly referred to as Doxy; Chloroquine; and the most controversial is Mefloquine, A.K.A. Lariam. It was developed during the Vietnam War to help protect the troops from other blood-borne diseases.

All of the drugs have a downside: Doxy gives you super sensitivity to sunlight, not always good in the tropics, and it has to be taken every day. Chloroquine is losing its potency in many areas of the world as the strains of malaria are becoming stronger and are mutating. Finally, there is Lariam. This one wins the award for craziest side effects, which include the usual nausea, vomiting, and/or abdominal pain but also includes a section on anxiety disorders, hallucinations, and delirium.

I, for one, love the Lariam dreams. These pills are taken only once a week and that day soon becomes known as "Malaria Pill Day" which is usually followed by "Lariam Dream Night!" On most of my African overland trips, we would all find out each other's malaria pill schedule and be sure to find out what crazy dreams everyone had the night of their pill. When I first started taking them, I would have the craziest, most vivid dreams the night I took the medicine, *Lariam Thursdays*, but as the weeks went on and my body was adjusting to the harshness of the Lariam, Wednesday nights became the worst. It was as if my body knew the potency was lower and was craving the next dose. Not kidding, I would wake up in the night, with *no* grasp of reality. Once I was dreaming that I could hear lions just outside my tent and that I was camping in a wildlife reserve in Africa, only to awake and realize that I could hear lions just outside my tent and that I was camping in a wildlife reserve in Africa. Then I was thinking, this all must be a dream and felt the side of the tent to make sure it was actually there - and it *was* a tent. This goes on for a few minutes until I can finally get a grasp on reality - I could hear lions just outside my tent and I *was* camping in a wildlife reserve in Africa. AHHH!

I have been on Mefloquine about four or five times in my journeys and am lucky to not have the severe depression that comes along with the dreams, but I still tend to get a bit more emotional than normal about situations. I cry while watching Father's Day commercials on the Hallmark Channel so you can imagine what this increased sensitivity has done to me. An example might be a typical interaction with a local in Africa. I would smile and chat and find out about their village, their life, and what makes *them* smile so much. Then I would turn away and begin to "bawl my eyes out." Is this because I am so sad to see such amazing people denied even the most basic resources, yet despite this, they are the happiest people I have ever seen? Or is it that I have an increased sensitivity because of the crazy drugs I am on? The answer is all of the above! The Lariam factor is that normally you could keep yourself from crying until you were out of their sight, only now, you just *HAVE* to break down, right there and then!

Secret to: Group Travel

MANY TRAVELERS OUT THERE have a strong opinion about whether or not to travel on an organized tour. Some feel that it is "cheating" and that to really get the most out of your time away you should do it *all* on your own. All I know is that I really enjoyed having the security of the group in the beginning to get my *travel legs,* if you will. There was always someone to tour with during the day, and nights were more social because I was with 30 other people. If you are budget conscious and watching your pennies, this is also a great option because with larger numbers comes economies of scale, so the tour companies can offer you a chance to see an area of the world cheaper than you could on your own. Not having to plan every detail is a plus too, sometimes.

I could list the cons of traveling in a big group, but I really relish the group dynamics and have been fortunate enough to enjoy my experiences more often than not. I do have a philosophy as to how to approach a large group atmosphere. It does depend on the size of the group and the number of days we will be traveling together as to how I proceed. If the tour is a shorter one, I am sure to *cut to the chase* and share more details of my life and travel stories, but if the tour is longer than a few weeks, then I know I can hold back and analyze a bit more. I like to spend a little time with everyone on the tour. Of course, it is easy to find the people that I "click" with, but I feel that I am meant to meet everyone for a reason, and by forcing myself to meet all of the group members I am able to get more out of my time with the group.

A fellow traveler and friend of mine, Natalie, has a philosophy of the "Rule of Six." She believes that even after you meet all of the people in your group and promise to be lifelong friends and keep in touch forever and ever, you will in actuality, only stay close to six people. I have to say that with all of her group travel experience combined with mine, we can confidently say this is the case. I have even started a tour and tried to predict on the first day which six that would be. Many times I have been surprised that I was way off! I recommend giving everyone a chance.

You could also end up traveling in a group of solo travelers, which is probably the best scenario of all. I have had many opportunities to be part of a large group that had formed at the "main hostel" and then decided to do daytrips and more travel as an "unofficial" group. Most travelers do have somewhat of an itinerary of where they are headed, so if yours matches with theirs you have instant travel partners. When the time comes for paths to split, you can do so without creating any hard feelings. I love the feeling of bumping into each other again along the path. It is crazy how it feels just like bumping into an old friend!

Jordan

I remember when I was booking my 35 Day Middle East Explorer tour, I was really excited about Turkey and Egypt, but was unsure of what I might see and experience in Syria and Jordan. I can say I was pleasantly surprised with all of Jordan. Now would be a good time to mention that this was the first time our guides Gavin and Christa had led this tour, so we were all learning as we went. We would prepare a few questions to ask Gavin about our next destination and he would always answer with, "We will see when we get there." See, group travel is not always boring and predictable!

We entered Jordan intending to set up a bush camp, but found the surrounding area to be too built up for us to set up camp for 22 people. Gavin used his Aussie charm and talked a small restaurant owner into letting us move the tables around in his dining room and let us put our swag down and sleep on the floor. The family was so excited we were there that they brought us drinks and Shishas (large water pipes that you smoke flavored tobacco from) and taught us the craziest version of Rummy I have ever seen. At one point of the night it was just me and three of the older men playing cards. Proud to say I was holding my own. I taught them the solitaire game that my Aunt Wanda taught me many years ago. They loved it. The men kept smiling and asking, "What is name of game?" I said "I don't know, my Aunt Wanda taught me." "AN TWANDA, good name!" So, from this point on we all called it the "An Twanda" game.

Jordan brings back so many memories and it is on the top of my "surprise locations" list. There were so many spots along the way that were not really planned, or anticipated, but happily delivered an unforgettable experience. We visited Mount Nebo and the memorial of Moses, hiked through the stone city of Petra, and swam in the Dead Sea - or rather floated in the Dead Sea. The salinity level is so high that you can't sink. They told us that if you get even a drop in your mouth it would make you get sick and I can't even imagine what it would feel like if you got any in your eyes. I could tell how strong it was by how much a little cut on my hand hurt.

I was one of the last to make it down to the water and plop in. As I did I realized that I was feeling an intense *sting* in the bottom region. Yeah, if you have ever traveled, you have had traveler's tummy and you know it requires a lot of time in the toilet. As I looked around to see if anyone else was feeling this same pain as I was, I heard Christa exclaim, "Oh yeah, we are all feeling the *burn*!"

The salt forms crystals on your skin as you are drying and it was necessary for us to wash off. Gavin had read the past guide's notes and said he would find us a freshwater waterfall to rinse off. How cool! Not so much! We pulled into a parking lot off the side of the highway that many locals were using as a picnic stop. The problem was, this is not a picnic stop; it has no garbage containers and the families would just throw their waste out of their cars and all over the ground. THE FLIES! Oh, the flies! They followed you everywhere; they would get in your eyes, in your ears, and they attached to any cuts you had. I had my sarong over my face and they still were getting to me. I have never been so close to a nervous breakdown in my life. Speeding away in the truck with the flaps down helped, but many hung on for the ride!

On to our next adventure, the beautiful Wadi Rum desert and a four hour desert jeep tour. This particular trip taught me that sometimes you just "pay for the tour." When you travel in a group, there is a mix of travel styles. People who don't read guidebooks, and people who buy every excursion and take the full day versus the half day just *because* it is offered. Some are on such tight budgets that they have to weigh the options each time, and sometimes they miss out of the best parts of the country because they are trying to save $10. This tour of the desert was well worth the price. We had lunch in the canyon, climbed rocks, and slept in the desert under the stars. The moon was so bright on this night that Christa and I didn't even need our flashlights to write in our journals.

Sometimes locations are memorable because of other people's experiences rather than your own. We were setting up camp just before sunset and thought we should all take a quick break and climb the rocks to watch a desert sunset. We all started scaling the rock face and going off in different directions. We noticed one of the couples on the tour, Manuel and Caty, heading off to a quiet spot away from the group. They were definitely our group's most romantic couple, so we gave them their space. The sunset was one of the most beautiful sights I have ever seen in my life. It was made even more special for us once we realized that Manuel had proposed to Caty as the sun was setting. He had been carrying the ring around for the whole month waiting until the right moment. Manuel, I would have to agree you chose well my friend, you chose well!

I will also always remember early in the morning of our departure we were packing up camp and realized that Steve, one of the group members, wasn't any where to be found. Somebody had seen him go on a "walk-a-bout" earlier in the morning and he had not returned yet. It is important to say that Steve had been late back to the truck on numerous occasions and the group was unsympathetic to say the least. "Guys, this is a desert, not a city. If he doesn't come back, we have to search for him; we can't leave him!" I pleaded. I can't believe the group decision was actually to leave him. They reasoned that there was a ranger station somewhere around where we camped and maybe he walked there. We would stop by on the way out of *the country* and see if he was there and if not, report him missing.

I watched every speck of the mountainside as we flew past looking for his bright blue jacket. Was I the only one that was worried? Note to self, never go on a "walk-a-bout" when traveling with a group, and get lost. They may leave you! As we were pulling into the ranger's station, a red pickup truck was barreling behind us, honking its horn wildly. I noticed it was Steve in the passenger seat, smiling away! He had wandered into a Bedouin cave, met a family, and had coffee with them and just lost track of time. Steve does not wear a watch. "OH, Steve!"

Onward and upward! This part of the journey becomes memorable for me because it wins awards in "the worst toilet ever" and "the longest border crossing ever" categories. We were heading across Lake Aqaba to Dahab, Egypt on a ferry. I usually like ferry crossings because there is more room than on the truck or a bus. You can walk around and they usually offer some kind of food and have accessible bathrooms. In the Muslim culture, it is customary to perform an ablution (washing of feet) before Salat or prayer, so around prayer time we found ourselves waiting to get into the toilets. As you enter, you notice water sloshing around all over the floor, women with their pant legs pulled up washing their legs and feet. The water was so deep we had to pull *our* pants up too. I am talking up to your ankles in water, and was it really just water? The toilet stalls were even deeper, so you were balancing on the sides of the walls to not slip into the sludge, all the while the door would pop open and expose your bare butt. The Muslim women found this very humorous and would push the door closed for us. However nice this seems, it was actually a hindrance because it would launch you forward and you would almost fall into the toilet. Wow, yet again, I wish I was a boy! The bathroom experience is not over once you leave the toilets because the water follows you out to the ferry floor.

Four hours later we arrived to a crazy, busy mess at immigration. Gavin had to organize the visa and paperwork for the truck so one of the other group members was in charge of getting the passenger visas we needed. It was dark outside but you could still see the masses of boxes filled with food products, linens and live stock. These people were waiting for that evasive immigration official to come by and approve their cargo. The entire place smelled of urine. I believe that the toilets here were just as disgusting as the ferry, so many chose to go outside.

The passenger visas were easy to secure, but Gavin ran into some trouble with the truck paperwork. Apparently a "new law" was passed just yesterday requiring more paperwork for the truck. He refused to pay the large bribe the officials were asking and so we were going to have to wait until morning when he could call the home office in London. We had two options, move on without him and pay for taxis into the nearest town, or hang out and sleep at the border with the truck. This was not a matter of money, rather of security. Even as a group, we would draw a lot of attention and thought it best to all stick together. Twelve hours later, after a night of sleeping outside on mats, and men with machine guns guarding us (or were they guarding the truck so we didn't leave?), we were on our way!

The reward for this leg of the journey - DAHAB! That means *gold* in Arabic, and boy was it ever: sun chairs, milkshakes, pancakes (crepes), sunshine and water….what else could one want? Me? Massages! I made friends with the massage man and acted as the liaison between the group and the massage studio. I received a free 90 minute massage for every three my crew paid for. Everyone was ready for massages and I cleaned up! I still wonder to myself if I flew directly into Dahab today would it be as magical and relaxing as it seemed after all we went through to get there? I hope I get to find out someday!

Family Travel

One of the first questions people ask me once they find out how much I travel is "Did you travel with your family a lot when you were younger?" That would make the most sense if I was raised in a household that traveled around, but we spent most of our travel dollars on trips to Florida where most of my mother's family lives. I remember thinking that I was very privileged to have traveled on an airplane when I was so young; many of my classmates had never even left Michigan. I did raise money and travel with my French Club to go to France, Italy and Switzerland when I was 15 years old. Even then I was "counting countries." I had been to Canada, America and Mexico, and by taking that trip I had doubled my number.

We started traveling as a family after I had already found my job that allowed me to travel nonstop. During my breaks from work, we enjoyed going on family cruises. Just after the September 11th attacks, we decided that life was too short and family was too important to put off spending time together, so we booked a Christmas/New Year's cruise of the Caribbean out of Tampa, Florida. On a day stopover in Costa Maya I wanted to visit the Mayan Ruins. I had asked both my brother and my mother to come with me, but neither was that excited about it. I hadn't asked my father yet, but there was no need as he really didn't have a choice because he was getting *the look* from my mother, so he "volunteered."

Mindi's Law was already in effect this early in my traveling career. We were waiting for the tour guide/driver to arrive at the port so we could leave for our day excursion and he was a little late. My father was not too sure about this adventure from the beginning and seemed to lose confidence once we realized that it was our driver's first day on the island. He was unsure how to get to the ruins and had to stop and ask the locals all along the way. My dad and I just laughed in between being launched in the air from the bumps on the road and stopping every few minutes. We finally arrived in one piece to the temple and then really started to laugh. It was a Mayan Pyramid alright, but it was just that, all alone in the middle of a cow pasture. We literally had to dodge stepping on cow poop as we made our way to the pyramid.

As we approach my dad said, "Oh, you are gonna climb it" meaning, we came all this way, make the most of it. I was about to climb when the guide came up and handed us his camera and asked if we could take *his* picture in front of the ruins. Priceless!

I am not sure what the exact explanation is for how well my family and I get on during travel, but I think it was a combination of my experience in handling difficult travel situations and the fact that at that point in our lives we didn't get to see each other on a regular basis so we tried to make the most of it!

Our family bond was put to the test during our holiday backpacking tour of England, Scotland, Wales, Amsterdam and Ireland. I was living and working in London at the time, and invited Mom, Dad, and brother Brent and his wife Amber for a three week backpacking trip. I thought it was important for them to see how I travel rather than just hear the stories and see the pictures. I did plan most of the journey just to save us time as they were only over for less than three weeks. My mom is a chronic over packer and I was happy to see she heeded my warning that you carry what you pack. We spent some of the time touring around London and staying in my flat. Other cities we explored were Edinburgh, Dublin, Amsterdam, Liverpool and St. Andrews. I surprised my brother and father with a Christmas lunch on the St. Andrew's Golf course, complete with Christmas crackers. We had a great time wandering around the town and really lived it up that night in the pubs of Edinburgh.

I was happy for my family to see what it was like to sleep in hostels and meet random strangers as roommates and bar mates - and did we ever! When I began traveling and mentioning that I stayed in youth hostels, my mom asked, "Isn't that where bums live?" I am glad she can now say firsthand how nice some of the hostels actually are. In our first hostel, our room was on the top floor, up 99 steps to my father's dismay. We had a girl in our six bed dorm that was staying in the hostel until she found a job and then she would find a flat. I explained the rules of keeping your packs locked and your valuables safe just in case our roommate was in the room when we were not. I really didn't have to worry about her going through *our* stuff; it was my mom that was the one to watch. She was "inspecting" the girl's clothes that were hanging on the bedpost and realized that she had a dress shirt for her interviews with the tag still on it! "I bet she is going to wear it and then return it!" My mom was proud of her investigation skills, while the rest of us were nervous the whole time that the girl would come back as my mom was rummaging through her things!

During our touring of London we set out to climb St. Paul's Cathedral. At the advice of Natalie, I always look for the tallest building, climb it and catch the view. St. Paul's has 530 steps to the Golden Gallery, and of course, I suggested we climb it. My father was still recovering from an ankle injury so he was lucky enough to sit this one out. My mom, Brent, Amber, and I headed to the top. The staircases were difficult to maneuver with a combination of winding stairs, tight spaces and some of the staircases offered an unwelcomed view straight down to the bottom. My mother was freaking out to say the least. She was sweating and climbing, complaining and panicking, and all the while, my brother was in her face with the video camera. She wanted to go back down, but the staircase was UP only and other climbers were coming up behind her. Sometimes, it is just too easy to enjoy those moments. Once she reached the top she was too afraid to even peer over the railing and just sat on a window seat and caught her breath. I captured this moment on film, and today it is still one of my favorite moments of the trip. Way to be brave, Mom.

My brother held his own as a backpacker- at least he had the basics down. We had a five hour stopover in Newcastle and we wanted to wander the city and get in a few sights. Brent was the first one to grab the map and start navigating. There was nowhere to store our packs between buses so we had to carry them around. I remember being at the back of the group and smiling. *This was my family and they were living out an adventure with me.* My brother also grasped the idea of "budget" which I thought would never be the case. We had taken a ferry from Holyhead, Wales to Dun Laoghaire, Ireland and had to make our way the short distance by public train to Dublin city center. The directions after the train were not clear. Brent suggested we walk it rather than take a taxi and use the money we saved for extra beers. I think it runs in the family! Budgeting - not drinking (well, that too)!

I am glad to have had the chance to spend that time with my family, showing them a glimpse into my lifestyle and creating the memories we still laugh about today. "The Actual!" My brother and his wife just had their second child and a trip to faraway places is off in the future, but as I explore the world, I am making a list of the places I will take them someday. Get ready for Africa, Amelia June!

Cousins' Reunion Tour

I flew straight from South America to Florida to visit with my Grandpa Stull, my mother's father, who was fighting a battle with lung cancer. They had told me that he was getting worse and that it would be a good time to come and spend some time with him. As part of my visit, my Aunt Mary, being the gracious host that she is, planned a family dinner for some of my family living in the area. As we sat around and chatted about life and all of our latest adventures, we quickly realized that this was the first time in many years that this group of cousins had gotten together.

Thinking of Grandpa being sick, and how fast life gets away from you, we decided to make a pact, a traveling pact. My favorite! My cousins Timothy and Casey were in for sure! We decided to make our first trip to be Las Vegas where our other cousin, Lynnea lives. We had all been to Vegas before but thought "not together," so we booked our tickets. It was just that easy. Casey and Tim used their Holiday Vacation points on a room from Planet Hollywood and we used many of Lynnea's local connections to really "take on the town!" We spent four days living it up in Vegas and the whole while talking about where Cousins Reunion #2 could be.

I told them that I was planning a trip the following January to Iceland, London, Spain, and then on to Malaysia to see Femi and finishing with a three month overland tour of Africa from Morocco to Nigeria. I knew that their schedules would be too busy to clear them for the entire journey, but to my excitement they were both in for the first three to four weeks. I knew that we were going to be able to travel well together. First of all, any time we are together, all of us or just a few of us, we always have a smile on our faces, so that is a good thing.

The emailing and researching began right away and once the tickets were confirmed, the only thing we had to do was wait! January came quickly and we were on our way. I was going out to New York to visit a very good friend of the family, Chelsey, who was living out there. My cousin Casey had a friend in NYC, too, so the two of us began our adventure a bit early. Now, I could write a book about all the fun we had in NYC, but will spare you the specifics and just say that we had a very good start to our reunion tour. We met Timothy in the bar at the JFK airport, and kicked things off with Coronas and Crown Royal shots.

Arriving into Reykjavik, Iceland about 9a.m. and it was still dark, we now realized that during their winter it is dark for about 20 hours of the day. We had from about 11a.m. to 3p.m. to have daylight and we vowed to make the most of it! We got checked into the Backpackers hostel and headed for...the Pub! We had to have our very first Viking beer. Only problem was, they didn't start serving lunch until 11a.m. and we were a few minutes early - another Viking then? Two beers, jet lag and a nice heavy lunch and it that was "all she wrote." Soon we were all back in the hostel, sleeping away our precious hours of daylight!

Iceland was a beautiful place; we enjoyed a Golden Circle day tour of the geysers, craters, geothermal plants, and the Pingvellir National Park was stunning. It was here that we saw the continental divide and we were able to check off seeing the world's northernmost capital! Kind of cool! Everyone from home kept asking all of us, "Why would you be going to Iceland? In winter?" We have plenty of answers to those questions now. We finished with a swim in the Blue Lagoon a truly unique experience. The geothermal water bubbles up hot and then the silica mud makes the water blue and milky. It is like swimming in a giant blue hot tub. We all got the in-water massages. You lay on a floating mat, cover up with a fleece blanket that is soaked in the water and this very large Icelandic man gives you a massage. He has to re-dunk you every few minutes to warm you up again as it is freezing outside of the water. The lifeguards were in full gear. We even got free massages from the massive waterfall and hid out in the cave hot tubs and steam rooms! A "Must-Do" in the world for sure!

Days were filled with wandering and touring, and the nights were filled with drinking and wandering! We found a British Pub in Iceland, funny that! And we also found SPIN THE WHEEL. This was a large wheel behind the bar and if you paid about twice the price of one beer (and in Iceland, that is a lot) you could take the chance at landing on a *winning* section of the wheel. Our first spin and Timothy won us a METER of BEER. Metric conversion are swirling and we were trying to figure out what a "meter of beer" would look like. "Isn't a meter distance not volume?" As we were pondering this notion, the bartender arranged ten pints on the bar and began to fill them all. Oh, a meter *long* of pint glasses - we loved this math!

The rest of the five days that we were in Reykjavik we did venture out and try other pubs and restaurants, but it seemed that as our crew from the hostel grew, so did the number of nights we had to show the "new person" how to SPIN THE WHEEL. In the morning when we woke with a slight hangover we would call it the WHEEL OF DEATH.

After Iceland comes London and Majorca, Spain. Well, because we were traveling in the "off season," Majorca was really quiet. We were in one of about four rooms occupied at the resort. Thanks again to Tim and Casey's Vacation Club points. We had a gorgeous condo with a rooftop patio and our very own winding staircase! The first night we thought it best to just eat in the hotel restaurant and find out from the locals what was happening on the island. Boy, did we ever meet the locals! One word: Sofia. She was the restaurant owner's daughter and was in charge of the place while her parents were away on holiday. Many of the locals had left the island to enjoy life somewhere else until the weather was better and they could return in time to greet the tourists.

Sofia was a "hoot" - partaking in the local beer as much as the other couple at the bar. We had so much fun chatting with her during dinner (which we thought she might drop at any moment) that we decided to stay after and have a few drinks with her at the bar. We were happy we did. I have always felt that meeting the locals in an area is the best way to get to know the place. Sofia and her partner filled us in on the few bars that were still open for this time of year, gave us ideas on how to spend the next few days, and helped us organize everything we needed to have a fun few days in Majorca. We could have kept to ourselves and possibly not found a thing to do on the island, leaving with a bad feeling about Majorca, but instead we had the inside scoop.

The next morning we decided to take their advice and hire a car to see more of the island. Along with the off-season comes off-season prices, and you know I love that! We hired the smallest of small cars I have ever seen in my life (Panda). I have a picture of Timothy standing by the car. His foot was as big as the tire. Now, my cousin Tim is a big guy, but this car was a matchbox car. We drove all over the island that day, pulling off at lookout points, taking amazing pictures, and enjoying the sunshine. I would just smile every time we wandered back to the car; it was just so…small!

Returning to ice cold London from Majorca was not easy, but it is one of my favorite cities in the world, so we managed. The old-fashioned pubs, fish n' chips, and plenty of pints helped us along as well! We spent a few days wandering around, playing tourist, and finished our time together in true *cousin fashion*. We knew we were all going to be getting together again soon for my cousin Lucas' wedding and were happy to know the reunions would continue!

My Last Truck

Well, after all of the group tours I have taken in my travels, I finally have to admit defeat. The "truck drama" got to me. I would like to think it was mostly the heat. I will let you decide. There was one day where we were traveling all day through Mali and arrived in a town called Nioro. The drive was daunting, and made worse because the only way to stay hydrated was by drinking *hot* water from our plastic water bottles, and it was becoming a bit too much. Even if you find a shop that has semi-cold water, within minutes of it being exposed to the heat of the day, it becomes too hot to drink. We would joke that we could just pop in a tea bag and have hot tea.

I was on cook group the night we arrived and had to go to the local market with my group to do the shopping for dinner. The market was so hot and it was filled with the smells of fish and red meat that had been sitting in the sun all day. I sat down to catch my breath but then *lost it.* My body was too hot and I started to have a little panic attack because I realized there was no way for me to cool down. My tentmate Kayelene was my savior, and she got me back to the truck. She and our driver, Mark, dumped water all over me and started fanning me. Here is a travel tip for you: if you are overheating and need to cool down quickly, pour water over a bandana or scarf and then drape it over your head. When the breeze hits it, it turns cool, even if the breeze is 100 degrees. I didn't believe it myself, until this episode.

That drama over, and another begins - group travel, you gotta love it! People were saying I just faked passing out to get out of cooking that night. Yeah, that was fun for me. I could have opted out of preparing the group meal, but cooked anyway just to prove them wrong, which looking back now, was a bad idea because I was totally exhausted. I ended up having it out with a guy on my cook group because he was being lazy and not helping with the dishes, AGAIN, and we both got yelled at by Mark, the driver, like we were five year olds. I had had enough and spent the rest of the night crying in my tent deciding what my next move should be.

The very next night the group was deciding whether to go down an even hotter, bumpier road than we had the day before, and this time it was *just for the adventure.* There was a perfectly good sealed road for us to take, but everyone who was new to overlanding was looking for that story to tell. I normally would agree, but this was the first month of the trip that many were on for nine more months. I tried to reason that they will have plenty of adventures in the coming months, when it was not so hot.

It was April in Mali, and even the locals don't move around during this month. Our highest recorded day was 45 degrees Celsius, roughly 113 Fahrenheit! I was drinking six liters of water a day (almost two gallons) and not peeing. So when the truck voted to go the bumpy road anyway, I took a vote for myself and got off the truck the next morning in Kayes.

First order of business, I checked myself into an air-conditioned room for two days and drank water nonstop. I felt much better after taking a proper shower and sleeping in a comfortable bed. On the Tuesday, I took the long, dry, dusty train from Kayes to Bamako. I remember feeling truly happy while sitting on that train because for the first time this trip I had to arrange my own travel plans, fight the crowds, and speak the language. Even with my French as bad as it was, I realized the Mindi I know and love was back in action. I was enjoying the scenery going by, at my own pace.

Once I arrived in Bamako I said a little prayer for a *"Travel Angel"* and as it always goes in travel, if you have good travel Karma, you will get what you ask for. This travel angel's name was Mahaman and his uncle owned the Auberge Lafia Hostel where I was staying in Bamako. He asked if I wanted a guided tour around the markets and the town, offering to take me on his motorbike. I was still a bit dehydrated from the train journey, so I opted for the motorbike tour rather than a walking tour. You have to realize how big of a step this was for me. When I was traveling in Vietnam, I went an entire three months protesting motorbikes because when I was there I saw a young man on a motorbike killed by a delivery truck. They are too dangerous for me. In Mali, I caved, mostly because it was bloody hot there and going fast on the bike at least made it feel a little cooler.

I met back with the truck to find out their plans and realized many were still holding a grudge against me so I decided to spend the next seven days off the truck as well. Mahaman was from Tombouctou (Timbuktu) and offered to be my guide through Dogon country and then take me up to his family's home. I found out from the group that the roads to Timbuktu were closed to tourists, or recommended that we don't go there, as some French dudes were kidnapped near there a week before. Sorry, Mom but I didn't tell you this part, as I didn't want you to worry. I laugh in the face of danger! Just kidding, but I did feel confident that Mahaman would get me there safely. The idea of staying in his family's home and experiencing the *real* African life was too attractive to pass up. That, and how cool is it to say I have been all the way to TOMBOUCTOU, especially since no one else in my group was going? Where was their sense of adventure now, when it counted?

To get to Timbuktu it was necessary to take a 4x4 truck as the roads were mostly just paths through the sand in the desert. Mahaman arranged for a truck that was leaving at night which meant we traveled most of road in the dark. I had sudden flashbacks of Masai Mara when we got stuck and had to get out and push. At least this time there were no lions in the bush, right? About half way through the journey the road breaks for the Niger River and it is necessary to take a car ferry across but we arrived at 1a.m. and the ferry didn't start running for five hours. So, where to sleep? The answer was not the one I was looking for - "in the dirt on the side of the road." Seriously? As Mindi's Law would have it, it was very windy in the desert that night and I awoke with sand caked in my eyes. Now I know where the *Sand Man* comes from - Timbuktu.

We were 12 in the truck with one riding on the roof, sitting on top of the luggage. I still can't believe that poor man had to ride up there the entire time. We almost rolled the truck two times and at one point everyone was praying out loud. I just kept saying, "We will be fine, it is going to be fine," the whole time picturing my head split open in the middle of nowhere in the desert in Africa. These are the adventures I live for. Not really - I could do without the life threatening flips. Our driver was great and gained control quickly, even pausing to check if the man up top was still holding on.

The stay with Mahaman's family was something I will cherish always. They opened their home to me. The head of the household was Mahaman's grandmother and she was such a strong lady. She was involved in every decision and made sure all who counted on her were cared for and that they had what they needed. She told me when I arrived on the first day they would consider me a tourist, on the second day, a house guest, but on the third day, I would be considered family. It was so cool to just lay around in the family room playing cards or an African version of the dice game "Sorry." The little girls loved my skin and my hair so they were constantly laying on me, touching me and massaging my head. The older sister did Tourek henna on both of my feet and one hand. Henna is a black dye that colors the skin. There is a special cream, and if applied each day, it makes the henna last longer. I was not complaining about the free hand and foot massages each day; I even received one from the grandma. I ate with them on the floor using only my hands and I have to say I got pretty good at *rolling* my rice. If you are ever there you will understand, and I am now big fan of peanut sauce, one of their local dishes.

This stay was a turning point for me in my life and in my travels. During my time with this family I realized many things about Femi and his culture. Even though the people of Timbuktu spoke French and were mostly of Muslim faith, they were still West African and I started to notice the similarities between this family and my husband's family. As an American, I was confused about some of the things Femi would say and do, not fully realizing the depths of his cultural background. Spending time in Mali with Mahaman's family allowed me to process the information without being too emotionally connected to the events.

A quick example of what I learned: when you grow up in an African family there is a strong sense of hierarchy, and a strict respect is given all down the line, obviously starting from the top. If you are the middle child, you have to respect the family members above you, but are able to request that the siblings below you, those that are younger than you, perform tasks for you. Some things might include running to the store and getting you something, fetching you a glass of water, or serving you your meal. So, the youngest child is constantly doing things for everyone in the house. This is opposite from how we treat the "baby" in the family in America. Before seeing this interchange, I always felt uncomfortable when Femi would send people to do things for him. It made me think he was being demanding and disrespectful; quite the contrary. One would think that after all of the cultures I have interacted with, I would have picked up on that one sooner. I am happy for my little adventure away from the truck because it gave me the clarity to realize I was ready to marry Femi.

Mahaman was such a great guide that I decided to have him take me into Dogon country. We trekked for three days and two nights through the small villages, stopping in the heat of the day for cold Fanta from an icebox powered by a generator. Along the way I even got a Dogon massage. When I asked what made it Dogon, other than the obvious location I was in, my masseuse said it was done with a special cream. It seemed like regular lotion to me, but I didn't really care, I was just happy for the break, because my legs were killing me.

There was a strong sandstorm brewing during my visit and all of my pictures turned out like I had a sepia tone filter on my camera. It was difficult to see very far in front of us on the treks, which takes away from some of the enjoyment of being "in the middle of nowhere," but I rather enjoyed the sand filter, as it also kept the temperature down. Trekking was quite peaceful except for when you would pass a local. The traditional greeting in Dogon country goes something like this (but in the local language): "Hello!" "Hello!!" "How is your family?" "Good, and your family?" "Good, and your wife?" "Fine, and your children?" "Okay, and your health?" "Fine, and yours?" After my guide explained that it is customary to ask at least seven questions, I started to pass the time by counting each time he greeted someone. It sounded so sing-songy in the local language and made me smile every time.

My favorite location was the Bandiagara Escarpment. The village is set high upon the hill and is one of the main entry or exit points of the area. My guide was quick to join the men of the village, sending me off to the women and children section of the camp. We were lucky (or unlucky) enough to arrive on a Sunday when the entire village gathers at the highest point of the camp and celebrates the week with their homemade millet beer. I have tried the local "brew" a few times in my travels and it always brings with it a case of "Delhi belly" so I politely declined. I seemed to be the only one not drinking it, and this included the children.

Children of all ages were lining up near the big pot and waiting for their portion of the smelly beverage. I looked around and noticed many kids segregated into groups, mostly by age, all with their own supply of the beer. Even small children, under two years of age, were holding their own cups or frantically trying to drink from their mother's cup. I even saw babies still breast feeding, taking a break from their mother's milk to partake in the celebration. At first, the children were running around, being silly and playing with me. I was bouncing them on my knee, giving "Horsey Rides" and playing "Peek-A-Boo" until I started to notice they were all becoming visibly intoxicated.

Children were running and falling down. One small boy hit his face on a rock and was bleeding. He came stumbling to his mom, who wiped the blood away and gave him more beer. A little girl was very fascinated with me and we were sitting together playing and then she started to become very violent. She was hitting me and yelling. The only thing that calmed her was...you guessed it, more beer. This was a scene that I quickly found disturbing, and made eye contact with Mahaman across the village and asked to go back. I have told this story to a few other travelers and they said, they too had similar experiences but they didn't think much of it. Of course, they were enjoying the millet beer a little too much themselves! Even writing this out for you all now, I still can't decide how I feel about it. I am putting it away in the little file marked "WOW!"

When I was finished with the trek, my plan was to meet back with the group and see if I could continue traveling with them. When I got back to the truck I wish I could tell you why the people on my truck were so dramatic, but it was just the stars were not aligned for me. I have had amazing group travel experiences until now. I had never come across such a group of controlling people. The two main culprits were female - imagine that, bitchy girls.

The most drama came from our cook groups, or the girls wanting to control everything. The big highlight for me was when we all voted to change our cook groups around. They had called for the vote, manipulated the group all week with secret conversations to be sure the vote went their way, and then the group changed direction during the chat and voted opposite of what they wanted. That was good for me because I was with all the people who didn't like me, well maybe it was just that they didn't appreciate that I was always having a fun time talking to the locals and playing with the children while they were listening to their iPods and reading their books, not even looking out the window. It really did start to feel like an episode of "Survivor" only without the option of voting people off! The only cure for this was to vote myself off once again.

We were crossing into Ghana and I had been waiting to get there for some time and did not want to miss out on enjoying the country by falling victim to group dynamics. So when my tent mate Kayelene said she needed to get a new passport in Accra, I was happy to volunteer to hop off the truck with her to help sort it out. We had a *secret plan* not to meet back with the truck until they were about to leave for Togo. After a few days away from the truck, Kay was ready to join back up, but I couldn't bear it, so I made another solo run. She had eight more months on the truck and she said she needed to just get on with it. I, on the other hand, only had six weeks left. I have to say this is the first time in all of my travels I was wishing the time away.

I had arranged with Mark to meet the group later that month in

Krokrobite, just outside Accra. This is the best place in Ghana if you ask me. I made sure I was a day early to sort myself out and look like the pro when the group arrived, not like any of my crazy truck mates would take my advice; most of them were too stubborn. During my time on the coast, I didn't have a chance to check internet and I had missed a message saying they were staying longer further up the coast and would be delayed in meeting me at Big Milly's Campsite. I can't say I was sad, especially since I found Ayeeko a.k.a. "The Rocks," and King Ray. He is a local musician, business man and all around African Cultural guide. He helps continue the growth of Ghana through his organization called www.ayeeko.org. He was my guide around Krokrobite and I was even invited to his recording studio session where he recorded a new track for his upcoming CD.

My only wish for Ghana was no mozzies with lots of breezy days ending in drum filled nights. I was rewarded with two of the three. There could be no drumming as a local village festival was going on and in honor of their past ancestors they have no partying and drumming, basically no loud noises for one month. It made the place a little quieter than I expected, but it was a perfect place to chill out and rejuvenate and get ready for the *pack* to return.

I had decided to finish the next two weeks with the truck to transit through Togo and Benin, mainly because this was the fastest way to get to Femi and Nigeria. Not to mention I was running low on money, and because my accommodation and food was already included on the truck, it was a better budget decision. I just kept a low profile and tried to ignore the *girls* as best I could.

So, my last truck on this latest trip from Morocco to Nigeria was just that - my last truck! Maybe it is due to the fact that I am slowing down my travel a bit (to get married in Nigeria) or that I have already had the chance to tackle most issues that come along with traveling in a group, but I realize now that I have run the gamut on group travel. I think that I have now found the style of travel that suits me best - on my own. I might give truck life a go again someday when I bring my family to Africa for safari; at least then we would have power in numbers!

Since the beginning of my traveling career I have taken: three Contiki tours; three African Trails' trucks; one Oasis Overland truck; a tour each with Stray, Paddywagon, and Baz Bus; and have traveled with various groups of my friends and fellow travelers. I have even traveled with members of my family, including my husband, and each and every trip has been a welcomed adventure in connecting with people, nature and culture.

Secret to: Connecting with People

A GUEST SPEAKER AT a training session I once attended talked about "connections." He was referring to connections in the service industry, but they relate to travel as well. He explained that we need to increase our interactions with people. As a society we are actually demanding that they decrease; ATM vs. bank teller, fast food restaurants rather than eating at home, even sending an email instead of making a phone call. It has been too long since we made sure we went to someone's house to visit them, now we just "shoot them an email" or worse - "Facebook them!"

We have to be careful not to say that technology is helping us stay "connected." It used to be a girl told her best friend she was engaged in person, not by putting a picture of her ring on Facebook. Or she told her parents she was pregnant with some formal announcement, not updating her status. I feel the same way when traveling; don't just go to another country, check into an all-inclusive resort and let your only interaction with the locals be asking Javier to bring you another Pina Colada. Interact; smile at people; ask questions, and learn!

In this section, I am sharing stories that have multiple points I am trying to make, but the overall take away should be the connections I formed with people along the way.

Zimbabwe Economics

Here is a little explanation of Zimbabwe Economics. First lesson: bank rate ("official" rate) versus black market rate. The bank rate when we arrived was 250 Zim Dollars (ZD) to the US Dollar. We had to change at least $20 USD to get a receipt that proved we changed money upon entering the country. In actuality, we would be trading the majority of our money on the black market. There were men that risked life in prison to sell us 3000 ZD to the US Dollar. (A pretty big disparity) I traded $50 US and got $150,000 ZD. At the bank rate, I would have had to trade $600 to get that many Zim Dollars. The reverse math is even more shocking and this is the part I still can't get my head around.

In our campsite, a soda is $2,000 ZD, less than a dollar at black market rate, but at "official" rate it is about $8 USD. The stores and markets set their prices based on the black market rate that is illegal. I paid $13,800 ZD for my burger and chips. That is $55.00 USD, and also a local's two week salary. So how can they afford to live here? A t-shirt in the shop was $50,000 ZD (a month's salary for a t-shirt). We were advised not to use our credit cards here because then we would get charged at bank rate and really pay $55.00 US for our hamburger.

Probably the most exciting money changing I have ever done! The tour group had to trade as one person, so here comes the math I so much enjoy. There were 20 of us trading at an average of $100 USD per person, so $2,000 US x $3,000 ZD = $6 Million ZD. The denominations were in the 500 and 1,000 notes. Can you imagine the piles of money? We had to have a secure back room at the camp because some people had a bag full of money when they came out.

So much for keeping a low profile and not being "showy" with our money. Usually this is a pretty easy thing to do., but not when the locals can't even shop in the stores for more than a few items like bread and milk. I would go to the counter and pay $10,000 ZD for a hunk of cheese; $40 USD in their system. But, no one blinks an eye, because the cashiers know you got your money on the black market. The total bill for our group meal was $300,000 ZD; a whopping $1,200 US if we changed on the up and up!

The government had just dropped a few zeros on the currency before we got to Zimbabwe. It was almost $300,000 ZD to the US Dollar. The money actually had an expiration date printed on it. They can't even guarantee that the money will be worth the paper it is printed on...literally!

We did an organized tour of the capital city, Harare, with a nice man who had been working with our tour company for years. He showed us all around the city and shared the economics and history of his government, but the biggest lesson I learned was from him and *his* story. He and his wife had four children. His wife's sister had passed away recently and left them with her five children. They were trying to feed and clothe nine children in a crazy, backwards economy. She was working a decent job by American standards; she was an accountant for a big company. I am not sure of the exact numbers, but she was making about $20,000 ZD per month. She was paid at the "official" rate because this was a business on the up and up! She could only walk in the store and buy two hunks of cheese, for the month! Her husband, our guide, had to take a job working with the tourists, so he could charge a rate that we would find acceptable and he would be able to make enough to survive. We were paying him about $3 USD each to be on this half day tour. From our group alone he was bringing in more than his wife could make in a month performing one of the top jobs in Harare.

Now, it sounds like our guide was rolling in the money. This was not so because the economy is so volatile that he was not even sure that the value of the money will stay the same by the next day when he goes to the market to buy food, or that the staple items like rice and flour and sugar will even be available in the street markets rather than the supermarkets! Instead of a tip, he asked that we go into the supermarket and buy him rice and flour for his family. That is one currency we all know the value of! We were all very happy to shop on his behalf. The few minutes we spent in the store shopping for the items he requested became a real eye opener for me. I had never shopped with the thought that I couldn't actually afford the basics. We all bought a few more things than requested, including some items to give to the children, and then handed them over to his wife, who was waiting outside the grocery store with tears in her eyes. She wasn't the only one choked up!

Syrian Shop Owner

I visited Syria while on a 35 day Middle East Explorer trip during the second Bush Administration. I feel this is necessary to explain as during this time tensions were (and still are) high in the Middle-East towards the Western world, namely America. Bush had said some pretty horrible things about the Syrians and their government. I was a bit worried about securing my travel visa at the border. There was only one other American on tour, Christa, and she was one of the guides, so she had arranged for her Syrian visa in advance.

I was hoping that the promise from Lonely Planet of getting get my stamp at the border would hold true. The group was given the visa application paperwork in advance so we could fill it out and make a timely crossing. That happened for everyone, everyone except me! First of all, we all had to be searched and questioned. They separated the women from the men. We were a bit nervous about that. It is just nice to have a safe male presence in case things get out of hand. I was traveling alone, but some of the women were very upset to be separated from their partners.

It turned out the only reason we were separated was for religious purposes. In the Muslim culture the women are not able to show their face or hair to men other than their husbands. This room was for security checks and passport validation. They had to be able to see the women's faces to match to the ID's. Also, the body check had to be performed by a female.

Crazy situation averted! We hoped now this would be the end of the border business and we would be sent on our way. Well the rest of the crew was stamped and passed through but they made me stay and fill out more paperwork because I was American. Thanks, George! The border crossing only took three and a half hours in the end, not too bad. I did apologize to a few of the border officials on the behalf of our "leader."

We arrived in Damascus and the thing to do there was shop. During the visits to the Souks (very large shopping areas) we would hear men yelling out to us, "Hello, where are you from?" "Australia? Sydney? Melbourne? G'day Mate," or they would try, "You are from Canada, eh?" I was nervous to tell people I was from America. It is always an internal struggle deciding whether to hide where I am from enough to be safe, but not hide it enough to feel like I am not proud to be from America. Some Americans go so far as to sew a Canadian maple leaf patch on their bag. In my opinion that is a bit unnecessary. We don't have to be as patriotic as Uncle Sam, but we should be able to defend our Nation, or at least ourselves. Many times, however, I was with an Australian, so when they guessed we were from Australia I just went with it.

I was in a little shop on the outside of the Souk and was looking at this shop owner's goods. We started chatting and he asked me where I was from. I almost said Canada, but looked in his eyes and said, "America!" "Welcome to my country, are you enjoying it?" I remember thinking that so many people have said that exact phrase to me - hundreds of people, actually and it never felt more sincere than at that moment. He then told me that he was very happy I did not tell a little lie like many other Americans tell him, that they are from Canada. I explained that it is not that I am ashamed to be American; it is just that my president says and does many things that I do not agree with. His response was perfect, and one I have thought about a lot on my travels: "I am not my government, and you are not your government, we are just people trying to make it in this world." I couldn't have said it any better myself.

The next two stories are my favorite connection stories and you can already see why by the title of this one.

How I Met My Husband

Every girl dreams of her Knight in Shining Armor riding up, sweeping her off her feet, and riding off into the sunset, right? Well, not me; not really. I mean, don't get me wrong, I have always wanted to find Mr. Right, but I was in no hurry to stop my traveling life to wait for him and soon came to hope I would meet him traveling, therefore upping my chances that he would like to continue a life "on the road!" The other people in my life seemed worried that I was not finding anyone. In America, being 30, unmarried, and no boyfriend was not an easy lifestyle to defend. On those days that I would feel a little lonely and wonder where oh where is the man of my dreams, I would talk to my mom, and she would always give me the same advice: "Everything happens for a reason, you will meet *him* when you are meant to meet him." My grandma also tried to be helpful and said that maybe my Knight was not riding a horse, maybe he was riding a bike; meaning it would take him longer to get to me! All I knew then was *I was meant* to travel, so I did!

I was living in London for just over a month when I was invited to a "Girls' Night" by a friend, Karma, who I had met on my Scandinavia-Russia tour. She was also living in London. Karma was having a few girls round and invited me to enjoy wine and nibbles. The surprise guest that night was a friend of hers from work who just happened to be a psychic palm reader. I have had my fair share of Tarot card readings and have always taken them as a means of entertainment, never too seriously, mainly because they all told me that I was going to meet "the man of my dreams" within the next six months; which obviously hadn't happened as of then. But this lady was different.

She was pretty spot-on in her assessment of me and my life. She told me that I loved to travel, (true), that I was close to my family and was missing them, (true) and that I was always up for adventure, also true! These are all things that one could guess when speaking to an American in London. However, she told me a few other things that really grabbed my attention. First off, she said that I would not live in London long term, but I had just arrived and was on a five year visa. My *only* plans were to live in London, so I was a little skeptical. Second, she said that I would "meet a dark skinned man and he would make me an offer that I could not refuse." I was kind of seeing this Australian guy and asked her, "Could he be a really tanned Australian?" She responded with a definite NO! Maybe this lady didn't really know what she was talking about after all. I enjoyed my time with her, jotting down a few other things she said so I could reference it later. I was about the fourth or fifth person to have a reading that night and good thing I took a turn when I did, because the rest of the night was kind of "fuzzy" as I drank more wine!

Strangely enough, the first prediction did come true in April of that year. The economy was taking a turn in London and companies were not using recruitment agencies all that much at the time, so I was let go. Mom's words were swirling around in my head, "Everything happens for a reason," and I agreed and took this as an opportunity to travel more. About five years later, in January 2009, I was traveling around South East Asia and found myself in Ho Chi Minh, Vietnam on the first day of the Chinese New Year. This was the Year of the OX which happened to be *my* sign. So, I set out with the mantra - "this is going to be my year!" I have to admit, I was still secretly holding onto the words of that psychic and throughout my travels was waiting for that dark skinned man to appear. Well, I was in South East Asia, so the chances of that happening were probably "slim to none." To my surprise, there were many African men in this area of the city. I let my mind wander, "What could they be doing here? Business? Studying?" All I knew was it was a big surprise to me.

I found myself in Vientiane, Laos a few weeks later, wandering the waterfront area of town. I was looking for a little lunch and a place to relax and read my newest find from a book swap. I noticed a little café with a few African flags and Bob Marley music coming from inside. I am always a fan of Bob, so I wandered in to check it out. I ordered my lunch and sat there for a while, quietly reading. As I was paying and about to leave, a taxi cab pulled up right in front of the restaurant. I noticed the guy in the backseat, thinking to myself, he is pretty handsome. I glanced over at him and he gave me this amazing smile that lit up the car. I should have taken my change and wandered back to my hotel, but something was keeping me there. I pretended to be looking around, like I was a little lost. Damsel in distress! He took the bait asking me if I was lost or if I needed help finding something. He explained that he was Nigerian, and was visiting his brother in Vientiane, and he was in fact living in Ho Chi Minh, Vietnam, at the time. I explained that I had just come from there and we started chatting about life in South East Asia.

His name, he told me, was Femi, and he invited me back into the restaurant for a Beer Lao. As you might have guessed by now, this is the dark skinned man that made me an offer I could not refuse! I said yes, and this began a wonderful traveling love affair. He had a few weeks free and was interested in what my plans were. I mentioned that I was finishing Laos and then heading to Cambodia. He was in the process of moving to Cambodia to try some business there and suggested that we travel around together for a bit. We did just that spending the next two months traveling and living together in Cambodia. Guess Grandma Stull was the closest on the prediction, but he didn't come by bike; he came by taxi cab!

My Aunt Julie told me that when I was in love, truly in love, I would do things that I never expected. Boy, was she right. I have rules when traveling. If you meet a guy, cool - but never change your plans. If he can come along with you, perfect - but don't miss out on what you were hoping to visit. Cambodia was country number 99 for me. I had planned to get to Indonesia, country number 100, at the end of March, but found myself still in Cambodia, living in the Tol Tom Poung area of Phnom Penh with Femi. I had a flight out of Bali, Indonesia at the end of April and finally *had* to move on, leaving Femi in Cambodia with the promise to keep in touch and to work on a plan to come back and visit. During the time I was away, Femi moved to Kuala Lumpur, Malaysia to takes classes towards a degree in business. I went back to Malaysia on my 2010 trip and spent another month with him. We traveled around Malaysia, discussing life and our plans for the future. We had decided that, yes, in fact, we would get married, but were not sure of the exact plan as he still had two more years in Malaysia to finish his degree.

My Nigerian Wedding

After I left Malaysia, I headed to West Africa. I would start in Morocco and end in Cameroon, or so I thought. As I traveled through the West African countries many things were happening to me. I was traveling with a group on an overland truck and it was not going very well, to say the least. I had really connected with the locals in this part of Africa, seemingly more than in East and South Africa, which was a good thing as my future husband was West African. I remember thinking how wonderful the people were and I was particularly taken by the hospitality shown to me, an outsider. Maybe it was a combination of the Lariam, the drama queens on my truck, and the amazing experiences I was having in my fiancé's homeland, but for the first time in my life I was wishing to be somewhere other than where I was. I was ready to get married.

I emailed Femi and asked if it would be possible to meet up with some of his family, and even better, if he would be able to make it to Nigeria during that time. When we were discussing the plans, I suggested that perhaps we could get married, early, in Nigeria. I mean, since we were going be there already and were getting the family together, why not? Femi kicked it into high gear, having only three weeks to plan everything. He had help and we both want to formally thank Uncle T for arranging the registry paperwork, and his younger brother Kayode for taking care of so many details. I hope we can repay him someday when it is his turn to get married. A big hug to his friend Taiwo; she is so beautiful and helped to make a special mark on our day as well.

Thank you to the rest of the family for rearranging their lives and schedules on such short notice to spend this special day with us. It was so easy to be the bride. I didn't plan a thing until I got to Lagos.

The only thing I had to do was make the call to my parents and tell them the good news. I knew that they would be supportive. Due to the short time frame, I was unable to have my mom and dad at my wedding. Mom and I had a typical "mother/daughter" conversation that went something like this: "Are you sure you won't be sad that you weren't there for the wedding?" "I am okay, as long as you are okay that I am not there!" "I am fine, too, but just want to be sure that you are fine!" "Of course, as long as you are not sad that I am not going to be there?!" Now that we had *that* settled, we could get down to business.

I tried to rewrite the day's events but couldn't put it any better than I did in my group email right after the wedding, so here it is:

JUNE 9, 2010

Well, I know in my last entry I left you all hanging that Femi and I had decided to get married...what I didn't tell you is that we were planning it for our time in Nigeria! I AM MARRIED... WE ARE MARRIED!!!!!! We didn't want to tell too many people until we were sure we could work out all the paperwork here in Nigeria, but God was with us and helped us to plan everything perfectly and we had our BIG day yesterday - June 8th, 2010. So our wedding date is 6-8-10. We wanted to make it easy to remember.

We got married in Lagos at the Marriage Registry with his two brothers, two sisters and father present, along with many of his friends and extended family. Actually, it was a small event by most standards. If we would have told more people, the whole village would have been there, but we wanted to keep it small. We had a little lunch reception with food and cake at a little deli called "Sweet Sensations" and it was perfect. Good news, Femi had the whole thing videoed so once we get copies most of you will be able to feel you were right there with me.

So what was it like to get married in Africa? Well, first of all, I didn't need to do the crazy wedding dress shopping. We picked out a wedding fabric and bought it for everyone attending. They then take it to their local tailor and have a dress or shirt and pants made. I have to say it looks so cool with everyone dressed the same. I loved the pattern we picked. I went to the tailor and flipped through African fashion magazines and mixed and matched the styles I liked until I had the perfect African wedding dress. I even got to wear a big head wrap and shawl that are traditional for his tribe. Femi's family is from the Yoruba tribe and his great grandfather was a chief in their village. The chiefs wore traditional beads that are orange in color and are worn as a necklace and bracelets to signify their status in the community. To honor this tradition, we both donned the beads.

I was smiling to myself all day. Some brides get so caught up in the details and get upset with little things like the napkins don't match the tablecloths or the flowers are not what they expected; I didn't even know what was going to happen from one minute to the next and I couldn't be happier! His friends and family made sure everything was perfect.

Many people have asked me some silly questions: Did you have to sacrifice an animal, perform some tribal dance, or be a part of any other crazy rituals? Part of me did want to mess with people and make up some crazy story, but no, it was all quite similar to our American traditions. It was a very special day that I will remember always.

Now, the sad news, I have to fly back to the US on June 11th and Femi flies to Malaysia. Honeymoon is over fast, eh? He has one year of university left and I have to work, but I am planning to go to my husband in September in Malaysia. Sounds crazy - My husband! FINALLY! Many of you have known me for a long time and know that I would have waited forever to be married if he wasn't perfect! I have found my "soul mate" and am so happy on this day!

I remember when I told my best friend David that I had met Femi and that we were going to get married he said, "It will make a great *last* chapter to your book!" This isn't the last chapter but it is one of my favorites! Who knows? You might be seeing another book from me called <u>Backpacking with Kids!</u>

Secret to: Connecting with Nature

Pacaya Volcano - Guatemala

MY TRIP TO ANTIGUA and the Pacaya Volcano, 19 miles outside of the city, is near the top of my "Top 10 Things I Have Seen in My Life" list! Not many people that I know can say that they were two feet away from flowing lava.

Antigua is a cute little town with all of the amenities to keep a backpacker interested and comfortable for a few days. Christa and I were ready for a good old fashioned "admin day" full of internet, banks, future trip booking and shopping. They even had a McDonald's there - perfect hangover food! We were in need after our "Big Night Out" at the Irish Pub. We met back up with a few guys we had originally met in Mexico City. One of the guys, Irish Joe, says a party can always be found at the Irish Pub. I have found this to be true all over the world. That is probably the best advice to give any backpacker in search of a party: if there is an Irish Pub in town, it is probably a good place to start. He introduced us to baby Guinness shots here! We *paid* for that one.

All of the guest houses, hostels and internet shops had signs out front offering a volcano tour, so it was pretty simple to plan our Pacaya trip. We decided to go on the 2p.m. tour so we could do most of the hiking in the daylight. They do offer a night tour, but we had heard from other travelers that the day tour was easier to hike and nicer to actually see the volcano.

Our tour company picked us up and then spent the next hour stopping at many other guest houses to collecting the remaining people for our tour, (Guatemalan time.) After a short drive, we arrived at the base of the volcano just inside the national park. The typical scene of children touts trying to sell you walking sticks, flashlights for the dark walk back down and a few horses in case you don't want to hike the mountain.

I said no to the walking stick, had my own flashlight and told them I might want a horse. Oh, I wish I would have paid the price up front and saved myself the torture. The hike was straight up for the first bit; they called this "San Francisco Hill." I did my best to keep up with the group. I was so out of breath. The guide would stop at a few points along the way to rest, but I was so far behind that by the time I reached the resting spot everyone was ready to move on.

Flashbacks of hiking up Mt. Sinai where I walked most of it but decided to pay for the camel for the rest of the way. (Actually, we were cheap and shared one camel between three of us) So, learning my lesson well, I opted for a horse ride the rest of the way. I felt a little stupid being the only one on a horse, but figured at least I didn't keel over and die. That would have been *really* embarrassing. I got off the horse after only a few minutes because the park gate was too small for the horses to go any further. Of course, my horse guide was not going to tell me that.

Either way, I enjoyed not having to climb for that short time. We had to walk a bit more over a grassy mound and then found ourselves navigating over cooled molten rock. It was very light and airy, and moved very easily under your feet. It was necessary to pay attention to your footing at all times. Once we walked over the peak, we could immediately see the hot, flowing lava rolling down the side of the volcano. I can't really put this experience into words; it is so unique. It was a crazy sight to say the least; tourists everywhere with long sticks trying to roast marshmallows over the lava, people posing for pictures, Christa trying to take mine with my hand over the lava, and all the while, lava just flowing by.

During our visit we even got to experience a large lava rock breaking off near the top and rolling down the volcano. It was a moment when I was thinking, this is really cool but it could go very, *very* wrong. It was rolling down the hill away from us at first, but it hit another rock and changed directions, rolling closer to us. Right at the last minute, it hit another large rock and changed directions again, rolling safely away from all of the tourists. That was a little wake up call. This is an active volcano that can erupt at any moment. Puts it in perspective a little hey?

Land of the Midnight Sun - Nordkapp, Norway

A trip to Scandinavia is not complete without a visit to the northernmost point in Europe. Some will argue there are others, but as far as in my travels this will be the closest I will get to the North Pole and the midnight sun. During the summer solstice, it was possible to see the sun at Nordkapp for 24 hours. The sun will still try to set around midnight, but when it comes close to the horizon, it is already on its way up again. Our group was there for almost three hours from 10p.m. to 1a.m. and witnessed the "dipping sun!" Many times the weather is really foggy and snowy, but we were fortunate enough to have a clear day, or night, I guess! One person in our group set up his video camera to the time-lapse setting and filmed for the whole three hours. Looked pretty cool when he sped it up! This place is one that reminds me of all our Earth has to offer.

Felucca Trip - Egypt

The felucca trip down the Nile from Luxor to Aswan was much anticipated by all on the tour. We had heard many stories about how hard it was to be a girl and sail because there are no toilets on board the felucca. We had also heard how amazing it was to sail down the Nile for two days and enjoy the sun and fresh air. So, 18 of us set off on a two day journey into the sunset. We decided to go with the felucca theme and buy Nubian dresses for the trip. Even the boys bought head wraps and gowns. We spent the first few hours of sailing doing a full-fledged photo shoot. We painted our toenails. We even painted some of the boys' toes once they fell asleep. The day was filled with reading, playing cards and just taking in the beautiful river scenery.

The bathroom ordeal wasn't as bad as anticipated. The captain would pull to the side of the river anytime we needed to use the "toilet." Actually, we just had to wander up the shore and find a bush. The worst part was that the locals were used to the tourists coming down the Nile and they would wait "in the bushes" in hopes to watch you pee. As if it isn't stressful enough to have to pooh in the trees, let's have people watching you, too! Oh, the fun of travel!

At night, we pulled over to create a makeshift campsite. We all slept on the felucca, but went ashore for the campfire and a session of Nubian drumming by the captain and the first mate. This is a life I could get use to. They offered the group to stay on one more night, but we thought it better to get on with the temples and pyramids. The captain did ask me to marry him and sail on the felucca with him forever. A marriage proposal and a new career opportunity - might have to give this one some thought!?!

Salt Flats of Uyuni- Bolivia

After finishing my share of adventure sports in La Paz, I was now ready for a little dose of nature. But first, another overnight bus trip. The hostel told me to expect about a 12 hour journey. We departed on time, around 9p.m., which is something I did not expect. I arrived the next morning at 8a.m. after a very bumpy ride to Uyuni, the launch point for the salt flats. I had booked my tour while I was in La Paz to be sure I could go on the tour the next morning. I was scheduled for an 11a.m.

departure. Now that's organization! Risky if the bus ran late, but this one worked in my favor!

I was in a Land Cruiser with six other people: three girls from Poland, a German girl, a Peruvian guy, and a Scottish guy! A good group, which was important since we would be crammed in for three days, freezing cold and eating nothing but junk food. The flats were so expansive, with white salt as far as the eye could see. They are officially 4,250 square miles and hold over 10 billion tons of salt. We visited the old salt hotel and had the option to stay in an updated version for $50 per person, but decided it wasn't *that* necessary. However, we did get to stay in our own Salt Hostel (salt blocks under our mattress and salt on the floor and we saved $50).

I wouldn't have minded a heater; it was bloody freezing. I don't do well with the cold, as the rest of the group will attest to! Man, it was COLD! On the second night of the tour it was so cold outside we had to sleep in all of our clothes, get inside our sleeping bags, cover up with three wool blankets, and wear a hat and gloves. I even had on two pair of socks. All this and I still had to keep my head under the covers and *breathe* for warmth. The next night my new cold buddy (one of the German girls) and I decided that maybe it would be best if we took Tylenol PM and "zonked" out for the night; at least if we were cold during the night, we wouldn't know about it! Worked - great night sleep, but small chance of hypothermia in the morning since the covers came off a bit and we *didn't* notice!

But, the sights were worth it! We visited Isla de Pescado and saw the gigantic cactus. The days were filled with driving for hours across the white desert. We visited Laguna Colorada and saw the flamingos. Some of the group actually swam in the Thermal Baths. It was minus 11 and you had to get out of your swimsuit back into clothes after the dip. Yeah, I could barely make it through the night with all the covers; I knew for sure I was not going to get....wet!

Peaceful Pisaq?

Part of the allure of traveling for me is the chance to "find yourself" and work on finding the answers to some of life's questions. What better place to look than in Peru? I had been to Peru five times with Walt Disney World as an international recruiter, and had a Peruvian roommate for 18 months, yet never found my way to Machu Picchu in all that time. My time had finally come.

Just like spending time in Panama City before booking the San Blas sail, it is also a good idea to spend some time in Cusco getting caught up on rest, Western Food and American movies. Many people also use this time to research their "perfect" Inca trail trek. Okay, a three to four day hike that includes a second day that is almost straight uphill, not my cup of tea, even if it is *coca tea*.

I have met so many other travelers who have done the trek and the one thing that I remember from each of them is when they finished the Inca trail and arrived at Machu Picchu, they were so tired they didn't even explore all of it. I wanted to spend my time wandering around this mystical place. I also opted to take the $6 shuttle bus to the top, where many hardcore travelers decide to save the money and add the two hour hike at the crack of dawn to the "bragging rights!" I know my limitations!

On the train the night before, I met an Irish girl, Cliona. We shared a room and planned to make the trek together. We were up early to catch the 5:30a.m. shuttle to the entrance of the ruins. A good tip we had both heard about was to head straight to the back to the entrance of the climb to Huayna Picchu as they only allow 400 people to the top each day. I was number seven and Cliona was number eight. If you take any advice from me, head to the top early. We were the only ones in sight and could go at our own pace up these massive steps. I am glad I had someone to help push me along - it was a tough climb!

We made it to the summit and only had to share the postcard spot with about ten others. We spent the time chatting, enjoying the views and taking pictures, full well knowing that the pictures would never do the place justice. At the top we met a Canadian girl and continued on the trek down as a threesome. We spent some much deserved chill time at one of the stone huts. While we were hanging out there, the Canadian girl explained to us that she had been mugged and lost most of her money. She was only one day away from catching her flight home but she was so close to Machu Picchu that she had to risk it and come anyway. She was down to her last Sol. Both Cliona and I put together some travel money and sent her on her way with a little renewed hope in mankind. We were happy to help a fellow traveler and I secretly hoped it would help in the karma department down the bumpy road of travel.

After nine hours of trekking, climbing, and exploring, I was ready for the bus ride down the mountain and was already dreaming of a hot shower. Too bad our $10 a night hotel does not include hot water. Once again, I surprise myself and take one of the coldest showers I have ever taken!

The next step on the "hippie trail" was Pisaq in the Sacred Valley of the Incas. I had already planned on partaking in a shaman visit before I met Joakim, a Swedish guy on my Galapagos boat who gave me the name of a shaman and told me how to plan a visit. I emailed and found out that they were doing one more ceremony for the season and then would not have another one for over a month. Timing was in my favor so I took this as a sign to continue on with the adventure.

Pisaq is a mystical little town surrounded by mountains, just screaming of days past. All of the people I met here had that look about them: the smile, the shine glowing around them, and most importantly the "twinkle" in their eyes. I felt like they were thinking, "I know something that you don't know." It's like the hippie who is in a daze and says how beautiful a flower is while staring adoringly at it. Out of context, one would think, "what is she on?" but here, it is part of the atmosphere, a contagious spirit.

My shaman visit was held in a little circular hut on the Shaman's compound and I was with about 15 others. We spent the hours of 9p.m. to about 4a.m. in an Ayahuasca ceremony. Ayahuasca (Eye-ah-waska) is a hallucinogenic vine that induces an amplified state of consciousness, and in this state it is said to be possible to find deep personal growth and to feel a holistic cleansing of the mind and soul. I am going to respect the ceremony and withhold my journey, but I have to say this is one of the most "magical" nights I have ever experienced. The "positive force" that surrounded me following the ceremony was undeniable. I noticed everyone in town seemed happy, peaceful and on a journey of their own. If this sounds like a quintessential hippie experience, it really was, in such a fun and happy way. Many people come here and get stuck. I can see how, because there was an instant community. I made so many new friends; we had meals together, played Extreme Jenga and spent time working on our hidden creative talents.

The days were peaceful and quiet and allowed time for staying under the covers and reading and writing, or listening to others play the guitar in the sunshine, or shopping in the fresh market for our group meal. However, the nights were not so peaceful. The family directly across the road from the compound had a few dogs that barked all night long. I figured they must be barking at the moon as there was never anything else out there. They were so loud it disrupted our sleep. The woman that ran the hostel found a solution; she fed them hamburger. Sounds nice, right? Well, she put sleeping pills in the meat. Is that the "Zen" thing to do? Yes! We all had to agree because that night we finally found a truly peaceful Pisaq.

Secret to: War Tourism

WAR TOURISM IS A controversial subject. Should people be visiting the exact locations of such devastation and loss? How do survivors and relatives of survivors feel about "tourists" paying to see these places that hold such painful memories? Does War Tourism help to educate a new generation of people with the hope of preventing these horrific events in the future? Can visiting the war torn regions of the past shed some light on the strength and courage of the people who had to endure these tragic times? I find it hard to put into words my experiences in places like, Auschwitz, or the Killing Fields, or Sniper Alley. These places mark such horror and pain. I am happy for the chance to visit them, pay my respects and learn about the travesties of the past, but I find it very sad and depressing, too!

War Tour - Sarajevo, Bosnia

When I am in a country where one of these monumental historical events has taken place, I try to take an organized tour. A lot of the time, as with Sniper Alley, the guide has lived through these events and can share his/her personal experiences. They can explain what it was like day after day, hearing the bombings, being scared to go outside and possibly be struck by a stray bullet. They can tell you how they managed to survive the shortage of food and supplies.

The area near the Holiday Inn in Sarajevo was called Sniper Alley because the Serbian fighters would shoot down onto Bosnian civilians as they walked through. At first, when someone was shot, an onlooker would run over and try to assist that person; but as time went on, the Serbs would just shoot the person who came to help, too. This stopped people from helping each other and many people would lie there wounded, but not dead. I spent a few days in Sarajevo taking in the beautiful city, but found it hard not to be reminded of the pain this community went through. The buildings all had bullet holes in them and the ground was splashed with red paint where bombs and mortars hit; an effort to memorialize those that were lost. These markings are called "the Sarajevo rose."

Part of the day tour included a stop off at the Sarajevo Tunnel Museum. There is a 60 foot section of the once estimated 3,000 feet of war tunnel remaining. The Bosnians dug the tunnel to the outskirts of the city in order to get people out and move guns, food and supplies in. This was the lifeline for a city that was under attack from the years of 1992-1995. The thing I have had to come to terms with about my country is how sheltered we are. I was in university at the time this was happening. I knew nothing of it. Was it my fault? Was I so caught up in my Tuesday Night $1 pitchers with the Sigma Pi's that I didn't read about it? Or was it the lack of coverage by the U.S. Media? Either way, don't feel too sad, America did help the refugees in this area; we sent them food and supplies…leftover from the Vietnam War (1973). Oh, so helpful we are! It was embarrassing to be an American that day on the tour. My only defense is that at least now I am out there exploring and I am making it a point to share these stories with my family and friends so they are able to learn from the past as well!

Stone Town, Zanzibar

We had just finished our Masai Mara game drive and were very excited about our sightings. I remember thinking, nothing can be better than today! Well, when we returned to camp we noticed that our driver, Gavin was nowhere to be found. Paulina (my Polish tentmate for over three months) and I were a bit nervous because we were the only two going all the way to Cape Town with African Trails. Our next destination was to be Zanzibar. We were worried we were going to be shipped off to another tour group.

Take the good news with the bad. The bad news was we *were* being transferred to another group in Zanzibar, but the good news was instead of at minimum 12 hours in the truck and an overnight in the crazy city of Dar es Salaam, we were being flown directly there by the tour company. A forty-five minute flight and we would be in paradise!

We had an organized tour of Stone Town as soon as we landed. This part is not as light and fluffy as Gavin's pancakes, so read on with caution. We did the Slave Tour. The guide led us into the dungeons where they would keep 75 women plus their children, all chained at the neck. The other side held about 50 men. The slave traders would keep them in the lower level dungeons for up to three days, with no food or water and only sea water rushing in to wash away their waste. They were unable to drink it, because it was salt water. Those that survived were considered the strong ones and were taken to auction for slave trade. At the auction, they were whipped, and if they winced and cried, they were sold for a cheap price, but if they could stand the pain, they could be sold for a higher price.

This was going on for like normal business trade from 1800-1873, yet another example of what we as humans can do to one another and what some people have had to endure. On my trip to West Africa, I visited the city of Ouidah in Benin on the Cape Coast. This is where The Gateway of No Return is located. Hundreds of thousands of African men and women were forced onto slave ships from this beach. During the tour our guide explained that the largest number of slaves were from the Yoruba tribe, because the men were thought to be of the strongest. This really struck a chord because my husband and his family are Yoruba. This is one connection with culture I wish I didn't have to make.

The Killing Fields - Phnom Penh, Cambodia

During the time that Femi and I lived in Cambodia we went to the S-21 Tuol Sleng Prison (pronounced: tool-slang) and the Killing Fields of Choeung Ek. This could be compared to visiting the concentration camps in Europe, but for some reason I was even more affected by this location. We had arranged to have a tuk-tuk driver for the day. I am sure that I paid more than most, but how do you negotiate a price on a day like today!?!

Let me start by telling you a little about the Khmer Rouge regime. Pol Pot was the main leader in the Angkor communist movement.

He had an idea to make everyone equal, but not in just resources; he planned to have a classless society where everyone had the same house. There was no longer a need for money because the people would work in the fields or his factories and at the end of the day they would be fed. So, in theory, everyone worked, ate and had a place to live. In order to get everyone to agree, his plan was to take the "city" people, the educated people, and kill them. He thought the rural people and those who could not read or write could be easily trained (brainwashed) into his way of thinking. Many believe the events that happened here were even more horrific than in Hitler's time because Pol Pot was exterminating his *own* people. From 1975 to 1979, under Pol Pot's rule, over three million Cambodians were tortured and murdered. I apologize if the following information is graphic, but this was how it was presented to us during our tour. There were actual pictures of the torture and many paintings depicting the horrific events. Here is what we saw that day:

We started at 9a.m. at the S-21 Museum. It was a secondary school with four large buildings, each having three floors. Each building and floor had different purposes. They evacuated the city of Phnom Pehn because they could not have people who were used to life in the city (the easy life) tell others of how it used to be. Pol Pot and his soldiers told the people, "Come with us, we will protect you from the United States; they are going to bomb the city in three days." That was a lie, although the United States did bomb in Cambodia during the Vietnam War. Pol Pot arranged for everyone from the capital city to be evacuated and brought to the S21 prison. There, they tortured them by ripping off finger nails, nipples and used electric shock to find out where their families were. Many tried to hide. Men, women and children were brought here, and at the height of Pol Pot's control, over 100 people were killed per day.

If the prisoners were not killed at S-21 then they were blindfolded and tied and brought to the killing fields. We visited one site, but it is said that there are about 343 others all around Cambodia. They dug shallow graves and brought the men and women to the edge of the grave and hit them over the head. They used bamboo sticks, axes and bayonets to kill them as bullets for this many people would have been too expensive.

There is a bone monument at the killing fields that houses the skulls of more than 9,000 victims, and you can see the evidence of how they were bashed in the skull! The way they killed the babies was what made me almost get sick. They would bash them up against a tree or throw them in the air and use bayonets to catch them. As many of us wonder... How? Why? Why didn't the soldiers try to change this? Well, just as with the followers of Hitler, it was kill or be killed. Many soldiers did try to escape to Vietnam but if they were caught they would be brought back to the killing fields and were beheaded in front of their comrades. Soldiers were instructed to use the palm branches from a young palm tree to saw off the defector's head. This was slow and painful and proved to be a very effective technique to deter any others from fleeing. Walking around the grounds, it was possible to see the clothes of the dead sticking out of the soil, with bones and teeth everywhere. During the rainy season, the water washes the dirt away and more bones and remains are found. I cannot explain the feeling I had inside that day.

So, as you can imagine the mood was sad and quiet. It is these visits that touch me the most, but are the hardest to explain in writing. These are places you must see for yourself and take your own feelings from it. I must say, I would much rather tell you about my crazy skydiving adventures or the times I saw some beautiful landscapes than tell you of such terror, but all of this happened in 1975-1979. Why were we never told of this in school?

There is still a lot of pain and poverty in Cambodia. The children are the worst victims, many are orphans and live in orphanages which are more closely watched now, but in the past men from all over the world would come here and "visit" little boys and rape and abuse them and all they had to do was pay a small fee to the people who were suppose to be protecting these children. The world is a crazy place. The girls have it worse, I believe. Many are sold into the sex trade by their own parents at the young age of 12 or 13. It is easier for a "brothel owner" to get more money if the girl is younger. The families sell the girls into the trade for about $1,000-2,000 US Dollars, then the girl has to earn enough to pay back that amount to the owner; then and only then, will she start making money for herself. The average price per session of sex with a paying customer is about $2 USD. I won't do the math for you. These girls only know this life and once their debt is paid, many have no choice but to stay in the business. This is still happening today.

Budgeting

BUDGET, BUDGET, BUDGET! This word is such a priority if you are a traveler on a long haul journey. By long haul I mean more than a month. It is possible to be on holiday or vacation and not worry about the price of bottled water, or how much a massage might cost. Even the littlest possible savings and cutbacks are helpful to stay on the road. If I spend less in each place, then I can go to more places. Plus, I am a numbers freak and I love the calculations.

I have come to have a pretty basic approach to budgeting. Not including the international flight to get to the region, I budget about $35 a day, or $250 a week, or $1,000 a month. Of course, some areas of the world are easier on the budget than others. I usually plan about $100 a day for London unless I am "dosing" on someone's couch!

I have a section in the back of my journal where I keep track of each item I purchase so I can be sure I am staying on track. After traveling with Christa in the Middle East, I adapted the budget tracking and would write down my expenses during the day *as I spent the money* so I wouldn't forget the little amounts. Some people tease me about my budgeting techniques but I always say, "You have to think like a local (in terms of price/value) or you will have to come home with the tourists!" Sometimes, if you compare items to what they would cost at home it doesn't seem that expensive, but you have to try and remember what locals pay for the same item and bargain from there.

I highly recommend using the "kitty system" if you are traveling together with a group of people. When I was in Estonia, Latvia and

Lithuania with Sally and Natalie, we each threw in a set amount of money at the beginning of each country into a special coin purse and this was used for any shared expenses, like ferry crossings, train tickets and basically anything that we all needed to pay for. The use of the kitty is helpful in many ways. It is much easier to have the correct change for three bus tickets than each of us trying to scramble to find loose change. The kitty also cuts down the amount of times you are all sitting around saying, "Okay, so I gave you 100, and you owed me 75, and then you borrowed 80 more and the train was 15 and I paid for you, so why don't I just pay for your bottle of water and the postcards and then we will be even!" "Wait, what?" Exactly! The kitty just makes for easier math.

Here are a few more of my best budget tricks:

- Buy nuts/granola/cereal and split into zip lock bags.
- Buy Laughing Cow cheese and crackers or bread: One eight triangle wheel nets me three meals.
- Make PBJ's: the peanut butter and jelly are heavy to carry but do not require refrigeration and bread is easy to find everywhere.
- If you are lucky enough to stay in a hotel that has a breakfast buffet included, try to "sneak" a few extras away to have for snacks, or even lunch. Careful with this one, getting caught might not be very fun!
- Sleep on airport floors the night before early morning flights. Sleeping on the floor at the Stansted Airport in London is a rite of passage, in my opinion!
- Book overnight trains, buses and ferries to save on a night's accommodation.
- Carry your own clothes washing kit and string the clothesline up in your room to dry clothes.
- I don't pay extra for air conditioning unless it is really miserable.
- I am not too worried about hot water and many places charge extra for rooms with hot water. If I am in a warm weather climate, most of the time I want cold water to cool off anyway.
- When hailing a taxi, I am sure to be on the right side of the road for the direction I hope to travel. The "turn-around"

can cost if it is a metered cab. In expensive areas, I am sure to negotiate a rate with the taxi driver in advance or insist they turn on the meter.

- Especially for Western Europe, the Museum Mecca, remember a student ID, many places offer discounted or even FREE admission. Not a student anymore? Don't have to be, there are many places to get an ID. I got my ISIC card in Nairobi - just have a passport photo and a little money and they print it on the spot. I had friends get theirs in Luxor, Egypt. Ask around, someone will be happy to help; for a fee, of course.
- Stay at the cheap place and then pay to use the services of the nice place such as beach chairs/pool/spa.
- Bring things to trade, especially in Africa. Old sunglasses, worn out t-shirts, and pens - they love to trade for pens. I always carry Crest White Strips with me to keep my teeth nice and white, and when someone mentions how white my teeth are I do a little advert for Crest and tell them about the strips. People are usually so amazed - I once traded for a free night stay with a youth hostel attendant for three sets of Crest White Strips. I also found that Lance Armstrong's charity Live Strong bracelets carry a great street value; I buy about 10 of them and trade along the way. Good for me and good for the charity!

When I first started traveling, the party budget was a lot higher than it is now. I usually try at least one of each of the local beers in every country. I usually don't drink if I am in smaller hostels and towns, but if I land in a party hostel then I know the cost of being social is a bit higher. I always have massage money in the budget because I will stay in a horrible hostel with a hard bed, but splurge on a massage. A little backwards, but massages are so wonderful! Well, some of them!

In the beginning, if the option was a 20 hour boat ride for $10 or a one hour flight for $70, I would take the boat ride to help with the budget and get the story. Now I have lots of stories, so I am more likely to take the flight. I met a guy in Ecuador, Ramon, and he taught me the phrase "Slack Packer." He follows a strict budget for six days a week, staying in larger dorms, cooking in self-catering kitchens and limiting the extras like Western food and snacks. On the seventh day he can stay in a nicer accommodation, eat out in restaurants and enjoy the fun extras. So, now I have adapted this style as well. I will still walk a little farther to save a dollar, and wash my own clothes, but when the journey time and comfort level are issues, I will be the happiest slack packer you have ever seen!

So many people ask me how I really afford to be away on these trips. "Vacations are expensive," they say. Well, first of all, I do not treat my time away as a vacation as you have just read. I am very serious about staying on track with my budget, but here is my overall philosophy on how this lifestyle can be maintained. I am currently working about six months of the year and traveling the other half. I can travel on about $1,000 a month, so if I make $7,000 while I am home, I can get back to the next working season with no worries. That means I really only need a job where I can earn about $400 per week and this allows me to save and still cover my living expenses and plane tickets.

Here comes the math that I love so much. If I was still living in Florida, working for Disney and living the "regular" life, I would spend about $800 a month on my mortgage, $300 a month on my car payment, $125 for car insurance, roughly $600 a month for utilities, gas for my car and groceries, $50 a month for a cell phone and finally a meager entertainment budget of about $200 a month. This adds up to about $2,100 for my monthly expenses. If you multiply out the $2,100 a month I would spend to "get-by" at home for a year, I would spend $25,000 on the basics. I make about $10,000 a year now, and spend only that amount. Those figures right there show you that I can live cheaper "on the road." Wow, I am actually saving money by traveling!

So, for my time at home, I live with my parents and have no car because I live in a small town and work two blocks from my house. I have no cell phone or credit card debt, so all of the money I earn; I save for my next trip. Thanks, Mom and Dad for the last few years of rent free living! Let's say you are wishing to live this lifestyle but don't have the option of living with your parents or walking to work. It can still be done! Just minimize your expenses as best you can. Maybe you can work two jobs, one to pay your bills and one to save for your trip. It might mean that you have to remain at home for a bit longer and or shorten your time away, but with a little budgeting, the sky's the limit!

On the subject of budget, I will leave you with this priceless story, an example of how budgeting can go wrong, very wrong! I was in Paris, France wandering around checking out the sights, Notre Dame, the Eiffel Tower, and the Louvre, basically taking in the city. I had noticed these giant coin-operated port-a-potties throughout my journey, but was never brave enough, or desperate enough to try them, but I did see two girls giving it a whirl. To operate, put a coin in the slot, open the door, do your business and when you are done, exit and the door locks behind you. It will reset and wait for the next person. These two must have had the same mindset as I do as far as budget goes, and they thought they would "trick" the system by holding the door open, and allowing the other girl in to save the 20 Euro cents. The only problem with this plan, once the door closes for the second time, the entire room gets washed down, flushed, with bright blue disinfectant. Are you with me? The second girl comes out screaming, covered head to toe in blue goo. I am sure she wished she had just paid the fee.

Just Pay For The Tour!

How many times have I said this in my life? As I just explained, time isn't money, money is time. If I save $10 today, that is an extra one-third of a day I get to spend "on the road." So, many times in my travels I have been extremely frugal with my spending. I have stolen bread roll sandwiches from included breakfasts to eat for my lunch later. I have eaten Laughing Cow cheese and crackers for three meals in a row to save from having to eat out in restaurants. I have even slept in some *nasty* places as you now know from reading that section of the book.

So, when looking at organized tours of certain attractions it would be an easy guess that a budget conscious traveler would forgo the expensive organized tour and try it the DIY (Do-It-Yourself) way. That may be true for some sights, but here and now I will tell you that sometimes its worth it to just "pay for the tour!" Here are a few examples when the "dollar" won out and a few examples of when I wished I would have just paid the extra five bucks for the tour!

First of all, my rule of thumb when I am traveling alone in a very large city is to take the bus tour! Some diehard travelers think this makes you less of a "traveler" but I say, what better way to see the entire city in one go, and then spend the next day or two exploring the bits you found interesting? There have been many times where I have landed in a large city and thought I would need three or four days to explore, booked myself the Hop-on-Hop-off All Day bus ticket, rode around on all the routes and found that I really only needed two more days. The money I spent on the bus ticket was now saved by not having to pay for the additional one or two night's accommodation. Plus, I am a sponge for silly, historic fun facts and these tours are always good for that. Remember to tip your guide if they made the tour extra special for you.

When I was visiting the Killing Fields in Cambodia I thought that getting a guide would take away from the time I would spend reflecting, but when we realized that the guide was a volunteer and had lost family in this tragic time, there was no question. Spending one hour with a man who was so passionate about showing you what had happened here was worth every penny we spent. He was wonderful and gave us our time to further wander the fields after the tour to take it all in.

Sometimes you are sure that you won't need a guide for an activity, so you think, why pay them $10 to drive me somewhere, because they are only going to make me stop off at a jade factory or a honey-making exhibit. But, here is one instance where I wish we would have just paid the money and been on our way. Christa, Emily, Stewart and I were in Cartenga, Colombia and had heard the legend of the mud volcano. Outside the city is a volcano that was said to have breathed the fire of the devil. A priest in the early times would make pilgrimages there and sprinkle the volcano with holy water and pray, so often that over time the volcano stopped spitting out flames and turned to the mud it is today. It is said that the Priest had drowned the Devil and drowned the flames. We heard that we could climb the volcano and get inside and bathe in the mud. Sign me up! The tour was $10 each, round trip from town, including entrance into the volcano. I was ready to go! But, since I was with three other travelers, we now had to "vote." One of the downsides of group travel: it is always a democracy! We had decided that since Stewart and Emily were fluent in Spanish and the local buses cost 50 cents to ride, we would make an adventure out of it and head out on our own.

I can't begin to tell you how many *wrong* buses we got on, buses going in the opposite direction, or buses that just left us standing on the side of the road. But, we all kept smiling because soon we would be swimming in a mud volcano. We found out from our last bus driver that it was still a two kilometer walk to the volcano. No worries, Stewart gets good directions and down the hot road we go. We are literally walking down the side of a highway. This is the moment when I start saying to myself, "Just pay for the tour!"

We walked down a path that opened to the volcano. No AHHH AH AH moment here! It looked like a man-made mud hole on top of a giant anthill. There was makeshift scaffolding all around it to hold up the sides, and wooden stairs that were built with hand rails so tourists could climb easier. We were disappointed to say the least. Stewart, so much so, that he refused to pay the $2 they wanted for an entrance fee. Well, I have come too far to NOT go in, so we decide to pretend it was another girls' spa day. The mud was amazing, you sink in a bit but then realize there is no bottom and you are floating. Little air bubbles would pop up while you were swimming around.

Part of the experience after you have been covered in the thick mud was to head down to the nearby river and wash off. We should have guessed that since this was such a tourist trap there would be more locals in on the action. Three ladies waited in the water with buckets to wash the mud off of us. We have been around enough to know that this is going to cost us something, so I decided "Budget Mindi" can wash herself off. I say "No, Gracias!" My lady would not take no for an answer, before I knew it she had the bottom half of my swimsuit off of me and was scrubbing the mud out if it. I started having flash backs of my Turkish bath in Istanbul. Meanwhile, back in the water, I was sitting with no pants on so I couldn't get up and get my bottoms back. I finally threw such a stink that she gave me my suit, and let me wash myself off.

I looked over and noticed Emily and Christa were enjoying their spa day. Not me! The priceless part of this experience was listening to Emily tell off my woman in Spanish after she tried to collect a tip from me for the services rendered. HA! Thanks, Em!

Travel Planning (or Not)

WHEN I FIRST STARTED traveling (United Kingdom for three weeks), I planned everything down to the train departure times, only to find the reality was that I crossed so much off my "itinerary" and added in new times and towns. Now, I have even limited my pre-trip prep to include only referencing an atlas to find the logical path. If I do too much *pre-search*, it feels like I have already been there. Besides, so many internet cafés are available nowadays; I can get info along the way as I need it! Even to this day, if I am reading a travel novel and there are stories about a place that I have not been to, I skip over it. I want to have my own "first impressions" and don't want them to be clouded by reading someone else's story. I do love to look at travel magazines, especially at the airport shops when I am trying to kill and hour or two. I am sure the cashiers love me because I look at all the magazines for about 30 minutes and then just buy a pack of gum.

Of course, there is always talking to others who have been there. "What should I see when I am there?" Two things will happen: one, they will tell you the *touristy* thing to do, which is good because you will hear about it anyway and probably want to see the major sight; two, they have a similar travel style to you and will share the "off the beaten path" ideas and help you to find a "gem." I take the same approach when others ask me advice about a place; I like to give as non-specific (non-opinionated/non-judgmental) advice. After all, everyone should go and find their own unique trip!

I have found that by purchasing a one-way ticket and "going until the money runs out" gives me the flexibility I like. I have had a general goal of visiting two or three cities in a country, and then, after talking with another traveler, boom, three more cities get added to my list! If you have the luxury of unlimited time, or do not have a pressing travel schedule, I say just pick a direction, north or south, and go. Last time I checked, buses, trains and boats all travel in both directions.

Pre-booking hostels and hotels and trying to plan everything down to the train times is sometimes just more confusing and stressful. If your trip is over a local holiday or weekend and you know accommodation will be difficult to find, of course, reserve something, but otherwise it just holds you to a sometimes impossible timeline. Plus, if you worry about time too much it will only cause stress, and aren't we supposed to be traveling to get away from the stress? That is why I have built the *waiting* into my travel style. I get early to airports. This is always a discussion with the people I travel with. Most want to wait until the last minute to arrive and then rush through. I love airports; it is all part of the adventure for me. I get checked in, grab a bite and a seat and play another round of The Departure Board Game. Besides it is not really as much fun to run for a plane, train or bus as if you are on the Amazing Race, especially since there is no million dollar prize if you catch it! Any time I have an extended wait, I have a long list of things to keep me occupied: do a few puzzles in my Variety Puzzle book, listen to my iPod, catch up on my journal, review my pictures on my camera from the previous leg of the journey, play a few hands of An Twanda card game, or read up on the next location in my handy-dandy Lonely Planet!

I have also purchased two "round the world" tickets. One was for my ten month trip across four continents, so this type of ticket made more sense. It did require picking departure dates months in advance, but it is a "soft" date and most airlines allow you to change as long as you give some notice. I even used my airline points and upgraded to Business Class on that journey; the extra cost was worth it for use of BC Lounges and large bed-seats for 17 hour plane journeys.

What day is it, anyway? When you are "on the road" it is hard to keep track of the date let alone the day of the week. Every day is a Friday, or better yet, a Saturday. If you are like Christa and I, you could have one New Year's Eve a week. See, we started our trip of Central and South America a few days before the actual New Year's Eve, and decided that we could have one night every week when we allowed ourselves to be "extra social" and spend a little more from our budget. Follow me for a little "Who's on First?" if you will? In Muslim and Jewish communities they go to the mosque or synagogue on Fridays, so that is their Sunday. So for them, Sunday is really Tuesday and you might want to take that into account when planning travel patterns of the locals and market days, etc.

I seem to be a pro at the "what day is it?" game because when I worked for Disney everyone had different days off so we would commonly have conversations about "When is your Friday?" "Oh, it is Saturday!" because I had Sunday and Monday off. Then you would hear me telling my staff on Tuesday to be nice to me because it was my Monday. So maybe I was born to not know what day it is, and the fun of it all, it doesn't really matter when you are planning a beach day!

Traveler's Gamble

I would say in general I am not a gambling person. I do go to the occasional casino, play a scratch off here and there but in general, I know that the odds are against me and would rather use my money somewhere else. Well, how does this translate into traveling? As a traveler you take risks and gambles every day with your itinerary. You have to choose where to go, how to get there, and how much you are willing to pay to see these places.

There is no set equation that I have found to ensure that you will enjoy your destination or that you will feel your money was well spent. But, I do have a lot of experience in this sort of gambling. Sometimes you make a lot of effort to get to a place and it turns out that it was all hype and not worth your time or money. On the other hand, sometimes you read the smallest passage in Lonely Planet and you feel the need to see that place. The gamble begins. You head out on numerous buses, boats and taxis to arrive at a location you would have gladly walked for days to find. The hard part is keeping yourself motivated to take the next gamble if the last one was not in your favor. Here are just a few of my most memorable gambles:

David, John and I were in Czech Republic and doing a bit of touring on our own. We had heard from a few other travelers that we needed to find the Bone Church. It is a small church in Kutna Hora, a small city just outside of Prague. This church is said to have been decorated with the bones of over 40,000 people. Legend says that during the plague there were so many bodies to deal with that the monk in charge went mad trying to dispose of all of them and started to decorate the entire church with the bones.

We were definitely intrigued, so we got directions and spent a full day navigating local buses and asking for more directions. We did enjoy the church but realized that we had spent seven hours roundtrip to spend 30 minutes inside. That is part of the gamble. This time it paid off!

Another one that sticks in my head happened during my trip to Estonia, Latvia and Lithuania with Sal and Nat. We had a fairly open schedule and were taking turns reading passages out of Lonely Planet and deciding where we would eat (in a windmill) or what we would visit. I think it was Nat that found "Europe's Widest Waterfall." Well, as a tourist, I guess you fall victim to the "World's most" anything. I mean, we were this close; we might as well make the extra two hour drive to Kuldiga (Latvia) and see this amazing waterfall. We diverted our plans, made the long drive and arrived to a small roadside park. Now, I guess I was expecting something like the welcome park at Niagara Falls, but this was just a roadside park. We all smiled and looked at each other once we saw the waterfall. It was no taller than we were, but yes, indeed, it did snake around a long way. Europe's Widest Waterfall at 249 meters wide (about 800 feet). Was it worth the drive? It was, because now we have the story to tell!

On this same trip we had found a passage explaining the Hill of Crosses in Lithuania. This hill had always been a pilgrimage for many Lithuanians to show their support of the Catholic religion. During the Soviet Rule, the soldiers would level this area, burn the crosses and forbid them to erect more. During the night, for many years, people would make the dangerous journey to replace all of the crosses that had been removed. Today there are hundreds of thousands of crosses at this site. I cannot explain to you what this place is like; you have to go there yourself. I am not a religious person, but you can feel the presence of positive energy there. We spent hours wandering around looking at all of the crosses and rosaries and enjoying the windy day. We all agreed that this was worth the trip!

It is discoveries like these that inspire you to try another "gamble" in the future. And so many times, I have remembered Hill of Crosses as I was "duped" into another tourist trap, point in case: Crimea and the Eternal Flames. This excursion was part of my Middle East tour, so I was already with a group and heading there anyway, but I know if I was traveling alone I would have tried to go there, too. Who wouldn't want to see the Eternal Flames? Fire that burns from the Earth 24 hours a day! Uh, Me! We hiked up a steep path in the dark with only our little flashlights to guide us through stumps and branches. Some of the group had traveler's sickness so they were not really enjoying the strenuous activity. We finally got to the top and looked around. There was another group already there sitting around what appeared to be little camp fires, roasting bloody marshmallows. These are the glorious Eternal Flames? I guess I was expecting something a bit more magical. The saying from this point on was, "they look like campfires, really!"

Sometimes a whole country can be a gamble like the time Christa and I were trying to get to El Salvador when we were in Central America. We had originally tried to cross over to El Salvador for a weekend trip from Antigua, Guatemala. We actually had a tour booked and found out three hours before departure that there was a landslide and the main road to El Salvador was closed. No worries, we diverted our path and made a weekend of it in Monterrico, Guatemala instead. We decided to try to get to El Salvador after we visited Honduras. So after the landslides of the prior month, we had finally made it to El Salvador.

What was there to see here? We didn't even know; we just didn't want to skip a country. I mean, we were right there, so we should see it. My vote is always a beach; if there is a beach, they will come! Well, evidently not Playa San Diego and not on a Tuesday. We arrived in the small one street town and were a little surprised at the lack of…well, anything! We found a little beach resort to stay at and found ourselves a true travel angel, Jose. It was his family's pensione we were staying in. He gave us the best room, ordered us take-way (Pollo Compero- it is their KFC) from a city that we must not have seen on the ride in, and spent time chatting with us about El Salvador, its people, and the future. The beaches were black sand and rather dirty, but we decided meeting Jose was the true jewel of this part of the trip.

We had not given up on El Salvador yet. Four buses the following day and three more the next and we were finally on the Route de las Flores (way of the flowers). Not so many flowers, really; just a butt formed like an old school bus seat. We arrived in Juaya, pronounced

WHY YOU A, and everyone was looking at us like, "Why you a here?" We were the only tourists around. Guess we were truly off the beaten path. The plan; enjoy the ice cream and nachos and head out of town the next day. Two more buses and another 12 hours and we were in Nicaragua. Not such a "bang" for our traveler's buck, but at least we can say that El Salvador has some of the friendliest people in all of Central America. Thanks, Jose!

So, to sum up the Traveler's Gamble: it is taking a chance, taking a chance that you will discover an amazing sight, something that will touch you personally and make you see the world as a better place. But, isn't that the reason we travel anyway, to take a chance and see the world? Even if at the time we feel we didn't beat the odds, upon reflection I bet we would all do it again. Well, maybe not the waterfall!

Another type of gamble we take daily as a traveler and not a tourist, is eating from local food stalls. To dine or not to dine is always the question! The sanitation levels of the food carts are usually what slows one from tucking in and trying the local fare. I would like to say that after so much travel I have "Guts of Steel," but that is not the case. I have developed a good eye for "cleaner" food stalls though and love to try the cheap and tasty local delights. The risk in this gamble is never of monetary value, it is more of the inconvenient kind. If you choose the wrong cart and get a case of "Delhi Belly" as it is called in India, it could slow you down on a travel day or cause a lot of frustration on a touring day. Sometimes it is hard to decide if those yummy flautas will be worth the struggle later. Imodium and forget it! Yum, flautas!

Unique Hostels Around the World

Well, I am sure some of you are reading this book hoping to get the "inside scoop" on the best places to stay across the planet. I can't guarantee that you will love them as much as I did, but these are some of the most memorable hostels/accommodation I have found throughout my travels. At least when you take a gamble you can hedge your bets. I always check out hostel locations on www.hostelworld.com or www. hostelbookers.com as they have pictures, traveler's feedback and the chance to reserve online in advance for only a 10% deposit. Not too much to lose if your plans suddenly change!

Rocking J's Hammock Hotel - Puerto Viejo, Costa Rico

Puerto Viejo is a little hippie beach town in Costa Rica. We had been searching for a beach town for a while and heard a few people talking about this spot. I had seen a poster in another hostel, "Come join us for Hippie Summer Camp - Rocking J's Hostel!" The hostel has 80 plus people staying there in tents, dorms and the ever-popular Hammock Hotel. You can rent a locker and a hammock for $3. Have to say it was not the cleanest of places, but the proximity to the beach and the chill atmosphere made it a favorite of mine in Central America.

Aqua Lounge - Bocas Panama

Aqua Lounge is a hostel that is located on Isla Bastimentos in Bocas del Toro. I can't say for sure what made me fall in love with this place first. The water is everywhere you look: out the windows of the hostel, through the floor boards and on three sides of this hostel that is built on stilts. The sun - we had the best weather every day we were there. The beaches - I had been searching for that type of beach with thick sand and crashing waves. A short boat trip to Wizard Beach is what I recommend. The drink specials, every night was Ladies Night somewhere. We crossed over to Isla Colon, the main island, to partake in a few free or almost free drinking nights! Or maybe it was the people! This is where we met Stewart and Emily and would go on to travel with them for two more months. We also met Sammy and Jason, short-time party mates, but they will be in our memories forever.

Slovenia - The former prison

Hostel Celica is located in Ljubljana, Slovenia. I had heard about this former prison turned hostel from a few travelers that were coming from Slovenia. They were all smiles when talking about this little place. I arrived in Ljubljana at about 4a.m. on a night train, since wandering through the streets at this hour might not be the best plan, I decided I would sleep at the train station in one of the waiting rooms until morning light. I was not the only one with this idea. I think most of the people there were waiting for a morning train, but I joined the ranks and slept as well as I could curled up on a bench.

The hostel was a welcomed surprise the next morning. The staff was amazing and let me check in right away so I could shower and rest a bit before exploring the city. My plan was to stay there for two days and then head on to Lake Bled. I met so many amazing people at this hostel. In the end, there were nine of us, all originally traveling solo that had banded together to party and explore Ljubljana. We would go out and eat dinner and party and then, saddened by the thought of some of us checking out the next day, we would rally and all re-up for another night. This happened until it was my fifth day and I really had to get a move on. I will always think back to that amazing place and smile. Visit the Skeleton Bar in Ljubljana. It is complete with a bathroom hidden behind a secret bookcase. Walk far enough down the narrow hallway and find pictures with 'eye-holes' so you can spy on the people in the bar!

University Dorms - Prague

There was nothing really special about the university dorm rooms we stayed in during our visit to Prague, but it is interesting that the universities are smart enough to make use of the dorms during the summer break. We did like the mode of transport that was needed to get to the school, a funicular. The train ride took you up Petrin Hill, where there are cafes, rose gardens and many spectacular views of Prague. Worth a visit even if you don't stay in the dorms.

Olympos Tree Houses - Turkey

A popular stopping point for the overland trucks on the Middle Eastern tours is Olympos, Turkey and Kadir's Tree Houses. It's not every day you get to sleep in a tree house - at least not as an adult. We were there for two nights. The big restaurant and easy walk to the beach was a plus. This was our jump off point for the canyoning trip where we spent the day swimming, hiking and jumping through the canyons. I was a bit nervous that part of this adventure would include having to swim into dark caves or under enclosed caverns. Luckily, the day was adventurous but not that scary. We did have the chance to jump off rocks and use the water chutes like they were slides.

Coffee Bay - Traditional Huts

During my tour of South Africa, I joined a hop-on-hop-off tour called Baz Bus. I bought a 21 day pass and it allowed me to hop-on and hop-off at any of the hostels along the way. One of my favorite places in South Africa and in all of the world is Coffee Shack in Coffee Bay on the Wild Coast. They give free welcome drinks, free Sunday meal and every fifth night is free. My rule when I am traveling, unless it is a very large city with lots to see, I only stay in a town for two or three days. This place was so welcoming and magical that I found myself seeing the fifth day and the sixth and seventh and had to force myself to leave before the ninth, because the tenth was free. Once you have had a free Sunday meal, it is tempting to stay again for the next Sunday. The dorms here are traditional thatched roof huts and the hostel does a lot with the community to make you feel like you are a part of it. They do offer the comforts that a backpacker is craving but also tie in the local flair. I was part of a Xhosa culture day that walked through the village and stopped over in a local home. We were able to sit with the family and ask questions about daily life and then end the day as many of the local villagers do, drinking their version of moonshine out of rusty tin cans. Can't say that it tasted very good, but I am guessing after drinking as much as these men did, you wouldn't know any different.

Generator - London

This hostel gets on the list just because I have stayed there multiple times. The Generator is an 800 bed hostel in the heart of London near Russell Square Station. As far as accommodation in Central London, the prices are fair, usually about 20 GBP (British Pounds) per night including a self-serve cereal and toast breky. They have their own hostel bar with a free welcome drink and have plenty of themed nights to keep everyone in the hostel on a cold blustery winter day. The ease of being on the Piccadilly Line (the dark blue line) is the biggest draw for me. I have always found everything to be at a high standard in this hostel and continue to visit this "old friend" every time I pop through London.

Panajachel - Jungle Hut

This hostel was memorable because we were in the mountains and jungles of Mexico. I did think that all of my journey in Central and South America would be tropical and steamy hot. Not really. Christa and I arrived at Panajachel late in the evening on a chicken bus (a decked out old US School bus, gangsta style). There was a sign on the reception that said they would return in the morning, so we wandered through the jungle paths until we found a little closed bar/restaurant area. During our time waiting, we were joined by a few other travelers in the same predicament. We spent the next few hours chatting and sharing travel stories and plans for our onward journeys. We were finally able to check in and we were all looking forward to a hot shower, a hot meal and a warm bed. You learn to live without a hot shower and it is usually easy to find a hot meal, but I never planned on having a screened-in room for my accommodation. Christa and I layered up in all of our clothes, crawled inside our sleeping bags and breathed ourselves warm. On a hot summer day, when the bugs are literally buzzing in your face, I think the jungle huts would be most perfect, just not on a rainy, cold Mexican winter's day!

Flintstones Caves in Goreme - Turkey

Another unique stop on the Middle Eastern tour was Cappadocia, Turkey. Our chosen hostel for the night was Flintstones Caves. We were joined by one other tour group so the place was very full. We were assigned general rooms in the seven person caves, but there are very posh single and double caves. The accommodation was not the only point of interest in Goreme. One of the fun cultural nights out was in this town. We all went to a "Turkish night" and enjoyed local foods, drinks and a twirling dervish show. The boys in our group even got to get up and show the Turkish men who was boss in a belly dancing contest. The dinner show was a hit because they place the bottles of alcohol on your table and you mix your own. OUCH! At the end of the night, or was it the next morning, I remember saying once or twice, "Which way to my cave?" This is a place I will never forget, or struggle to remember.

Finding Your Travel Style

I SPEND A LOT of time thinking about other travelers and their travel styles. I have met people who were riding a bike around the world, or volunteering, or even strictly camping in a tent and think that maybe *my way* is not as hardcore as I thought. I want to make the point that you should not apologize for your style or make excuses. Everyone is unique and therefore they will have an individual travel style.

My style is always evolving. I started as a "newbie" and very green in Western Europe, then transitioned to "hardcore" in Eastern Europe and Africa, and then to "old pro" in Central and South America, and now to my current state of "slack packer" in South East Asia and India. I went back a little "hardcore" with my last trip from Morocco to Nigeria, and booked the overland camping tour. Not really that bad since I had done a few other overland tours before, but still not cushy hotel travel! I then adapted the "holiday mode" for my Honeymoon with Femi around Malaysia. We still utilized long-haul buses, but once we got to our resort, we joined the land of "package tours" and "All-Inclusive." Gotta mix it up a bit, right?

It is very possible to change styles throughout one trip. I try to change it up with group travel and solo travel, and when I feel brave I might even travel with friends. This always sounds like the best option, but it is similar to the advice you receive when you start your freshman year in university: don't be roommates with your best friend - sometimes a little space is good! So many people wonder why I like to travel on my own. I have come up with a pro and con list.

PROS:

I can eat when I am hungry, sleep when I am tired, and move on when I am ready. I can stay on the beach for a week or in a museum for hours.

I can go to random places that may be far off the tourist trail and not worry if they are worth the journey or not. When I am traveling with others, I feel like I have to entertain them and there is more pressure than just entertaining myself.

I can meet other travelers and travel with them for as long as it makes sense and I can split with them with no hard feelings. If I set out traveling with someone for a set period of time, it is not easy to separate "on the road" if I feel the need to!

I love traveling alone because I can reinvent myself with each encounter. When traveling with someone who really knows me, I may not be able to avoid certain "stories" and they seem to expect me to act a certain way.

CONS:

When I am traveling alone it can be lonely in some parts of the world. It is nice to be able to choose a quiet hostel rather than a loud, party hostel, but in some areas of the world, there is no option other than hotels, making it harder to meet people. I just try to limit the time spent in these regions and use that time to catch up on reading or journal writing.

Dining alone can become boring, especially if there are themed restaurants and dinner shows to be seen. Occasionally I meet locals or other travelers at these events and once they find out that I am traveling alone they seem to feel the need to take me under their wing. I gladly accept their hospitality and enjoy the conversation until it is time to move on.

Traveling solo can be more expensive, especially with accommodation. I usually have to stay in large dorms to keep on budget, but when there are two or three people traveling together we can upgrade to a nice room with our own bathroom. Staying in large dorms also limits the amount of "good" sleep I can get!

When I am moving around a country on buses, boats and trains there is no one to watch my pack while I use the toilet or buy food.

I always have a random person sitting next to me on overnight buses. Sometimes I win the travel karma lottery and get a fellow traveler to share stories with and find out what is next on The List. It is the time I get the smelly local man that uses my shoulder as a pillow that makes me wish I had a *chosen* travel partner.

Other travelers are serious about their "travel style" and feel the need to tell me how I should travel. The most common comparison is between Tourist and Traveler. Originally, I had planned to define the difference between being a traveler or a tourist because it is a real debate on the road, but with all of my recent reading, it seems as if everyone has taken a stab at it, even as far back as Mark Twain. Although, I think Rolf Potts' *Vagabonding* says it best: "Just keep it real." So, whatever *real* is for you is the best answer.

I hope that we (the travelers of the world, and by that I mean those who leave home to go somewhere else) *never* define it in writing. Isn't that the point, to define it for yourself? Pick your wine and drink it. If the world only liked one wine, why would winemakers try other varietals and get creative with bottling?

Another popular debate is "to guidebook or not to guidebook?" I am a fan of *Lonely Planet*. I am not much of a planner, so it is comforting to know that I have the "Getting There and Away" section to help me plan my route as I go. I love using the local maps and the language section to assist me in each country. I do agree that you have to take it with a grain of salt and realize that just because the restaurant or hostel is listed in the guidebook, doesn't mean it is the *best* option, but rather an opinion. Other travelers call it "Lonely Liar," because many times the edition you are carrying is outdated and even in some of the most underdeveloped areas of the world, the tourism trail develops quickly and information changes.

When comparing travel styles with other travelers the concept of "admin days" is discussed. I classify any day that I spend most of it doing laundry, sending emails and uploading photos to my website as an admin day. I used to think of them as wasted touring days, but now I have come to realize that this time is needed to regroup, catch up, and connect to the rest of the world! My only advice here is not to spend a large amount of time in internet cafes and on Facebook. I was not a Twitterer, Blogger, or a Facebooker until this year. I had to finally cave, not because of the social pressure, but because I really wanted to sell this book!

So, I guess I can't "Just Say NO to Facebook" anymore! However, I still believe that if you connect with me enough to exchange personal details, then it should be just that, a personal interaction. I would appreciate the opportunity to receive an individual email not just a post on my *wall*. I have heard so many other travelers talking about Facebook and comparing how many friends they have, and I notice them spending half their time updating their status rather than actually getting out there and doing things. Or worse yet, checking on what everyone else "at home" is doing. Isn't that part of the reason to travel is to be out on the road exploring, not worrying that you are missing something at home?

Of course, this is just my opinion! All I ask is that if you are out there and meet a few unique souls that refuse to be on Facebook, don't worry about trying to change their mind. I promise the next person you bump into will be more than happy to join your "I want to share my life in a fish bowl" group, no questions asked!

Back in the beginning when I first started traveling, there were very few internet cafes. It reminds me of the people who say they backpacked Europe in the 70's before there were youth hostels. It is always great to relive the olden days, as well as embrace the changing world, but I think that we are now spending more time in touch with technology than in touch with people and the world. I traveled for years without an MP3 player or iPod and with only playing cards and puzzle books to entertain me on long journeys. I only shared my photos with friends and family on SmugMug, my personal photo website. I sent group emails to my friends and family every few weeks, only sharing the important details. I have gotten so many group emails from other travelers that share a few too many details about their daily routine. In my opinion, group emails are *not* the journal version of events. I don't care what you had for breakfast unless it was a caterpillar or something culturally freaky.

Travel is Like Wine

I have not always been a wine drinker. When I first started out in the restaurant business as a manager many people would tease me because I didn't eat seafood, drink wine or even drink coffee. They would say I was in the wrong business. I would counter with, "I know what it should all taste like, smell like, and look like and I am great at hospitality, so I am sure I will be fine!" I am glad that over the years I have pushed myself to expand my palate. Although, I still don't drink coffee.

I think that at first I was very intimidated by wine. There is so much to know and so many varietals to know about. It wasn't until I helped open Spoodles on Disney's BoardWalk, that I realized I could learn about wines and I actually liked the taste. We had a wine list with over 150 wines and during our new hire training we were encouraged to try them all. Bring on the wine!

Since then I have made it a point to go to wine tastings and enjoy as many vineyards as I can find. So, after many years of traveling and of drinking wine it is a natural thing for me to want to compare the two. In the "wine world" there are so many levels. There are the people that know everything about wine, those who know nothing about wine and many that are somewhere in between. The same can be said about the "travel world," too! There are people that are travel experts, visiting over 100 countries, those that only take their two week holiday every year and those floating somewhere in the middle.

Some travelers are on a strict budget and others spend their money like it is their last few days on earth. Same with wine drinkers; I am happy to enjoy a bottle of red wine on half price Wine Wednesdays at Mulligan's that doesn't break the bank, but can sure appreciate the taste of an expensive glass of wine (or bottle) from time to time. Thanks, Uncle Tim!

I think it is important to find a balance in your travel lifestyle that suits your comfort zone. I believe travel, like wine drinking, is a personal choice that only you can make, and only you can decide what you "like." So, go out and enjoy whatever makes you smile! I have come to find out in my wine tasting that I don't enjoy whites as much as I enjoy reds. That doesn't mean I don't enjoy the occasional Sauvignon Blanc, but I make sure that it is not heavily oaked. You need to explore your travel style until you find what fits best for you. Maybe you don't like traveling with groups, but you do find yourself on a city tour from time to time. Red wines are an acquired taste. Some can be strong and heavy like a Cabernet Sauvignon or nice and smooth like a Merlot. For me, Western Europe is my Merlot and India and Africa are my Cabs!

The approach to wine can also be compared to the approach taken when traveling. Many people can suggest a wine that they really enjoy, like a place they visited, but only you are the one who can truly "taste" it for yourself. I love to hear other people's take on a place to visit, and even if they share that they had a terrible time in that location, if I am interested in going, I will still go. And I will visit with an open mind.

Once you open a bottle of wine you can "let it breathe" or drink it right away. The same can be said about how you approach a new city. I like to take it as it goes. In some cities I have nothing but time and slow myself down and savor all that it has to offer. In others, I realize that I would much rather move on and enjoy another city, so I speed through it. The point is you don't have to know *everything* about everything; you just have to be willing to learn and enjoy getting the experience. The more wine you drink the better it will taste! So, what is to be said about people who drink beer? Who knows? My advice is always to "do what makes you smile." If you are smiling, you must be doing something right! But, I want to know who came up with the idea to "spit" out the wine at tastings? I don't agree. I say "Get drunk" on travel!

Don't Be a Barbara or Barry

> *"To feel at home, stay at home. A foreign country is*
> *not designed to make you comfortable. It is designed*
> *to makes its own people comfortable."*
> -Clifton Fadiman

I have created two characters out of need to explain my displeasure of meeting other Americans on the road who just don't get it. If you are always wondering (out loud) why everything is "not the same as in the USA," then I suggest you go back…to the USA! The female is Barbara and the male is Barry. They are usually 45-65 years old and pretty used to their cushy life as an American, but since all of their other friends are out seeing places, they figure they better get on it too!

During my travels I am usually the only American on tour with many Aussies, Kiwis, and Brits. To be fair to potential American travelers, especially the young ones, I have to say the travel culture is built into the lifestyle of other countries like Australia and Great Britain. They actually have a year in between their equivalent of high school and university called "gap year" and they are encouraged by their parents, friends and educators to take this year to "see the world!" So, we are a bit behind in the culture game, and we are unfortunately "sheltered."

So, as the only American on tour, I sometimes have to answer for the Barbaras and Barrys that bump into our group. Said with a high nasal tone and very loud "BARBARA, where are we supposed to meet our group?" "BARRY, the guide said to be at the bus stop at 2p.m. SHARP!" When you bump into these Barbaras and Barrys you can see everyone else rolling their eyes, and they turn to me (the fellow American) as if to say, "you are one of them, make them be quiet!" To cover all bases I know that there are usually Barbara's and Barry's from Canada, too, I just call them Bill and Betty.

These are the characters that you will hear on the bus talking loudly into their camcorders, narrating over the guide. They are the ones negotiating in the markets for a higher price than the person even began asking. "Oh, $10, that is *so* cheap, I will take three!" Thanks, Barbara, the going rate is actually $3, I could have gotten three for what you paid for one! The Barbaras and Barrys are usually on the tours that stay at three star and above hotels and eat in restaurants that have only "western" food. "Why isn't there ice in my glass, don't they know we are American, and we like ice with our drinks?" Oh, Barbara!

Want to search out and find Barbaras and Barrys, head to a McDonald's. That is the mother-ship for American travelers. But, hey, I am not going to apologize for being "that American" that goes to McDonald's. I have to say, I hate seeing the Golden Arches in remote parts of the world because that means everything is changing, but they do have clean toilets! And I am known to eat a Big Mac, or for sure get a 30 cent ice cream now and then!

That was not what it said in the Brochure!

Have you ever picked up a tourist brochure for a location, studied the pictures and thought to yourself, "I wonder if this place still looks like this?" If you are going to be traveling a lot you better get use to thinking this way. With the exception of maybe Walt Disney World's brochures, I have a rule of thumb never to trust them completely. I have become hesitant with terms like "newly renovated." When? Twenty years ago, when it was built? And just as postcards show the most exciting thing to see in town, the brochure will show the ONE nice thing on the tour and skip all the other crazy things you will have to see.

Sometimes entire destinations have such dazzling marketing about them, you cannot help but get swept away. This happened to me with Belize. I had heard from a few people I could give it a miss, but in true explorer's fashion, I wanted to make my own decision, and besides, it looks pretty nice in the brochures. HA! Christa and I arrived in Caye Caulker, a revered backpacker haunt, boasting of hammocks and great eats, walking without shoes in the sand. "Wait! Stop there! What sand, what beach?" Where is the beach that we saw in the brochure? The reality was that the little island only had about two feet of beach down on the split. There was a cool little bar there that tried to make the most of the small beachfront by putting picnic tables in the water. So, I guess the advertised barefoot and sand was really barefoot and dirt, all over the roads of the town.

These are the times that test if you are a Barbara or a Barry. Barbara would complain the entire time saying this was not what was in the brochure and get caught up in that mentality. For me, I met some cool people, laid in the sun (be it on a picnic table in the water) and chilled out for a few days. I am happy, however, that Belize was part of a bigger trip and not my destination. Had it been a honeymoon brochure I was looking at, I might have had to be Barbara for a minute or two!

Just remember, my fellow Americans, we are the ambassadors of our country and we already get a bad enough rap for our political mishaps. Smile, take in the culture, don't ask why it isn't like home, and embrace the differences. Besides, it just makes returning home that much more enjoyable!

Things I Love to Hate about Travel!

Time (departure and in general)

IN THE BEGINNING, TIME is the hardest element to adjust to. Every culture treats time differently and definitely has its own concept of time. For example, in the afternoons in Spain from 3p.m. to 5p.m. it is "siesta time!" Shops close, children go home to have lunch and rest, businesspeople come home from work. This means that dinner isn't eaten until about 9p.m. or 10p.m. and after it is perfect to go out and dance the night away. The shops and businesses open the next morning at about 9 o' clock. I remember thinking I could get used to that lifestyle after spending almost one month in Spain.

Time in other countries is not as important as it is in America. Maybe that is okay, because life is hectic enough. Why do we have to have buses on time and have our food arrive within five minutes of ordering it? Stop and enjoy life. You know you are a true traveler when this no longer annoys you.

With Spanish time, it just takes a few days to reset your clock from American time and then everything falls into place. Now African Time is probably the hardest to adjust to. In Africa, it happens when it happens. They do have shop hours, and they do have departure times for buses, but many times, things will happen and time slips away. So the stores open when they get there and the transport departs a few hours later. When I was traveling on my own before my African Overland trip, I was leaving Nairobi to visit a small island called Lamu. I pre-booked an 8 a.m. bus ticket. I was told the journey time would be about six hours. Figuring that would put me on the island about 3p.m., perfect to get accommodation and to get to know my way around before it got dark. Eight o' clock came and went; people were lined up everywhere, loading large cartons of dry goods onto the top of the bus. Children were running and playing in the streets, vendors would stop you one after the other to ask you to buy "their" sunglasses or travel food items.

At 9 a.m. and then 10 a.m. - people were still loading cargo, live chickens were now in the mix, women with three or four children, trying to make their way on the bus and filling the already overflowing seats. Finally at about 11 o' clock, the bus slowly chugs out of Nairobi. Only three hours late, "Oh, it is African Time! No worries! Hakuna Matata!" A popular saying on the continent is TIA - This is Africa! I had heard of the bumpy roads in Africa and the bad shock systems on the rickety old buses. I had even heard about how some people get "brain shake" if they ride on bumpy buses too long without a break. Yet, here I am riding on an old bus down what can only be described as a washboard road. Well, I recalculated the arrival time. I shouldn't have done that, as now we were pulled over at a rest stop for almost one hour. I wondered to myself if this hour was built in, or was the driver just enjoying his visit with his friend so much that he has lost track of time? I fear the latter!

It was 2 p.m. and we are only about two hours outside of Nairobi. The roads were now bumpier and wetter. They had some heavy rains in this area, bridges were washed out, roads were a mess and you could see signs that the local people had picked up and moved to drier land. There were makeshift plastic shelters all along the high road. If you looked farther back into the brush you would notice their permanent housing structures (huts) with water rings about midway up the side. The road conditions were now affecting the driving and the speed at which we could travel. I was just about to doze off when I felt a sharp turn and then a sudden stop. You guessed it, bogged!

In order to get out of the hole we were in, we needed to push the bus. Simple? Not really, there were too many people on the bus, so most of the men and a lot of the women had to get out of the bus so we could make it lighter and to help push. I didn't want to sit there like a true *Mzungu* (Ma Zoon Goo - white person) and wait to be rescued;

I wanted to be part of the team that got us out of the muck. I hopped out with everyone else!

Bad idea, as I got covered in mud and it was caked on my shoes and made it nearly impossible to even walk let alone get leverage to push. We pushed and dug and pushed some more; almost an hour more. Cheers came from all on board as the bus raced away without us. The driver was taking no chances and drove the bus a quarter of a mile down the road to drier ground. Picture us all running after it with about three inches of mud on the bottoms of our shoes, well my shoes; many of the others from the rescue team were barefoot.

I had lost track of the time we should arrive; the journey took over eight hours after the three hour delay in the departure and it was now about 7 o' clock. We were getting off the bus and onto the water taxi to finally land on Lamu. As a Mzungu, it is not hard to find someone to help you with your bag, or buy a ticket, or even get that pair of sunglasses you have always wanted. I was on the boat, bag semi-secured, and eating a bag of mangos within minutes. I say semi-secured because it was lying on top of everyone else's and seemed dangerously close to falling overboard if we hit a big enough wave. Oh well - TIA! Now we were moving along. Well, we had to wait for the entire boat to fill up and just the people from our bus were not enough. I understand the price of gas is high and if they are making the trek, they might as well take a full boat, but I was hot, tired and was sure I had a small case of the "brain shakes."

I have never been happier than right then! The boat was moving after almost another hour. The sun was still out, beating down on us. I settled into a spot with a bit of shade. The boat driver said the ride should be about 20 minutes, factor in African time, possibly one hour. Maybe more! As we were trolling across the brown waters towards Lamu, I noticed the boat was taking on water, through cracks in the bottom of the boat. I looked around nervously and no one else seemed alarmed. There were two other men who were helping the driver by scooping out the incoming water with the bottom half of plastic jugs. I was amazed; this bailing of water was part of the daily routine.

We finally docked at the port, I take back what I said; *now* I am the happiest I have been all day. It was about 8:30p.m., and I was so hungry I could cry. I spent the next seven days on Lamu adjusting to island life. The time there did move even slower, "pole, pole" as they say in Swahili, and I loved every minute of it. I found it hard to leave that place, but maybe it was the 12 hour return journey that was keeping me there. I will admit to you that I bought the $100 plane ticket and flew back to Nairobi. The plane was only *one* hour late but I was back in Nairobi within two hours, not 12. Hakuna Matata! No Worries!

Power Outages

Lamu was not just a lesson in Africa time; it was a true slice of African life, especially island life. Resources are limited in Africa, and the power to run the generators was no exception. I was checked into a nice hotel-style hostel called the Bahari. In Swahili that means sea, and it *was* right by the sea. One night I was gazing out my window and admiring the bright moonlight. Such a beautiful sight! Just as I was getting my camera to capture this moment, the power went out in my room. I took my moonlight photo and then grabbed my flashlight and went to the front desk area to enquire about how long they thought the power would be out. "Maybe one hour, maybe longer," said with such normalcy that I knew I would be showering in the dark that night.

Well, maybe showering in the dark was not such a bad thing. Most showers I have found when I am traveling are rigged so that only cold water comes out, but a portable electric water heater is attached to heat the small amount of water that can pass through the tiny filter. Genius? Well, only if there were not bare wires hanging all around the faucet. I showered in the dark, and in cold water, but at least I didn't get a shock of a lifetime from the faulty shower head. That would come a day later when I was turning on the water and felt a shock run through my hands and into my feet. Good thing I was standing on a rubber floor mat! Ouch!

Power outages in cities and islands have now become routine for me. I have had so many nights by candlelight, filling in my journal holding my flashlight in my mouth. Until I discovered the head torch! In southern Laos, 4,000 Islands has a scheduled power outage at 8 p.m. every night. The entire island goes pitch black. I remembered the outage but underestimated how long the walk back to our bungalow would seem.

Even when they are planned, things can still pop up and frighten you. I was planning on walking back from my evening meal one night on Gili Air, a small island off Lombok in Indonesia. I loved the idea of a small island, few people and the quiet nights. The lady at my front desk had told me that the power would be going out around 9p.m., so if I was at the other end of the island for dinner, be sure to bring my flashlight. I had learned my lesson in the past, tripping over tree stumps or rocks, so this time on my walk to dinner I carefully studied the trail for my dark walk home.

I was just about one-third of the way back to my bungalow when the batteries in my flashlight went out and I was now surrounded in darkness. There were no other people around; remember, I wished for this. I started to walk very slowly, letting my eyes adjust to what moonlight there was. I am feeling for sand in front of my feet and when I felt the grass I would divert my path a bit. You wanted adventure - you got it! This trek was almost impossible with no light. I could hear things moving in the bushes and thought to myself, if it steps, or slithers out in front of me I am going to scream *so* loud. Hey, maybe then someone will come to rescue me?

Rescue me! Enter, Travel Angel - a woman was riding behind me on a bike, a bike with a light on the front. She slowed when she saw me walking two centimeters a minute in front of her. At first when the light was enough for me to see the ground, I just started to walk really fast to make the most of her light, but then I realized I was not as close to home as I had hoped. I called to her and asked if I could run behind her to use the light as my batteries were dead. She was a French woman, and didn't speak much English, but my situation was pretty clear. She rode slowly to the main port, turning around and smiling every so often to be sure I was still there. I still had to make the short trek back to my hotel from the port, but this was a cakewalk after what I had been through. I think I might still be out there had she not come along.

Showers

So, I have mentioned the dangerous mode of heating the water in many showers with the electrical contraption. Now I guess is the time to tell you the other things I have come to love-to-hate about showering when I travel. Cold Water! I have to say sometimes the trade-off for not being electrocuted is the cold water, but I have definitely taken more cold showers in my life than warm. You have to be efficient. I remember a time when we were on a camping tour in Europe and to conserve hot water they made you purchase hot water tokens. There were little coin slots in the shower stalls and when you put in your token you had about three minutes of *warmish* water. I would get my hair wet and shampoo in cold and rinse in warm. Three minutes is not a lot of time, and you know I was on a budget!

The only time I can remember having too much hot water was in South Africa. The campsites would run hoses under the ground (only about six inches underground). The residual water in the lines would be scorching from the day's sun. In most campsites, the truck pulls up and people run for the shower blocks to get the only hot water for the day. In this camp site, those first patrons were mighty surprised at how hot the water actually was. There was no cold to be found! Can't win for losing!

Quick-dry towels that never dry: other than the fact that they are smaller, come in a little mesh pouch, and fit nicely in the top of your back pack, they are crap because there is nothing "quick-drying" about them. Sure, they dry faster than a terry cloth towel, but then they should name it a semi-quick-dry towel. Here is Mindi's travel tip for drying off after a shower on an early morning departure: I use the pillow case from the hostel as my towel. It works just fine and I don't have to have my damp towel packed away for the day's journey.

Showering in flip-flops is another skill that you master the more you travel. So many shower floors are nasty and moldy, so I don't think it is any surprise that you should shower with shoes on. It is just being sure you get the flip-flops that have a little traction. This is the most important when you are hopping around while trying to put on pants in a wet shower. I have gotten pretty good at getting my jeans on in a 2x2 shower stall. I am thinking of having a Backpacker's Olympics and this would definitely be an event.

Bucket Showers: This is actually the most environmentally friendly method of showering and the one adopted in most African countries. It is not out of the love of the environment, but out of conserving water as the source may not be so close to the house. I don't mind the bucket showers as much as I do the open air cubicles that are usually provided. If you are too tall, you may be showing off more to the locals than you had hoped!

Public Toilets

Speaking of the pant legs of jeans, the first thing I think you learn about public toilets, especially the ones at roadside stops - they are nasty and you don't want any part of your clothing or body to touch any part of the toilet block. A true bonding moment among women travelers happens during the bathroom stops. Of course, there is always a longer line for the women's toilet than the men's and we get picked on for this, but if we could stand up to pee, we wouldn't have to roll up our pant legs, bring our own tissue and have thighs of steel to balance while we hover over the toilet.

In order to be the "most effective" in a squat toilet, Turkish toilet or "hole in the ground," whatever you want to call the toilet that requires you to squat down and *aim* into a hole while your feet are up on pedestals, there are a few key techniques I can share with you. I want to share them with you so in case you come upon one of these many "toilet options" in your travels, you can avoid the splattering of shoes and pant legs that came with my "rookie attempts."

Rule # 1: On the walk to the toilet, roll up your pant legs, tucking them inside your socks is not an option.

Rule #2: Be sure to have tissue with you as it is almost never provided, even in those nasty toilets where you have to *pay* to use them (Don't get me started on that one…what are we paying for?) Good travel karma: always have lots if tissue and share when others do not have any. I promise you, there will come a time when you don't have any yourself and you will really need it. Travel karma will return and someone will be there to save you!

Rule #3: Get good at balancing, and don't touch anything in there, remember other people splatter, too! And probably the most important rule of all…

Rule #4: If you are going Number One face forward, so you pee straight into the hole and if you are going Number Two, face backward so, well you get the idea right? If you do Number Two the wrong way, you better hope it is a powerful flushing machine, or they provide lots of water!

The hardest adjustment I have had to make with toilet abroad is the "not being able to flush the paper" thing. First of all, we are so trained to throw the used tissue in the toilet; and second of all, that is just nasty! I understand that most of the sewer systems can't handle the paper, but that does not make it any easier. I think the funniest part is that after about three to four months of putting the paper in the bin, I guarantee you will return home and your family will ask why you are putting used toilet paper in the garbage can. That, and you will always have a little spare change in your pocket in case you have to pay to use a toilet! Reverse culture shock!

Crazy Travel Foods

I am definitely a person that tries the local fare. I tried the kangaroo in Australia, the ostrich in South Africa, I even ate caterpillars in Namibia, but sometimes you just want to eat something that you recognize. Careful what you wish for. Sometimes all you can find are Snickers and Pringles and that might sound amazing after caterpillars, but not when that is *all* you can find. I should have bought stock in Laughing Cow Cheese and Jif Peanut Butter before I started traveling because I cannot count the number of triangles of cheese I have eaten or the number of PBJ sandwiches I have made, although Christa and I did keep a tally in the Americas. It is funny how pizza and nachos make it on every menu on the tourist path. Sometimes this is a bigger gamble than ordering the local dish. My worst nacho experience to date: Copacabana, Bolivia. I ordered nachos at a Mexican themed restaurant thinking I would finally get those amazing nachos I have been searching for. Not today! They were literally Doritos with chopped up hot dog and pieces of sliced cheese topped with a runny imitation of sour cream. The search continues.

Hostel Living

This section is the hardest to write because if you have ever stayed in a hostel you have your own list of things that drive you crazy about the other 30 people you are crammed in a room with. Here is my quick list of common distractions in almost any hostel:

Plastic bags: Sorry, I am one of the culprits; I know it is annoying at 6a.m. when you have just returned from the previous night out and the person next to you is packing and unpacking every single item in their bloody pack, but they do keep the smelly clothes from infecting the clean clothes. I just try to be courteous and get the things I need out of the bags the night before and even try not to do too much of the "zipper mania" thing either.

The random snorers, or worse yet, night-farters: I shared a room with an older guy from Greece when I was in a hostel in South Africa. We were chatting away before bed and had said our good nights and then I hear this loud noise. I know immediately what it was and hoped he didn't feel the need to apologize. That might have been a normal night, one not worth writing about but he continued to fart all night long. The first few times it was all I could do not to bust out in laughter. I knew he was sleeping at this point because the farts were semi-drowned out by his snoring.

I met a Canadian traveler in a hostel in Krakow, Poland. He was my bunkmate and the loudest snorer I have met to date. He worked in the airline industry on jet engines and had easy access to industrial ear plugs, so part of his introduction to his new bunkmates goes something like this: "Hey, I am Guy, from Toronto Canada, I have been traveling around Europe for about two months, I snore, these are for you, and I am buying the first round of drinks downstairs for the inconvenience!" How do you hate a guy that gives you ear plugs and buys you beers? Smart strategy! Oh, I was on the top bunk and he on the bottom. I felt like we were *on* a jet engine. Thanks for the beers, Guy! Wouldn't it be cheaper and easier to just get a single room, but then again, I wouldn't have this story!

The smell of hangover: This is one smell I cannot get used to. Even if you are one of the ones that were out all night on the town ripping it up, the next morning an eight bed dorm smells like a beer brewery. If it is a hostel with an actual heating unit, look out because this smell just hangs in the air until the first person out of bed opens the door or some windows. That person is usually me!

Sex in the dorms and it is not you: In doing research for this book I read a lot of other travel stories and a few of the books cover this phenomenon in depth. I am sure you can imagine the scenarios, but let me just tell you the patterns that I have observed. There are three types of offenders. First, the sneaky yet not-so-sneaky - they are the ones that try to come in the room all quiet, get in their own beds first and then after about five minutes, crawl into one bed and go at it. Second, the blatant couple - they actually don't care if people know; they are actually talking about it out loud and letting the rest of us know what is happening play by play. And finally, the third couple, the so drunk "I don't even realize I am having sex in an eight bed dorm room" couple - this is usually a boy from my room who has snagged a random girl from another hostel. She figures she doesn't know anyone in this dorm and he figures he will wake up and be a legend so they just go for it! All this is fine if it is happening across the room, but Mindi's Law provides that it is in the same set of bunks as me! Oh hostel living!

Truck Life

Toilet stops: When you venture out and start traveling on an overland truck, the first thing that you have to get used to is going to the bathroom outside. There is one simple rule: girls on one side of the truck and guys on the other. This rule is usually overlooked after you all have been traveling together for more than a month. You start to realize it is too much work trying to find the perfect place to hide on the side of the road. I have the mentality that if you really want to stare at my butt while I am peeing, then have at it. I still get a little embarrassed when I have to "take the shovel" to do a poo while at a bush camp. There are two or three designated shovels hanging on the door of the truck that are used to dig holes for the #2's, a very important rule so that you don't find someone else's treasure in the dark, if you know what I mean! Chances are if you found a "good spot" someone else thought so too!

Hygiene: Yours and everyone else's. On the longer Africa overland trips there are always the guys that decide to not shave, or grow out that porn star moustache they have always dreamed of. I am fine with this, it is the ones who decide to try and see how long they can go without bathing who add an unwelcome dimension to the trip. There are times when we are all limited to baby wipe baths, and it is hard enough to keep the truck from smelling of body odor, so it is not nice adding those smelly boys to the mix! The upside about the lack of hygiene on a truck is that you don't have to keep clean shaven legs at all times. Who cares about a little hair? Not me! And, although there are all kinds of bugs you have to keep an eye out for while camping, bedbugs are usually non-existent because the filth you are laying in is always your own. The best advice I can give to anyone going on an adventure in Africa - bring baby wipes, and lots of them!

I wish I only had to worry about keeping my body clean on the truck, however, I am usually the only one who worries about the cleanliness of our dishes. I was a Girl Scout and know that there is a proper way to sanitize dishes while camping, but most people don't seem to want to make the extra effort to add sanitizer to the water, or even heat water for that matter. It seems like it would be common sense that we are just getting each other sick by sharing our dishes and sharing our germs. I usually just buy some Dettol and add it myself, and give the dishes a good cleaning once a week when I am on cook duty. The cook group usually sets up a row of three wash bins. The first one is for rinsing the main goop off, the second has soap in it to give a proper wash and then the third is for rinsing. After a few people have gone, it is difficult to tell which is which! Gross!

Flapping: This is the common way to get your dishes to dry. A proper flap: hold cup and silverware in one hand and plate in the other. Walk around swinging arms wildly using the air flow to dry your dishes. Be careful to hang on tight; it is no fun when dishes go flying and land in the dirt. Now the process must start over! If there is a good fire going, some opt for leaning over the flames and using the heat to dry the dishes. I tend to like this one, too as I feel the added heat *has* to help the sanitation issue. That is, until the person is not paying attention and *dips* the plates in the ashes. Oh, well, it gives the next meal a nice smoky flavor!

Internet Connection or Lack Thereof

When I first started this traveling life of mine, I wasn't even checking an email account on a regular basis. It was 2004 before I even signed up for a free Yahoo account and I only did that because the private email company I was using was giving me trouble when I was trying to log in from overseas. Internet cafes were almost non-existent outside of Western Europe, but technology has come a long way since, with cyber cafes popping up in many little corners of the world. I started to send group emails on my first big trip around the world, and this was more to have an electronic journal than to communicate with others, but it worked both ways. My family liked reading about my experiences as they were happening to me, even though my mother still does not know how to reply to one of my messages to this day.

Fast forward to 2010 and everyone and their brother is on Facebook and Twitter and who knows what else. But you still come across the old, outdated computers with the slowest connection known to man. Fellow travelers, you know the ones when you are at a computer so slow you that you type a word and then watch as the letters appear one at a time. Forget adding pictures to your site in most places - I was online in Africa for one hour and got three photos loaded. We have gotten so spoiled at home.

Sometimes it is not the connection as much as it is a strange keyboard like the Arabic or French kind. I love the ones that test your true typing ability because they are worn down and are missing many letters from the keys. I also seem to find the magic button that erases my entire email I so eloquently composed just as I was about to send it, leaving me sad and upset. I have sent so many rewrites with little to no detail, just to get an email out to everyone. I still wonder where those perfect versions went.

Shopping, or Rather Bargaining

I don't love to hate this, I just hate this. I don't get too caught up in "how we do things in America," but I do have to admit the price tag is a glorious invention. The store owner sets a price and you buy it if you think it is a fair price. None of this, "What is your first price, or what is your *best* price?" It is a simple, "What *is* the price?" I find myself cringing when I actually find something I like and want to buy it. No matter how many times I have been forced into bargaining, I still find it awkward when the store owner says the first price and it is a ridiculous amount. I know this is the technique, shoot super high, then the customer can cut it in half and then probably end up paying half of that amount. So much work when both sides know the game! Plus, I feel so rude offering my best price when they start so high.

But, one thing I have learned, they will NOT let you walk away if they are still making money. If they let you, then maybe you are driving too hard of a bargain and you can up your offer at the next stall. As you know, they all have the same offerings! I have some patience when bargaining for souvenirs, but absolutely none for taxi or tuk-tuk rides. When the driver starts with a "stupid" amount, I just walk away. They will usually immediately drop to the going rate, if not, I continue walking; there will be someone who wants the fare. I am careful not to be too rude in areas where taxis are scarce, remembering they have the upper hand in this situation.

"To shop or not to shop?" Whether your trip includes a day in a Souk, night market, or Bazaar, you have to decide what your travel style is regarding souvenir shopping. I am not much of a "shopper" at home so this one was easy for me. I am content with buying postcards, jewelry, and trinkets, as long as the items will fit easily in my pack and do not weigh too much. I did go through a spell in the Middle East where I thought I needed to make some big item purchases. I learned my lesson from buying overpriced Turkish carpets and Turkish ceramics that I had shipped home only to have them never make it. My polar opposite in this arena is Natalie who will have a house full of items from overseas, including crystal from Prague and dishtowels from Lithuania. I plan to visit her home and relive my journeys through her purchases!

One thing I do love about shopping is the creative shopkeepers and their amazing sales pitches! Probably the most effective sales people I have come across are the Egyptians. Come rain, or shine, or tour bus or solo traveler, especially in the Cairo Markets, it is their *duty* to get you to interact with them. They are shouting at everyone, calling to them to "just look, no charge for looking!" "Where are you from?" or "You need a beautiful scarf?" Sometimes, after a long day of "marketing," the traveler's patience can start to run thin. I am always conscious of this and try to maintain my cool.

One day I was wandering the markets of Cairo, in the touristy section, and was tiring of all of the questions and shouting, so I just ignored the men when they asked me several questions in English. Finally, after they wouldn't let up, I mumbled, "Habla Espanol," thinking this might give me a few minutes peace as I wandered away from him. Nope! The man yells at the top of his lungs down the market to the rest of the upcoming stalls, "ESPANOL!" Then the men all started greeting me in Spanish. Amazing! Well, let's have some fun! Now I change to "Spreken zie Deutsch." This man yells onward, "DEUTSCH!" And the greetings continue in my "native" language! Well, I can see I am getting *nowhere fast*, so I change to Liechtenstein as the answer to where I am from. "Leichten? Lichten? Excuse me? Where?" We have a WINNER! I strolled along the rest of the way smiling, not even paying attention to what language they now chose to ask me to "look for free!"

It is sometimes necessary to change your approach to the hounding. This scenario finds us in Egypt again, I've told you these Egyptians they know how to sell! As part of my Middle Eastern overland truck, we found ourselves in Dahab. It is a small little beach town with a main strip of restaurants and shops arching around a bend of the beautiful Red Sea. The problem here is that there are about 20 restaurants and they are pretty much all the same. So they have guys out front to entice the customers to choose their particular restaurant over the one before it or after it. I am sure they get a little "cut of the action" for each patron they bring in. Well, we arrived in a group of 21 strong and the word was out! We had just arrived and were excited to check out the scene. We were bombarded with "Hellos and Welcomes" which normally isn't the worst thing that could happen to a traveler, but they were followed by the "sales pitch" and when you are not even in the market for a restaurant at that particular time, it becomes a bit much!

I found a "gentleman" who was very persistent in trying to get me to eat at his place. He was pretty creative, too, trying to "woo" me with pet names and telling me how beautiful I was. I have to admit, this part wasn't that hard to take, even if I knew he only wanted me for my Egyptian pounds. He was calling me "Morning Star" in the morning and "Sunshine" in the heat of the day and his "North Star" in the evening when I would pass. Before you think I was purposely walking by just to hear these words, there is only one street in the town and it is necessary to pass there multiple times a day! Really!

Anyway, I did need to eat in his restaurant at some point, but with a large group, the decisions were not always entirely up to me! I thought I would play with him a bit! I told him that if he could come up with a nice name for me each time I passed, different each time, then on the last day I would convince my entire group to dine at his restaurant. He was up for the challenge. I told him that I would be keeping track and that if he repeated himself even once, the bet was off and he had to just let me pass without saying *anything* to me! A quick hand shake and an "Of course, my American Beauty," and we were on!

He held his own for a few days, and with only one more to go I thought that he was going to force me to hold up my end of the bargain and get my group to dine with him! The last day, I was wandering by and heard him say "Good Morning, my Morning Star." AHA! I got him; that was the one he used the very first day! I turned to tell him the deal was off and to my surprise, he was not speaking to me, he was chatting up another tourist. As I turned to look at him, I must have looked almost heartbroken that I was not his *only* Morning Star, (not quite that devastated really but for dramatics) because I caught his eye. He realized that I had just heard him calling another by MY name and instantly started to ramble on and on how I was his *ONLY ONE* and the *LOVE OF HIS LIFE* and the *WIND BENEATH HIS WINGS* and the *PILLOW UNDER HIS HEAD* and…and…and, I yelled "The deal is OFF!" and tried to act very hurt that he was cheating on me! He looked so defeated!

I head quickly back to my hotel to round up my crew for dinner; they had already agreed to dine there after hearing the story a few days ago. He was all smiles as we, 21 strong, turned the corner and chose *his* restaurant for dinner that night! He made sure the restaurant owner knew who I was and I received a FREE appetizer for the table and a FREE bottle of water. On the way out, we smiled at each other and nodded. I knew that he was on to his next "love affair" and I was happy to have known him, my worthy adversary!

An Honorable Mention for the "Worst Sales Pitch in the World" came as I passed a clothing stall in India: "Women's Jeans! Don't worry we have BIG sizes!" You What? "Most Creative and Clever Award" was said to me while wandering the markets of Jaipur, the pink city, in India after I said I was not shopping today, only taking pictures! He says "then take pictures of my shop!" Clever! India seems to be the leader, or maybe because it was my most recent trip, but another was: "Where are you from madam?" I say, "America." He says, "Me? I am from India!" It did bring a smile to my face, but I didn't go into his shop.

In Brazil, they have a restaurant style called Churrascaria. Servers come around with large skewers of meat and carve it onto your plate. There are about 12 different people coming around offering various cuts of meat. They have little markers on the table, one side is green and the other side is red. When you arrive at the restaurant you turn the marker to green, signifying "Bring it on!" They will continue to come by and offer you what they are carving until you turn the marker over to red. This tells them you are ready for a little digestion period. It is up to you how many times you flip between green and red. I wish we could wear little green or red badges on our clothing when walking through the various tourist markets around the world to tell if we were in the mood to shop or not. It would save the tourist a lot of hassles, but then again, what would be the fun of that?

And a few others...

Which direction is the traffic coming from? I suggest looking *both ways*! London is smart enough to paint LOOK LEFT on the cross walks to inform their tourists. Also, if they drive on the opposite side of the road, they also walk on the opposite side of subway passages, sidewalks and in supermarkets. I ran into every other person in the grocery store in Kuala Lumpur when I lived there. Here I think it is them being *rude,* and then realize it is just me on the *wrong* side of the aisle.

Then there are times when you find NO assigned seats for the airplane, e.g. easyJet or other budget airlines force everyone to shove in when it is time to board. An added bonus comes when the airline shuttles passengers to the plane on a bus, everyone gets to race to get on the bus, and once the doors open, race again to the plane. So, there is no need to assign seats on a plane, but they find it necessary to pre-assign seats for the *movie theaters.* Not good for the late arrivers who have to sit in ROW 1, SEATS 3 and 4. You have to put your head straight back to even get the movie to come into focus. Although, I guess that is where you would end up sitting if you were late to arrive in an American cinema, too!

The crazy thing is, all of the things listed above seem like "inconveniences" at the time, but I actually look forward to them after I have been home a bit. Even funnier is when I first get back out on the road, I smile as the predictability of backpacking sets in, as it is now my reality and I am in love with this lifestyle!

Keeping a Positive Attitude

THIS SECTION REALLY IS about a good attitude towards life in general and not just traveling, but I think it is most important to remember on the road. In everyday life we have interactions with people and how we approach each situation is up to us. I am a true believer that positive energy attracts positive energy. This is most important when you are traveling in a foreign country because sometimes all that you can understand of each other is a smile.

One of the hardest regions to keep smiling was in the Middle East. The men are full on, to say the least. Cat calling to the Western women, it is like a constant construction site. Many of my fellow female travelers would get so angry and yell back at the men, and act upset. The men actually like that more. I took the opposite approach. I smiled and made eye-contact. When they asked me to marry them (and believe me, they will ask) I would counter with "How many camels?" In the Middle-East, the men have to give a "dowry" to the father of the bride and camels are a strong currency. (About $8,000 USD each) When I would ask "How many camels?" they might come back with ten; I would act shocked and say "Only ten?" I would continue smiling and say, "I was offered 20 yesterday!" They would smile too and the negative situation was averted. I could go on my way in peace although sometimes I would stop to shop. I tell you, I have received many *free* gifts that way. Plus, it is better to send positive vibes out to the world anyway! Just a thought: should I be offended my love is only worth $80,000? I guess from a random stranger who has never met me, it might actually be a compliment!

I have done quite well to remain positive in all sorts of situations. First thing I do is remember I am not in my country, the rules are different, and I am a visitor. If that doesn't work I start to hum a song from Crowded House, "Take The Weather With You:" Everywhere you go, always take the weather with you! Just reminds me that I can make a positive out of a negative if I just try. I think it is also due to the fact that I have renamed Murphy's Law to MINDI's Law. Remember, if something is able to go wrong, it probably will. Some people think that this might be thinking negative, but if you think the worst and prepare for it, then you can hope for the good, but are still ready for the bad. Example, a bus journey is supposed to take six hours; if I plan for eight or ten, then I am prepared either way.

Getting lost, being lost or getting bad directions is par for the course when you are exploring another country. It is important to remember that you are doing just that, exploring. I was raised with a grandmother who constantly gets lost and takes wrong turns, but every time as we were finding our way or turning around she would say "At least we get to see something we wouldn't have seen otherwise." I have heard this since I was a little girl and it has followed me through life and my travels.

I *also* have the worst sense of direction of anyone I know. My friend David laughs at me all the time because I will never turn the right way out of an elevator, or out of the hostel. I guess if you know your limitations or are comfortable with them, then you can adapt your style to fit your weakness. I usually just get a map of the city, and then just wander until I am lost and see if I can find my way out. A good plan is to always have the address of the place you are staying at so if you truly get lost, you can just jump in a cab! I take one of the hostel's business cards and put it in my day pack.

When everything goes wrong and I am all out of positive thinking tricks, I usually just go with the thought that when you run into a road block, just change roads! If I was planning to go to El Salvador, but there were landslides, then I changed roads and went to Honduras. If you have a plan B and C, then A might just work out in the end.

My advice to you, when someone tells you about a location you have dreamt of visiting, but they hated it, it was dirty and smelly and the trains were never on time; GO! Try it out for yourself. I have met many travelers along the way who have told me similar stories and it is still one of my favorite parts of meeting new people, finding out where they have been and what they suggest/or don't suggest. Not everyone is going to have the same experience. Just remember that it is all relative! That is why travel is so personal. Of course, some places are just what they are, but it is *your* approach and *your* attitude that will make the world of difference!

Staying Excited about Travel

"Once the travel bug bites, there is no known antidote, and I know that I shall be happily infected until the end of my life."
Michael Palin

My thoughts on the travel bug: I believe it has the ability to bite everyone, but some people put up better repellent than others. I knew when I was young that I wanted the travel bug to bite, and I was actually waiting for it. I think there are different levels of "infection" and I might just have one of the worse cases out there! Some people are happy to be infected for a short period in their lives and then they slip back into the mainstream lifestyle. I am one who has made traveling part of my mainstream, and I will live this way until I can no longer get on a plane, train or bus!

Although I feel traveling is my destiny, there are times when I need to pump myself back up and get ready for the next adventure. I have a few tricks that keep travel and trip planning top of mind! I play the Departure Board Game. While I am waiting for a flight, I sit in front of the departure board and see how many places I have already been, then take note of places I have not! This, of course, adds to The List! I love testing myself and trying to see if I know the location of all of the places on the board.

I study atlases, maps, and globes; it is almost like an obsession. I have my own collection, but I am always looking in libraries and book stores, too. I have taught my four year old niece that the atlas is "Aunt Mindi's Favorite Book" and she loves to look at it with me and hear stories. I love the travel section of any bookstore. On many trips, especially if it is rainy and cold, I will find my way to an international bookstore and spend most of the day flipping through Lonely Planet guidebooks to places I have yet to visit.

The hardest time to keep up the motivation to travel is just after I get home from a trip. The first few weeks are marvelous. I get to eat my mom's cooking, go out in my town and see everyone I have been missing, have drinks and dinner at Mulligan's, and share my crazy stories. However, once I am used to the "routine" again, I start to get restless. I try to keep myself inspired by staying in touch with the many travelers whom I have met along the way. We share emails, stories and pictures. There is no better friend than a fellow traveler who lets you live through them while they are on the road, and responds to your group emails when you are on the road. It is quite possible that you have not seen these friends since the first time you met them a few years back, but by keeping up on each other's travels, you stay connected.

I am a very visual person and like to have my pictures posted to my website and find myself looking through them when it seems like it will be months before I will get out there again. I also put all of my photos and brochures into scrapbooks. I have scrapbooked every trip I have ever taken, including my international recruiting trips with Walt Disney International Recruiting. I have a rule that I need to print my pictures and get them into scrapbook form within two to three weeks of returning home. This assures I actually will print the pictures, especially in the age of the digital photo. No one seems to print their pictures anymore! I find it easier to remember all of the details to make a scrapbook while they are still fresh.

I love to flip through my scrapbooks and relive my adventures. It helps get me from trip to trip. A little secret - I watch how others look through my scrapbooks. So many people flip through quickly, not really looking, just browsing. I take note of the people that truly "look" at my photos, ask questions and want to spend time hearing about other cultures. Those are the people that I know I can go to when I have been home for awhile and want to tell some of my stories. I am sure the same thing will happen with my book. Some of you will skim this book, or just read it for pleasure but some others will hopefully gain a bit of inspiration. For those of you who "just get it," I hope our paths will cross someday out there on the road!

Travel Rituals & Travel Hints

Travel Rituals

I TAKE PHOTOS OF the local beer in each country and if possible remove the label and save it for my scrapbook. I try to save some coins or small denomination bills and take pictures of the larger bills; originally, I tried to keep one of each denomination for each country but I that was becoming an expensive souvenir! I take a picture of the country's flag; if you do this, please be careful not to take pictures at the borders or official buildings. They get a little upset and usually make you delete the photo. I have seen someone get their camera taken away from them by police in Russia - beware of the KGB!

I try to look at the postcards as soon as I land so I can see what there is to see in that area.

I always keep a brand new, fresh pair of socks to wear on the trip home. Nothing feels better after six months of wearing "not-so-clean" clothes every day.

I try to learn two words of the local language per day I am in that country: I learn hello, please and thank you first – these are the three most powerful words in any language. The level of hospitality in a country will speak for itself. If you can learn hello and thank you without having to research it, chances are the country is a very welcoming one. On the other hand, if you don't have to look up "no thank you" then there probably too many touts bothering you because there are too many tourists.

Travel Hints: Packing

I am not going to provide a complete packing list as many other travel books tend to do because by performing a quick Google search you can have all the information you will ever need. There are a few things that do make every trip with me. I have a few superstitions as to what to bring, similar to a baseball player that is on a winning streak and continues to follow the same pregame ritual. Many things I bring so I won't *have* to use them, like antibiotics and first aid supplies, and a rain coat. Mindi's Law; if I have one it won't rain the entire six months, but if I forget to pack it, monsoon!

Here is a short list of not-so-typical items:

- 2-3 disposable cameras - I bring these cameras on *big nights out* so I don't lose my digital camera. My favorite trick is to break apart the disposable camera once it is finished and remove the AA battery to use in my alarm clock and then all I have to carry is a roll of film.
- Biofreeze - a type of pain relieving gel you can get at the chiropractor's office or from a masseuse. This is helpful when I have sore muscles from carrying my pack or sleeping on bad hostel beds. I recommend the roll-on kind as it is less messy. A bonus: is it cools your body temperature down, so it is great to use on a hot-sticky night in the tent.
- Head torch and extra batteries - especially for camping trips to Africa. It is much easier to erect a tent in the dark using a head torch to than trying to juggle the traditional flashlight while pounding in tent pegs.
- Cloth beach bag - I got mine in Thailand and it folds up to the size of a pair of socks. It is a great addition to the day pack for beach days or even dirty laundry.
- A knife-spoon-can opener combo - great for making PBJ's, cheese and crackers or make-your-own supermarket sandwiches.
- I am brand loyal when it comes to my travel shoes and my backpack! I have only ever worn Teva walking shoes. I am on my fifth or sixth pair. I buy the Omnium style that have a closed toe but are still sandal-like so I can hike in them,

but also walk in mud and water, and they dry quickly! I usually order them from www.zappos.com. When it comes to my backpack, I have had three since I started traveling and all were Kelty – www.kelty.com. My first pack was a top-load design and I found it very difficult to locate the item I was looking for, so I have since changed to a front-load style. The Red Cloud line is amazing because it has separate place for sleeping bag, shoes and also has a top pack that comes off and can be a hip pack for hiking. Kelty's site is also great for sleeping bags, sleep sheets, roll mats and rain gear for the backpack!

- Things I can't go without: puzzle books, sarong, playing cards for the "An Twanda" game and at least two books to start out so I am able to swap at the various book exchanges along the way.

Travel Hints: Currency

Check your currency; be sure the bills do not have excessive writing on them, tears or rips. Try to change money for the first time in a country with a proper exchange bureau (e.g. Travelex). I usually take the commission hit and the bad exchange rate at the airport for a small amount just to have cash on me for that first bus/taxi ride. This also allows you to see what the currency looks like. Sometimes if you change money on the street, the guys are trying to pass old versions of money that are no longer accepted in banks or supermarkets, or worse yet they are trying to pass counterfeit money.

If you are changing money at a travel agent-cum-money exchanger, always ask for a business card (especially if you are changing a large amount) and keep your receipt that way if anything goes wrong when trying to use your newly changed money, you have a place to go back to if it is fraudulent.

When traveling in Africa, be sure that your US Dollars are dated from 2001 or later. This is one I learned the hard way. It is best to have the most recent possible print date. Old bills are rarely accepted anywhere in Africa. If you happen to find yourself "on the continent," and have outdated bills, you will feel like a criminal, being sneaky when trying to "pass" old bills. When I was traveling with Christa the first time, she went through her remaining US Dollars and traded me out, as she was on her way back to the US and could obviously spend them there. Simple little transaction between two travelers, but stress reliever for me for sure!

The Currency Game - for those travelers that were out there before the inception of the European Union-(EU) and the common currency throughout Europe (EURO), you know this game. Trying to balance the right amount of your own currency to change over to the local currency for the number of days that you have in that country, without changing too little or too much. After many multi-country (currency) trips, I have become pretty good at this. See, the math skills are helping again. I have had many border crossings that consisted of me, the equivalent of about $3 US Dollars and a little food stall. I try to get as much as I can, for the little I have left. So, do I get one big pack of Pringles and spend the whole lot, or do I try to get as many little packs of peanuts and cookies as I can? Either way, it is usually spent on things that I really didn't need, and in my case, I always favor CHOCOLATE!

Now, I didn't say once the currency was exchanged that the conversion was easy! Some countries have *fun* currency. For instance the Vietnamese Dong, (the name in itself makes me chuckle), but the first time you try to take money out of an ATM and realize that you have to take millions, literally *millions* of Dong, the smiling stops there! You get a little nervous and hope that you are remembering the exchange rate correctly, otherwise you may have just cleaned out your bank account! The rate was about 16,000 Dong to 1 USD the last time I was there, so think about taking around $100 USD; you are now a "Millionaire!" 1.6 million Dong! WOW!

Separate your money in a few places. Keep an emergency cash fund of US dollars, Euros, or British pounds. There have been many times I have been in places which don't have ATMs, don't take credit cards, and the banks are closed for some random holiday I didn't know about, and I was stuck without money for a few days. Also, remember to replenish the fund if you did have to break into it. I don't use a money belt, but many travelers do. I feel it is the first place the robbers will look. Plus, for a long time I was traveling on my first passport and I had to have pages added twice, and it was becoming too thick to carry in the money belt, so I stopped using it. (Not to mention I didn't like having the added bulk in my mid-section.)

Travel Hints: Passport Control

If you are like me, you don't want to be separated from your passport for any reason. Some youth hostels/hotels may require you to leave your passport at the front desk while you are staying with them. I suggest you don't if you can help it. First of all, it just increases the chances that you could forget it there and not realize it until you have made it to the train station, or worse, the airport. Secondly, it is just not good practice to allow someone else control of your passport. I usually just say "Oh, I would rather not leave it with you, thanks!" You will find out quickly if it is a solid requirement (some governments do require it of the hotels) or if they just prefer to keep it.

Some tricks to getting your passport back in your control: Have extra photo copies of your passport and give one to the front desk. It is smart to have a copy scanned and saved to email in case you lose it - you will have all the details. Keep extra photo copies in your day back and journal. Carry a second form of ID, for example, driver's license or student ID. They will usually take this as collateral as they are probably just assuring you pay upon checkout. If you can tell they are worried about payment, sometimes paying in full at the beginning of your stay makes them a little less worried about keeping the passport.

Travel Hints: Security

Secure your backpack zipper sections with rock climbing clips otherwise known as carabiners; it's not a lock but makes it harder for the random person to undo your bag while you are standing on a crowded bus or train. This happened to me in Albania before I started using these clips. I was taking a bus to the main bus station. It was a very packed local bus and there was no room to put my big pack down so I was forced to wear it. A young guy behind me must have thought this was a great opportunity to snag whatever he could out of my front zipper section. His plan was foiled by an elderly woman who saw what he was doing and screamed. It was in Albanian of course, so everyone on the bus knew what was happening before me. He jumped off at the next stop. I did an inventory and didn't notice anything missing. I was lucky!

Travel with your own padlock; I suggest the wire combo kind. The keys are too easy to lose and the wire comes in handy when the locker rings are small. Regular padlocks are too thick and don't clamp on many small lockers. I have the Swiss army reinforced wire lock.

Travel Hints: General

DON'T DRINK THE WATER! Use bottled water to brush your teeth. Remember not to rinse your mouth with the water when you are in the shower. Sounds crazy, but a bad case of Delhi Belly and you will know what I mean; take all precautions!

When doing hand washing of your laundry, be sure to rinse thoroughly. On my first backpacking trip I was doing my washing and an Australian guy was asking how to "hand-wash" and said that he didn't have any laundry soap. Seeing that he had been wearing the same t-shirt and board shorts the entire trip, I thought it best to help him out. I handed over my soap and continued on with my washing. Later the next day, we were all walking around Rome sight-seeing and I noticed he was "lathering up" in the crotch region of his shorts. I am guessing he didn't give the shorts a good enough rinse.

Travel Karma & Travel Angels

I GUESS YOU COULD say I am a bit superstitious. I think about walking under ladders, seeing black cats and I feel certain that some numbers are lucky or unlucky. I also believe that you get back what you give and you can create your own destiny. But, the most important philosophy I try to focus on is travel karma.

The normal rules of karma apply but are intensified by life on the road. You shouldn't litter, you should leave parks and beaches the way you found them, and you should treat others the way you would like to be treated. These are basic rules we learned in kindergarten. I believe travel karma has a point system. You can gain points by helping other lost travelers find their way; not leaving a mess behind for the cleaning lady; watching someone's bag while they use the rest room; or simply by helping someone with their bag on the bus.

I am always the most nervous about other travelers who are sleeping at the airport. Not the "tough" ones that are hunkered down with a roll-mat and sleeping bag, and chances are they have an alarm clock, too. It is the ones who are passed out in the uncomfortable airport chairs who seem to scream, "I have too long a layover and I just happened to fall asleep!" What if they miss that flight? Should I wake them up? I'd just finished my trip to India with my friend David and was returning back to Malaysia. The airline had already switched our departure gate once so I was watching the screens carefully in case they got any other bright ideas. A fellow traveler came and sat beside me. We just carried on waiting, both reading our respective books. When I realized that the airline did in fact, change the gate again, to one that was much farther away, I turned to see if she noticed as well. She had fallen asleep! There is always that moment when you think, I don't want to be embarrassed if she really isn't on the same flight as me, but in the name of travel karma, I had to try! I nudged her and it took a few times, she was really out, I asked her if she was traveling to Kuala Lumpur on Air Asia and she responded, "YES!" "They changed our gate and we are boarding!" Bonus points for me and an unmissed flight for her! I just hope she repays the favor to someone else in the future. We gotta stick together out there!

Just like in Greek Mythology there were gods of love and fortune and power, I believe there are gods that spend their days watching over travelers. They are the point keepers, if you will. You appease the Travel Gods by helping others, giving off positive vibes, and keeping a great attitude. I think there are ways to piss off the Travel Gods, too, by getting "cocky." If you expect things to go your way *all* the time, chances are they won't. Don't tempt fate: keep things locked up, stay alert. If you get lazy, the Travel Gods will take the opportunity to "sock" it to you! You will know when the Travel Gods are messing with you: if things are going too well, you should be peeking around every corner for something to go wrong, and when it almost does you shout, "Aha, I beat you" or "Okay, I will take that, I have had good travel karma until now."

The Travel Gods also have Angels that they send to you as a "bonus" for all the good karma points you have earned. That person comes along just at the right time…to answer a question, give you their cab, or walk you to your train platform. I happen know the names of some of my Travel Angels, but many, I do not. I try to "pay it forward" and be someone else's travel angel (even if they don't know it).

Sometimes the Travel Angels are fellow travelers that offer up their homes for a free place to crash. Free accommodation is like winning the lottery. It is amazing how fellow travelers open up their homes and cities to you with little or no thought. The rule I try to live by: it's okay to ask for a free "spot on the floor" from fellow travelers and their families but, just be prepared to open your house in the future. When you have, give! And when you are staying with someone, be a good houseguest! Sometimes they have housemates; respect them and go about your touring; your mates will join you if they can and want to! It is funny how fellow travelers know how to host each other. It is the small things mean the most, like a fresh towel, laundry service, home cooked meals, and I promise you that all of this is better than a five star hotel.

Early in my travel career I was searching online for a Contiki Tour of Spain and Portugal. The company's website offered a forum to chat with other people that might be joining the same tour. I found a fellow traveler that was going it alone, too, and we thought we could band together. Le Le and I exchanged emails and thoughts on our trip, but when it came time for the departure, we realized that we were unable to start the trip on the same date. I was moving to London and had to get my life set up there. I felt bad leaving my new friend without a travel partner, so I offered my flat in London as a pre- and post-trip stopover if she was interested. Now remember, I have never actually met her in person. She happily took me up on a *free* place to stay in London, as it is an expensive town. I can still remember walking out of my flat to meet her at the Tube station thinking, *I don't even really know what she looks like and she is going to be living in my apartment for one week!* Le Le and I had a wonderful week swapping life and travel stories and promised to keep in touch in the future. Six years later and we are still in contact. It is amazing what a little *travel karma* can accomplish.

Traveling allows you to ask for things and watch them show up. If I am lonely and I would like a travel partner, I just write about it in my journal or ask for one out loud! Who will I get? Am I ready for that person? How will I act? And what reaction will I have to them? Throughout my stories you have heard me make mention of the Travel Angels and how they have helped me through a tough situation. This section of the book is to pay homage to all of the Travel Angels that have helped me through the years. I hope I have made you proud!

Addis Ababa, Ethiopia

Ever had a strange feeling about a place before you even get there? Ethiopia was a nightmare in my planning. First of all, I was due to go there as part of my 18 week African overland tour that was cancelled. The tour company suggested that Americans get their Ethiopian travel visas in advance, so I had taken all the steps, paid $150 and secured the visa. Now that the tour was cancelled I had to decide if I was going to go it alone or not. I had the visa already, so easy enough right? Not!

I had been in contact with Ethiopian Airlines (EA) to try to secure tickets in advance. With the limited amount of time I had and the distance between the points I wanted to see, I had decided to try to book the tickets before I arrived. I had the perfect itinerary worked out with the lady at EA, but when it came time to issue the tickets, she never responded to my emails.

I decided to go anyway and work on the internal flights when I got there. I arrived in Addis Ababa, which means "new flower," in the early afternoon and was on a mission to change money, sort out a hostel and book a few flights. All of these are the usual post-landing rituals, but nothing about this trip was going to be *usual.*

I collected my bag and passed through customs with no issues, headed for the ATM and realized there was no cash machine in the airport. I walked to the taxi stand and explained to my taxi driver that I had no BIRR (the local currency) and if he could drive me to a bank I could pay him after. One hour and a half later, the fifth bank (no one takes Master Card and the one that did, the phone lines were out), second hotel/hostel (there was no vacancy anywhere we stopped) and no BIRR, I was becoming frustrated. My driver was so amazing, even with all the trouble to get money and still no luck, he even drove me to the Ethiopian Airlines Office and waited with me for one hour. I waited in the packed lobby for my number to be called, only to find out that they could get me a flight to Lilebela but couldn't guarantee a return ticket to match with my departure back to Kenya. See why one-way tickets are a good idea!

Four days to hang out in the capital, with little or nothing to do was not how I envisioned my adventures in Ethiopia. I was about to cry, literally. Alex, my driver, was my savior. He just kept smiling and drove me to another hotel, this one cashed traveler's checks and gave money from Master Card. With the money sorted, he suggested his friend's pensione for my three nights. Usually I would be wary of this, as you never know what the place will look like, but I was at his mercy. He drove me to the supermarket (the pensione had a self-catering kitchen) and then planned my itinerary.

He would be my personal driver for the next three days, taking me to the National Museum, Entoto (the old capital city), a tour of all the monuments, a day trip to Sodere to swim in the natural springs and he even arranged for me to see an Ethiopian Dinner/Dance Show that served authentic Ethiopian food while you watch the dancers from the different regions perform. The tour even included meeting his wife, three year old baby, and brother. I really felt comfortable and happy. It just goes to show you that even when things are going wrong, smile and push through it.

We would need to use this advice one more time during our time together. Because Sodere was outside the city limits, Alex had to go to his boss and get a special permit to drive the taxi out of the city. He secured the permit and we were off. The drive was breathtaking. The countryside was different than that of Egypt and Kenya, a sort of blending of the two. From dry and dusty, then lush and green; to camel farms, day markets and bumpy roads! We had found the hot springs with no problems and were heading back to the city. Alex stopped at a road side gas station, gassed up and we ate a bit of lunch. As we were leaving the gas station a police car pulled us over. While we were stopping, Alex quickly explained that the police are corrupt and will try to get a bribe from him or even worse, try to get *me* to pay a bribe. He said "No matter what, don't pull out your money!"

What happened next was my first of many experiences with bribery and extortion. Alex was talking to the policeman and going back and forth and finally got out of the car. I was trying to watch but not get caught watching. I saw Alex give him some Birr. I didn't know the bills well enough to know how much it was. Sometimes a few dollars for them to buy their lunch is all they are after. Fortunately, that was the case this time.

On the return drive Alex explained to me that he has heard stories of police seeing a white passenger and asking for a large amount of money. When the passenger and the driver refuse, the police threaten to take the driver to jail for being outside their permit area and tell the passenger that they will have to find their own way back to Addis Ababa. I can see how one would dish out the money for the bribe.

So, overall, the trip to Ethiopia was not what was planned or expected but thanks to Alex my wonderful tour guide, it became more than I could have ever hoped for. When it comes to Travel Angels, Alex is on the top of the list!

Malindi, Kenya

My given name is Melinda, and so when I saw the city named Malindi on the map of Kenya, it seemed only natural to head there for a visit, and for an added bonus, it was on the coast. Sometimes this is all it takes to help design my travel itinerary. I knew I had to endure another daunting bus ride to get there, but never in my wildest travel nightmares would I have imagined what was going to happen to me on this journey.

The bus departed only about one hour late at about 8a.m. - pretty good for African standards. This bus was going to Mombasa. I loved saying this name and would say it like they say Mufasa in Disney's The Lion King, "Muuufaaaasa, oooooooh!" You can take the girl out of Disney! I was told this bus would take about ten hours, and then I still had to take the 120 kilometer journey from Mombasa to Malindi. I had a backup plan to spend the night in Mombasa if the ten hour bus ride turned into a 15 hour journey.

The first leg of the trip was pretty basic; four people to each seat designed for two, vendors selling everything from some kind of juice in a bag to live chickens, and two or three quick stops to pick up more passengers. The bus would stop alongside the road at a junction and pick up those waiting from surrounding villages. I was "busting for the loo" but afraid to get off because the bus might leave me. I was traveling alone so I had no one to hold the bus for me until I returned. My poor bladder, it has gone through the gauntlet on my journeys.

We arrived in bustling Mombasa just about 7p.m. and again I was pleased with the timing. I mean, it could have been so much worse! Mombasa is quite a large city and it didn't look like a very easy city to navigate, so I decided quickly to search for the next bus to Malindi. I collected my bag and tried to ignore the massive amounts of touts trying to sell me their wares. What I needed was a travel shop or bus station. I looked around and saw a lot of *nothing*. I noticed a traffic cop in the middle of a small intersection directing traffic – well, moving her arms around to put on a good show. The drivers were not really listening to her whistle or paying attention to her signals. It is everyone for themselves in Africa. I told her where I was going and asked the best way to find transport. To my surprise she got on her mobile phone and made a call. Was she ignoring me, or being *extremely* helpful? Lucky for me it was the latter. Her brother was a bus driver and was taking a special chartered bus to Malindi that very minute, and she was calling to find out if there was space for one more. My fare would have been gravy and she probably would get a little *somethin' somethin'* for referring me. That is how it works in Africa, and this time I was on the upside. She left her post and drove me on her motorbike around the corner to her brother's bus.

Add random traffic cop to the list of Travel Angels please! Within five minutes of getting off the first bus, I was comfortably seated on the second. Her brother explained to me that I would have the bus to myself until we reached the little village just outside Mombasa. Could today get any better? Uh oh, I spoke too soon. I hate when I do that! We pulled up to a building that looked like a small school. This is where we were getting the other passengers. I watched as almost 30 women football (soccer) players boarded the bus all of them in their red team jerseys. They were probably just as surprised to see me as I was to see them.

They all settled in and we were on our way. Some of them had to double up in the seats, but they graciously left me a seat all to myself. This too would change; about 20 minutes down the road we stopped at another school. No way, couldn't be? Yes, at least 20 more players, this time with blue team jerseys on. The bus was definitely getting crowded now, and I was forced to share my seat with a player from the blue team. I could not script this if I tried. We stopped for a third time and picked up another 20 women, in yellow jerseys. Now we are three to a seat and my face is pressed right up against the window. So much for leg room, I was sitting on my left butt cheek only. This was now extreme torture on my very full bladder. I still hadn't gone to the toilet all day.

With all of the commotion I lost track of how far we had actually traveled so I was unsure how much longer I would have to be crushed up against the side of the bus. Had seating not been an issue, I would have had a lot of fun. This was one of the liveliest bus rides ever. The three competing teams were taking turns *shouting* their club songs and taunting each other about the upcoming competition. They were even tossing around a soccer ball from row to row at one point. The girl next to me was trying to make small talk and asked me where I was staying in Malindi. She was shocked when I said that I would be sorting that out once I arrived. There was a statewide football tournament and she was sure that the hotels would not have any rooms available. I just sat there in the middle of all of these shouting women and took a moment to think what this meant to me.

It was almost 9p.m. now and we were still about 45 minutes outside of town. What have I gotten myself into? I should have stayed in Mombasa. She could see that I was a bit worried and she offered me a solution. She informed me that the three groups on board were staying at three separate hotels and maybe as the bus dropped each group off, I could get out and see if there was a room available for me. She took it one step further and offered to let me sleep on the floor of her hotel if there was nothing available by the last stop. For a bad day, I was getting a good dose of travel karma. Luckily there was space at the second hotel. Eden Rock was *way* out of my "backpacker's budget," but sometimes you just have to bite the bullet so to speak. It was $40 US a night, so not too crippling. I thanked the remaining players and just smiled back at them when they sent me off with a big cheer.

First order of business: TOILET! After I dropped my bag in my gorgeous room, fully equipped with a four poster bed and mosquito net, I went in search of some much needed food. I asked the hotel about their restaurant but they informed me it was closed. I tried to bargain for a few slices of bread, but had no luck. I had a splitting headache and needed food. I decided I had to at least walk a bit to see if I could find some biscuits or crackers. As I was walking outside of the hotel gates, an Eden Rock resort van pulled up next to me. The driver was smiling and trying to make small talk. I was in "no mood" to deal with some man hitting on me at this point in my day. Once he saw I was having none of it, he asked me where I was going. I explained my situation and he assured me there was nothing within walking distance, but he knew of a place that was still open and he would drive me there. Mom, don't worry it is not my normal practice to jump in a car with a strange man in the middle of the night! He was driving the resort's van so I decided to go for it. His name was Samson and he brought me to a little restaurant and bought me Chicken N' Chips. The *best* chicken and french fries I have ever eaten!

Samson asked what my plans were for my time in Malindi and I explained I just wanted to chill on the beach. He explained that he ran a tour company and wanted to know if he could be my guide. I explained that because I was staying in the resort which was out of my budget, I would not be able to afford any "cushy" extras. He offered to drive me around the next day to check out a few smaller guest houses that might still have rooms that were more within my budget. Now you are speakin' my language! He also offered me the last remaining seat on his tour bus in two days time. He was taking a group of Italian tourists around to the local beaches and said I could ride along for *free* since they had already paid for the fuel costs, etc. He just asked that I don't tell the tourists that I didn't pay. As the Go-Go's would say, "My lips are sealed!"

I found a nice, cheap room at Dagamas Hotel for the next few days and joined Samson on the tour from Silversands Beach to Angel's Bay on the Indian Ocean. Angel's Bay, a coincidence? I think not! This turned out to be one of the best adventures, even though it was a bit rocky from time to time. I have to thank my Travel Angels for pulling it off - the traffic cop, the loud and crazy football players, and most of all Samson, for feeding this starving Mzungu in the middle of the night!

Future Travel List

The true sign of a person who is "hooked" on travel is the constant updating of their "List." I have a list in my last journal, my current journal, near my bed and even on scrap pieces of paper in my purse. Every time I look at an atlas, travel book or research places on the internet, I update my list. I have even been known to find future destinations while doing a word search or crossword puzzle. The departure board at the airport is the biggest threat. Remember my Departure Board game?

Sri Lanka/Nepal/Maldives

Return to Indonesia (Java and Komodo Islands)

More of West Africa - Senegal, Sierra Leone, Cote D'Ivoire

South Africa coastline from Durban to Johannesburg including Lesotho/Swaziland

Finish South America-Venezuela/Suriname/Guyana/French Guiana/Uruguay/Paraguay

Cuba/Caribbean islands (including Dominican Republic and Haiti)

Northern Territory of Australia and Great Barrier Reef

North Island of New Zealand/Fiji

Western Ireland/Isle of Skye/Isle of Man/Guernsey

Antarctica/Falkland Islands

Tran-Siberian Railway

Finish North America and Canada (in an RV)

So, as you might have guessed by now, I want to see as much of this world as I may be blessed enough to see! Now let's just hope that Femi's list is the same as mine!

Countries that never seem to fall off "The List"

I have such a strong desire to visit so many places in the world and as you know I have been keeping a "list." Some places tend to make The List and then within a few months fall off again. Booking those trips just seemed to fall into place. However, there are times when it is just "not in the stars!" I have many places in the world I have missed: missed due to geography; missed because I ran out of time; missed because plans changed at the last minute and even missed because the tour company I booked with forgot to pick me up!

Western Ireland is an area of the world that I have tried to get to a few times, but to no avail! I lived in London for over a year and thought that Ireland would be my weekend playground. When I left the UK earlier than expected, I had to make other plans. After traveling with my friend David and his family in Italy and finishing most of Eastern Europe, I flew from Croatia to Ireland. I was short on time and had been traveling on my own for over a month and was ready for a tour. I really needed a tour at this point because I was tired of planning everything myself. Sometimes it is great to wake up and have someone else tell you what the plan is for the day! I picked the Paddy Wagon Tour! I did a 10 day tour around the "Ring of Kerry" in the south and it was a great craic - that's Irish for I enjoyed every minute of it! Highly recommended for sure!

Upon my return to Dublin, I booked a second tour with the same company for the western portion, another seven days in Ireland. How exciting! That is, until they never came to pick me up at my hostel. I was waiting patiently and on time as always, but the green paddy wagon never came. I asked the people at the hostel reception to please call and verify that they were aware I was there and waiting. By the time we called, the tour was already 30 minutes up the road and would not return for me. I was disappointed to say the least. I spoke with the company and of course they refunded my money, but now what was I to do with the next few days, after all I had been to Dublin a few times already. They offered me a free day trip to Northern Ireland to do the Belfast City Tour. Did you say FREE? I am in! Belfast and Northern Ireland - CHECK! But, to this day, Western Ireland still remains on The List!

All 11 Disney Gates

As you have probably realized by now, I love lists, especially checklists. So it is natural that being a Disney girl, I would want to make it one of my goals to visit all 11 Disney Theme Parks.

I worked at Walt Disney World in Orlando, Florida from 1995 to 2004 so I was able to visit the Magic Kingdom, Epcot, Disney's Hollywood Studios, and Disney's Animal Kingdom Park more times than I can count. The fact that we could play in the parks for free was a big bonus for me! I was also able to be an unofficial tour guide for the countless many that came to visit me while I lived in Florida.

On my International Recruiting trip to China and Japan in 2001, the company flew us through Los Angeles, so the other recruiter and I took advantage of the one night stopover and visited the two parks in California (Disneyland and Disney's California Adventure Park). As cast members we were entitled to visit all Disney Parks for free.

In 2003, during my six week unpaid leave from Disney, I visited Paris as part of the Contiki camping tour. We had a few free days to explore the city and I was happy to take three friends from the tour with me to visit the two parks in Paris (Disneyland Paris & Walt Disney Studios) I was still considered a cast member and carried my Main Gate park pass, so entrance for me and my friends was once again free.

I purposefully scheduled my ten month trip around the world to come home through Tokyo, Japan. I was no longer an active cast member so these were the first two parks that I had to pay an entrance fee. Seemed strange, but seeing these two parks was well worth the money. So, as of 2006, I had seen ten of the 11 Disney gates (Tokyo Disneyland & Tokyo Disney Seas).

The Disney Company built the 11th gate in Hong Kong in 2005, and it took me until 2009 to visit Hong Kong Disneyland. I was visiting South East Asia and used Hong Kong as my stopover on my way back to the USA. It is always a pleasure to end a long backpacking trip with a little Disney luxury, and of course, impeccable service.

I had the opportunity to experience the resorts as well as the parks in Tokyo and in Hong Kong. I stayed in Disney's Hollywood Hotel for two nights near Disneyland Hong Kong. I arrived at the resort early in the afternoon on my first day and immediately headed to the park. They had a ticket special going, buy one day and get a second free. So,

I wandered through the park slowly. It was quite quiet and I was able to get most of the big attractions in, but had a few loose ends for the next day. I decided to just eat in the hotel restaurant that evening, but much to my dismay, I was very ill that night and all the next day. This was during the beginning of the swine flu outbreaks, so I was unsure if I had food poisoning or flu. I was unable to leave my room the second day of my visit and I still needed to do a bit of shopping and had hoped to at least make it to the fireworks that evening.

I called down to the front desk to inform them that I was not feeling well and that I had eaten in the hotel the night before. They assured me that no one else had called to complain of food poisoning, but they would check with the chef. I mentioned how I was unable to leave the room and they asked me if I was in need of anything. I explained that I had wanted to purchase a Mickey and Minnie remote control car for my niece's birthday but couldn't get to the shops. They packaged one up for me and sent it to my room along with a signed card from Mickey himself with get well wishes. They even sent along stickers and pictures of the characters for my niece. There was a second knock on the door and it was the Chef with crackers, toast and some homemade soup.

I was doing my best to rest up for the evening so I could get to the fireworks, but I was still not feeling up to it. The manager of the front desk called and asked how I was feeling and wanted to know if I would be making it to the fireworks. I explained I was still feeling very ill. I told her I used to work for Disney and was very sad to miss the fireworks because this was the last park on my list. She said that she would arrange a fireworks viewing from a suite on the top floor and I could rest in that room during the show. The room overlooked the park and with the television set to the *Magical* station, I could hear Mickey and friends announcing the show and watch the fireworks as they were choreographed to the music. At that very moment, I felt very special and all of my happy memories of the Walt Disney World Company came flooding back. I can always say, "Disney does it right!"

I just read that the company signed a deal with the French government to open a third park in Paris, but according to the contract they have until 2030 to complete it, so maybe I can take my children there someday! Add another location to my list!

Secret to: LIFE

LIVE life like there is no tomorrow,
but DREAM like there is a future!
Sidewalk Graffiti - Ireland, 2005

I WISH I COULD say that I knew the answers to all of life's questions, or that by traveling the world I am any closer to understanding the mysteries of life. I can't - but the one thing I can say is that my life is fuller and richer because I do! Just know that life is a journey; you need to continue to push yourself forward, analyze your actions, learn from others and always notice the "good" in life. Challenge yourself to be "better" everyday.

The Lessons I have Learned from Traveling

- Be kind to the environment/nature. It is slowly slipping away from us; we have to preserve it!
- See the "good" in people: locals and fellow travelers.
- If something makes you smile is a good clue that you are on the right track.
- Don't be afraid to "ask" for things out loud. Everyone is entitled to good travel karma if they earn it.
- Take love when it is given and give love when it is needed.
- We spend half of our life wishing away time and the other half commenting on how fast it went. Live in the moment!

- Travel can't always be events, sometimes it is just… traveling!
- Don't be afraid to cry.
- Roll with the punches.
- Don't travel with someone who has a different idea of "budget" than you! It will only add stress and possibly end your friendship.
- When traveling, try not to have strong opinions about what to eat for dinner or where.
- Be flexible: Nothing ever goes as planned, especially if you *need* it to.
- Less IS more! We don't really need all of the materialistic things we have. Give something to your favorite charity today!
- The definition of "poor" is subjective.
- Traveling allows me to be me, only better.

Things I Ask of You:

- Get out there and travel; even within your own country.
- Do some solo travel. You owe it to yourself to discover how strong you are.
- Don't litter! This world is in enough danger, be part of the solution not part of the problem.
- Don't be a graffiti artist in museums, forts or monuments. At the risk of sounding cheesy, "leave only footprints and take only memories." I can't think of anything worse than wandering through a historical sight and seeing "Joanie loves Chachi 1988" carved into the side of a statue.
- Respect cultural differences.
- Be your country's Ambassador; let others see the good, not the bad and the ugly.
- Look for the beauty in life: in what Mother Nature provides, and in the people you meet along the way.
- Bring home your experiences and share with others!

Ways You Can Find "The Secret"

> *"Since life is short and the world is wide, the*
> *sooner you start exploring the better."*
> Simon Raven

Start small - Maybe you have always wanted to travel the world, but have not been able to get up the nerve to do it. Maybe you are happy with your career, but want to make the most out of your vacation time. Maybe you can't afford a large "around the world trip" right now. Start with a few trips in your home country; get your feet wet in English-speaking airports, youth hostels, and tourist attractions. Then, after you get your travel legs, venture out a bit. Take a two or three week mini-adventure, then plan longer trips each time; before you know it you will be looking forward to taking a longer, more intense trip. If you are a first time traveler, between the ages of 18-35, I recommend starting with Western or Eastern Europe with Contiki, or if you don't want to mess with the group travel thing, stay in larger hostels at the start of your trip. You will meet lots of other travelers and if your itineraries match, you can wander together. Work your way up to an African Trails overland trip and then go to India. I promise if you "get your feet wet" in the easier locations, you will have a better time as you grow with travel.

Organize an internship, find a volunteer opportunity, or get creative in finding a job that will pay you to travel - There are so many opportunities out there. If you are blessed enough to come from a culture that provides a *gap year,* make the most of it. If not, maybe you can create your own. If you are still a student, spend a semester abroad; heck, do a semester at sea. My friends at Yummy Jobs have amazing programs for students, non-students and graduates. Check them out at: www.yummyjobs.com Take a little advice from an ex-recruiter: employers will be more likely to give you an interview and hire you if you have studied abroad, participated on a work program and/or completed one or more internships. In a tough job market, it is even more important to stand out in the crowd. Build your resume (CV) as best you can, and why not see some of the world while you are at it?!

Always look at a map/atlas and watch the Travel Channel - The more you start to familiarize yourself with the world, the more you will want to get out there and explore it! Start your own list today!

Tell people you are doing it - Even before you have convinced yourself, start telling your friends, family, or anyone that will listen. The more you tell people, the more you will convince yourself. I remember being so nervous to actually go to Africa, but I knew I really wanted to go, so I just started telling everyone that I was planning a trip. People will keep you honest. They will ask how your saving is going, so you better "be saving," and they will ask you if you have booked your ticket, and I am telling you, you will do just that! You will book your ticket! There is no better way to show your commitment to a trip than to put money on it! Once you have saved the money and are able to purchase the ticket, nothing should stop you!

Don't be afraid to "break the mold" - Many people told me to keep my house and to get married, have kids and do what everyone else was doing. Maybe we (the travelers) are not "out of line," maybe it is the world. The idea that we all have to live a "normal life" is becoming outdated. I think the "right path" is the one *you* choose for yourself, whatever that may be! I have learned now that you can travel with your children, too. Travel is a life experience that cannot be taught in school!

I am not saying "good-bye"...

Since the very beginning of my travel adventures I have always found it strange to meet people "on the road," connect quickly and then have to say "good-bye" knowing full well that you may never see that person again. One could get very depressed and upset with all of these sad good-byes! That is why I adopted the strategy to *not* say good-bye, but rather "Safe Travels!" Deep in my heart, I can then hope that someday, I *will* see them again! To quote the American writer and cartoonist, Dr. Seuss, "Don't cry because it's over, smile because it happened."

I am a little sad that this "chapter" in my life is ending. I will miss the traveling for self discovery. My wish is that travel will still play a part in the next chapter of my life!

I hope my book has given you at least one "AHA" moment, or at least a few laughs out loud, but most of all I hope it has inspired you to

TRAVEL. Even if it is just a short trip outside of your comfort zone! If you found this book at some faraway place, at some random youth hostel, in a little corner of the world, then…you already knew the "SECRET" before you read the first page! Trade this book happily for another "hidden treasure."

And from one traveler to another,
SAFE TRAVELS!

Acknowledgments

MANY THANKS TO MY family who has always supported me: Mom and Dad, there are no words to tell you how much you have done for me. You have encouraged me my entire life to be the best that I can be, you have tolerated the nonconventional way I tend to do things and have always shown me such strong love and support. Oh yeah, and thanks for letting your 30 something daughter move back in with you for the last five or six years to make my dreams possible.

Brent and Amber, thanks for giving us two of the most beautiful girls I have ever seen, and in turn giving Mom and Dad the grandchildren they were waiting for, also allowing me to be on the loose for a bit longer! Thank you for posting pictures of the girls so I didn't have to miss them growing up while I was away.

Thank you to David for your undying love and support! You allow me to be the "truest" form of myself. You were the one that helped me "jump-start" my traveling lifestyle and have always helped to cultivate it by getting creative with the jobs we could do to make money and still be together and travel. You are a genius! I am looking forward to many more trips together in the future. Also, thanks for your help with the photos for this book; I may have never figured it out!

To the Ingersoll Family and Mulligan's Restaurant: Not only did Cheboygan need Mulligan's, but I did too. I can't tell you enough how much all of your love and support has meant to me. You are my second family and knowing I always had a great seasonal job to come back to made my adventures possible. Ann and Leon, thanks for letting me borrow the "Dyna-Ride;" without it, my first weekend getaways to write would not have been possible. Just one more selfless thing your family has done for me!

Thank you to Tracy Lindsay for volunteering to be my editor. You have always shown an interest in my travels and shared yours with me. I am glad we had the chance to work on my "life project" together. We had a tight deadline and I appreciate your dedication. I will be sure to call you if I decide to publish another book!

Along the way I have met and traveled with some amazing people I can now call my friends. They not only opened up their lives to me as a fellow backpacker, but they have all opened their homes to me when I was a wandering traveler. Thanks to Karma, my trip to Melbourne would not have been the same without you as a host. Thanks to Julie and Tim for letting me have the run of the house while I was in Sydney. I had never chased down a missing parakeet (outside) and caught it until I stayed with you. Thanks to Michael and Mary in Perth, Australia for giving me my own room and personal tour of Swan Valley. You are two of the coolest people I know. I will be back to visit someday. It says something that I was in Australia for six weeks and I only had to stay in a youth hostel for three nights. Thank you, everyone!

Jason and Lexy: Where do I begin? Thank you for helping me make the transition to international living. I loved my time at Yummy Jobs and most of all in London. Jason, we go way back to Disney days and you still continue to surprise me with your ideas and wisdom. I started out being your mentor, but I think the roles have reversed now! Thank you for all of your support for this book!

Carly, you crazy girl! Thank you for allowing me to see a little of myself in someone else and realize that I am not alone in this crazy world. You were my Travel Angel, helping me to get organized after my tour of Africa was canceled, and a star for inviting me into your home only days after you returned home yourself. Thank you to the MacGechan family in Brisbane, Australia for making me feel so at home; if you are ever in the United States my home is open to you. Thank you to Stewart and Emily for having me on my many stopovers in London. Our journeys together are just beginning, and I look forward to many more. Another trip to Madrid may be in order!

Finally to Natalie, you earn the TOP award, mate! I have stayed with you so many times I can't count anymore. No matter what is happening in your life at the time of my visit, you always make me feel so at home and you definitely made my London life fun and exciting. Thanks for organizing all of the interesting bank holiday trips. And thank you to the Zweck family in Adelaide, Australia for sharing your daughter's time home with me, and letting me taste your wonderful pastries and drink your amazing wine. You are wonderfully gracious people.

A quick shout out to Aunt Julie and Uncle David at Johnson's Studio and Camera Shop. Thanks for always keeping me "outfitted" with cameras, memory cards and letting me print my photos. I know you have "given" me many more photos than I have paid for.

To Marlene, thanks for helping me to top-up the songs on my iPod at the beginning of every travel season; to Carrie, Lexi and Zack for adding in "cool" songs for me to take as well!

To Aunt Philly (Phyllis) for making sure my mom and dad could see my photos, read my emails and for helping me with my administrative tasks when I was on the other side of the world.

And a big thank you to those who continually questioned this lifestyle! It was you who gave me the push to keep going and prove it could be done.

I have one last person to thank, and that is my beautiful husband, Femi. He has been so patient with me while I "figured" out that my crazy travel life *can* be intertwined with love and marriage. He makes me a better person just by knowing him and I look forward to many more "chapters" of life with him by my side.

261558BV00002B/2/P